TURNING AWAY FROM THE COUNTERFEIT LIFE

EXPOSING THE ENEMY'S TACTICS AND THE WAR BEING WAGED OVER YOUR CHOICES

ANN BERNARD

TURNING AWAY FROM THE COUNTERFEIT LIFE:
Exposing the Enemy's Tactics and the War Being Waged Over Your Choices

ISBN: 979-8-9994757-0-1

For information about this title or to order additional books and/or electronic media, contact the publisher:
Ann Bernard Books
Email: ann@annbernard.biz

Printed in the United States of America

Contents

*Chapters about the Author's Personal Experiences

At the Judgement Seat

———•———

The Moment of Revelation

She stood in radiant light, yet felt no warmth.

Everything around her was still. Not cold, not harsh—just quiet. Too quiet for someone like Elena, whose life had always been filled with the sound of voices. Patients, nurses, volunteers. Laughter in the hallways of her care home. The hum of activity. The whispered thank-yous of families at the end of their grief-stricken journeys.

She had done good. She had built something that mattered.

As she looked around, waiting for someone to greet her, a screen—or perhaps a veil—parted before her. She instinctively stepped forward. She thought it would be a review, a celebration. Perhaps a replay of all she had done. But it wasn't her life she saw first.

It was someone else's.

A woman. Strong, calm, radiant. She looked like her, but different—more whole. This woman knelt beside a dying man, not just holding his hand, but praying over him. There was power in her voice. She wasn't just comforting—she was ushering him into eternity.

Elena watched as this version of herself moved through hospital rooms, neighborhoods, and church basements—not just caring for bodies but speaking directly to spirits, declaring healing, breaking chains, saving souls.

This woman hadn't just built a home care business. She'd birthed a movement of compassion and boldness. She trained other caregivers to not only meet physical needs but to be ambassadors of Heaven. Her nonprofit wasn't just a home for the dying—it was holy ground, a sanctuary where the lost were found in their final moments.

Tears rose unbidden in Elena's eyes. *Why does this feel like me... but not my life?*

And then, the answer came.

"This is the life I authored for you."

The voice was unmistakable—tender but firm. God's voice. And it pierced her deeper than any rebuke.

"But I did good," she whispered. "I loved people. I helped. I gave my life to this."

"You did good. But you stopped seeking Me. You stopped listening. You followed a voice that was not Mine."

Memories flooded in: the quiet prayers she used to say, not to Jesus but to her grandmother. The dreams she interpreted as signs from those who had passed. The "guides," she thought, were watching over her—comforting and familiar. She had never questioned where those voices came from. She just... believed.

She remembered the times she felt a stirring to speak the name of Jesus and didn't, the times she felt moved to pray for someone but chose silence instead. The nudge to go deeper, to trust more, to surrender completely was always there, always pushed aside.

She thought she was spiritual. Enlightened, even. She thought her love for others was enough.

It wasn't rebellion that led her away from God's design. It was comfort, success, and doing just enough good to never notice she had missed God.

Her knees gave out as the weight of it settled on her.

She hadn't lived a wicked life. She had lived a counterfeit one.

And now she saw the difference—clearer than ever before.

What Could Have Been

The Bible tells us that *we will all appear before the judgment seat of Christ* (2 Corinthians 5:10) and *give an account of ourselves to God* (Romans 14:12)—our actions, our choices, and ultimately, the life we lived.

Many believe that in that moment, we will not only see what we did, but also what could have been—the life God authored for us. Similar to the example above, the *movie* that will play out for us will not be the one we lived, but the one God had planned for us from the beginning.

And like those on their deathbed who are most burdened by what they didn't do, we will be pierced not just by our mistakes, sins, and wrong choices, but by the revelation of an entire life's worth of divine appointments, relationships, breakthroughs, and transformations that were forfeited. This life will be marked by the impact we were meant to have, the influence we were designed to carry, the good we were created to do, and the difference we were meant to make in the lives of others.

We'll see the appointments we missed, the moments that could've been miracles if only we had chosen differently.

Deep down, we already know that our decisions shape different paths. We see glimpses of the promptings we ignore, the fear we give in to, and the choices we make for the wrong reasons. But what we often fail to see is that every choice isn't just between right and wrong or better and worse; it's between God's authored life and the counterfeit life the enemy subtly offers.

The Nature of Our Enemy

The Bible is not vague about who our adversary is. Satan is not some abstract force of evil or a character of myth—he is real, personal, and dangerously active. He is called the father of lies (John 8:44), the one who has twisted truth from the beginning and continues to use deception as his primary weapon. He is described as the deceiver of the whole world (Revelation 12:9), operating not just through blatant falsehoods but through carefully crafted illusions that feel right, sound wise, and even appear helpful. He is the thief who comes only to steal, kill, and destroy (John 10:10), though he often does so without a sound, without an explosion—just a quiet erosion of faith, clarity, or purpose. He is also the god of this world who blinds the minds of unbelievers (2 Corinthians 4:4), keeping them from recognizing the light of the Gospel, dulling their spiritual senses, and distracting them with temporary fulfillment.

And perhaps most disturbingly, he masquerades as an angel of light (2 Corinthians 11:14). His deception doesn't always come dressed in darkness.

Often, it wears the disguise of enlightenment, progress, prosperity, or love. He whispers through spiritual-sounding language, cloaks lies in half-truths, and presents counterfeit paths that seem compassionate or reasonable but are void of God's truth.

Unseen but Not Uninvolved

This enemy runs underground in truly wicked and unthinkable ways—ways the world is just beginning to acknowledge, but God has long exposed. Through secret societies, occultic rituals, and elite networks, he orchestrates manipulation and domination, trafficking souls and bodies alike. Hidden behind wealth, influence, and institutions, he fuels agendas that are anti-God and anti-human, thriving in shadows where silence and power protect him.

His presence is also clearly visible in the overt atrocities that shock our conscience: human trafficking, child exploitation, mass shootings, racial genocide, sexual abuse, domestic violence, addiction epidemics, and systemic corruption across politics, healthcare, education, and media. We recognize these things as evil because they are grotesque, violent, and tragic. They make headlines. They stir outrage. But what's far more unsettling is how much of the enemy's work never does.

The Real Battle Is Subtle

What many fail to see—and what this book seeks to illuminate—is that the enemy's most effective strategies are not always brutal or barbaric. They are subtle. Spectacularly subtle.

He is just as active in the boardroom as in the back alley, in the classroom as in the courtroom, in the hallways of our homes and churches as much as in the halls of government. He inserts lies not only into our newsfeeds, but into our thoughts. He whispers in moments of hesitation, convinces us to stay quiet when we should speak, to compromise when we should stand, to delay when we should obey.

And so, the life he offers isn't always full of despair. Sometimes it's full of comfort. It's familiar. It looks safe. It even looks *good*. But it is not God-authored. It is counterfeit—designed to detour you just far enough off-course that you never become who you were truly created to be.

Why I Wrote This Book

I wrote this book because I've seen—up close and personal—how the enemy works. And I've also seen the power of God to set people free.

This book is born out of the work God called and anointed me to do. I teach people how to become personal storytellers—not just to share what they've lived through, but to *understand who they are* and *author who they are becoming*. Through a Holy Spirit–inspired framework, I guide people to extract meaning from their experiences, identify what shaped them, and recognize the deeper forces—both divine and deceptive—behind the choices they've made.

It began as a method for communication, connection, and personal development. But over time, God revealed something deeper: the very process I was using to help people grow was also *exposing the enemy*. As I walked people through their stories, I saw patterns repeat—stories of identity confusion, emotional pain, spiritual drift, and relationships fractured by silence, shame, and offense. What looked like ordinary struggles were actually spiritual strategies. Division, loneliness, and stagnation weren't just emotional or relational issues—they were the fallout of targeted attacks.

And so, personal storytelling became more than a tool. It became a weapon—a means to reclaim territory the enemy tried to steal. A way to help people welcome God, the Author of our lives, deeper into their stories—to let Him move through their memories, heal what was broken, restore what was lost, refresh what has grown weary, and rewrite the parts the enemy tried to define.

This work is also about rebuilding what's been broken. It's about families reconnecting. Communities healing. People remembering who they are in Christ—and seeing who others are too. I do this work in obedience and under the anointing of God, not only to help individuals grow but to call us into unity as the Body of Christ. This is Kingdom work. It's restoration, healing, and warfare all at once.

But before I could lead others in it, I had to walk it myself.

As I share in Chapter 20, God refined me in the fire—through suffering, surrender, and the renewal of my mind. I faced spiritual attacks that left me exhausted and overwhelmed. I cried out to God, and in His mercy, He reminded me who I was. He didn't just comfort me—He commissioned me. That was the moment I understood: I'm a warrior.

One of my favorite scriptures is Psalm 27:13:

> *"I believe that I shall look upon the goodness of the Lord in the land of the living!"*

I believe that—not as a wish, but as a declaration. Because it's not just God's goodness we were created for—it's His Kingdom. On earth as it is in heaven. We were given dominion, and through Christ, we've been empowered to live in alignment with His will. This book is an offering to the Body of Christ—to equip, awaken, and unite us in the battle for truth, freedom, and life.

An Invitation to Wake Up

Throughout this book, we will not only explore stories of counterfeit living—we will expose the tactics behind them. Each chapter presents a scenario, walks through the key choices at play, and pulls back the curtain on the spiritual dynamics involved. You'll see how the enemy subtly works to deceive, delay, distract, or derail us, often using what feels safe, familiar, or even wise. What may seem like a small or noble decision can, over time, lead to a life that looks full—but is spiritually off-course. By tracing these moments back to their root, we'll uncover how counterfeit lives are formed—and how we can reject them before it's too late.

This book is not just a discussion of good versus evil—it's a confrontation with the deceptive power of "almost right." It's a wake-up call to recognize how often our most routine decisions—what we tolerate, what we delay, what we rationalize—are shaping either a life authored by God… or a life crafted, inch by inch, by the enemy.

The real danger isn't always in the glaring evil we can point to. It's in the quiet compromises. The delayed obediences. The decisions we dress up as wisdom that are really rooted in fear, pride, or unbelief. These aren't harmless. They are the slow and subtle sabotage of the enemy, working behind the scenes while we tell ourselves everything's fine.

This book is meant to raise awareness of the critical importance of our choices—not just the big, dramatic ones, but the small ones we make every day that shape our identity, our direction, and our legacy. To see how the enemy moves, how he manipulates what we think is harmless, and how easily we can be led away from truth without ever realizing it.

It's a challenge and an invitation. A challenge to ask yourself honest, soul-searching questions:

Who am I listening to?

Who is really leading my life?

Is the story I'm living the one God authored—or one the enemy has quietly rewritten?

What's In This Book

Each chapter introduces a series of choices through a fictional scenario or personal experience. These are meant to feel real—because they are. They reflect the kinds of choices we all face in relationships, careers, identity, calling, and faith.

After each story, we'll explore what's happening beneath the surface. We'll name the choices, reveal the enemy's tactics, and expose the spiritual dynamics at work. You'll see how the enemy uses what is almost right to pull us just far enough from God's truth. And you'll see how God invites us—again and again—into clarity, courage, and obedience.

Section I

But before we dive into those decisions, we must start with the true story that frames them all. That's why the book begins with the Fall and the redemptive work of Jesus. Chapters One and Two lay the spiritual foundation for everything that follows. Because you cannot understand what's been stolen unless you first understand what was given. And you cannot reject the counterfeit until you truly grasp the life that was authored for you.

Section II: Counterfeit Selves — The Ways We Drift From the Truth

Section II exposes the drift—how the enemy subtly shapes who we become when we stop anchoring our identity in Christ.

In this part of the journey, we begin to see how performance tries to replace intimacy, how pride mimics spiritual maturity, how shame disguises itself as humility, and how culture quietly rewrites conviction. We face the temptation to resist refinement—not because we don't love God, but because we may not yet trust His process.

These chapters don't just address what we do—they uncover who we're becoming. And that's why they matter. Because the most dangerous counterfeit isn't always marked by obvious sin—it's often a life lived with the right language but the wrong foundation. When we believe false things about ourselves, we stop receiving the fullness of salvation. We may be saved—but we're not yet free.

Section II invites us to confront the roles we've adopted, the labels we've worn, and the false selves we've protected. And in doing so, it prepares us for what comes next: the internal war we must face to break those agreements and walk fully in truth.

Section III: The War Within — Spiritual Pressure and Personal Pain

Section III brings us into the depths of the internal battle—where spiritual warfare targets not just our actions, but our emotions, thoughts, and inner identity.

Here, the enemy doesn't attack with obvious rebellion. Instead, he exploits exhaustion, pain, disappointment, and unhealed wounds. We encounter the pressure of depression, the spiral of doubt and worry, the erosion of joy through bitterness and anger, and the torment of condemnation. These are not just emotional struggles—they are spiritual strategies designed to wear us down, distort truth, and keep us from living free.

This section reminds us that the war within is not weakness—it's where the real fight for faith unfolds. And while these chapters may expose vulnerable places, they also shine with the hope of transformation. They show us how the Word renews our minds, how the Spirit breaks strongholds, how truth dismantles lies, and how community restores what isolation has eroded.

Section III doesn't leave us in the pain. It leads us through it—into healing, wholeness, and deeper intimacy with God.

Because these aren't just battles to survive. They are invitations to overcome.

Section IV: Counterfeit Connection — The Enemy's Attack on Relationships

Section IV shifts the focus from the internal war to the battleground of relationships—because the enemy knows that if he can fracture connection, he can fracture the Body. These chapters explore how counterfeit connection forms when we avoid truth, suppress conflict, isolate out of fear, and protect our image instead of pursuing real healing.

In this section, we see how the enemy doesn't just attack marriages and friendships with obvious division—he sows strife through unspoken offense, fuels gossip masked as discernment, promotes false unity that avoids accountability, and convinces us that spiritual independence is maturity. We meet believers who are still showing up, still praying, still serving—but beneath the surface, they're disconnected, disillusioned, or quietly resentful.

These aren't just relational issues—they're spiritual strongholds.

Each chapter unearths the high cost of avoiding truth in community. We see how pain is perpetuated when we withdraw instead of press in, when we perform instead of confess, and when we settle for shallow peace instead of pursuing real reconciliation. But we also see what's possible when we confront the lies and walk in Spirit-empowered truth.

Section IV is a call to brave connection. It teaches us to engage with love, speak with grace, and stay rooted in God's design for authentic, truth-filled relationships. Because you can't live the life God authored for you in isolation—and you can't reflect Christ to the world while disconnected from His Body.

This section prepares us for what comes next: the life of influence we're called to live—not for ourselves, but for the Kingdom.

Section V: Counterfeit Decisions, Eternal Consequences

Section V brings the journey full circle. These chapters don't focus on dramatic rebellion or visible sin—they expose the quiet compromises that slowly shift the trajectory of a believer's life. The enemy doesn't always lure us into disobedience with blatant temptation; more often, he uses exhaustion, delay, logic, and fear to guide us into a life that's *almost* obedient—but not fully surrendered.

In this section, we meet believers who didn't set out to disobey God. They were tired. Discouraged. Uncertain. They were waiting on God and didn't see results. They felt like their efforts weren't bearing fruit. So they made small, subtle shifts—taking breaks, making "wise" decisions, chasing stability, delaying obedience. But each seemingly harmless choice opened the door to spiritual drift.

We see how striving replaces surrender. How logic drowns out trust. How the waiting becomes a breeding ground for the enemy's lies. And how delay, if not handled in faith, becomes disobedience in disguise.

Section V reveals that the most dangerous choices are often the ones we justify. The ones we label as temporary. The ones we make when we're weary or disillusioned. But each of these choices carries eternal consequences—not just in terms of salvation, but in the fruitfulness, peace, and purpose available to us here and now.

This section doesn't just diagnose the problem—it calls the reader to a deeper, more resilient obedience. It challenges us to choose trust when we can't see, to stay faithful when it costs us, and to wait on God with holy expectancy. Because every act of obedience is a seed, and every seed has a harvest. This section reminds us that eternity is shaped by the decisions we make daily—and the invitation is still open: choose the authored life.

This book wasn't meant to be read once and shelved. After finishing Section I, you don't have to read every chapter in order. Instead, take a look at the Table of Contents and ask the Holy Spirit to highlight what's most relevant for you right now. Start with the chapter that speaks to your current battle. Come back when a new struggle rises. The enemy rarely uses the same tactic twice, and as his strategy shifts, so should your response. Let this book be a companion in the fight—a resource you return to when the lies get louder, the pressure intensifies, or you simply need to be reminded of what's true. Victory is possible, but it requires awareness, repentance, and Spirit-led resistance. You're not alone in this war, and you don't have to fight it blind.

Section I

---•---

CHAPTER 1

The Fall — How the World Became Counterfeit

———•———

"He was a murderer from the beginning... when he lies, he speaks his native language, for he is a liar and the father of lies." John 8:44 (NIV)

Before the fall, before the deception, before the world became counterfeit—there was creation. And at the height of creation, God made man. "Then God said, 'Let us make mankind in our image, in our likeness...'" (Genesis 1:26). Humanity was not an afterthought; we were God's intention. Male and female, He created them—formed from the dust, yet breathed into by the Spirit of the living God. We were made to reflect Him—to bear His image in the earth, to rule with authority, to create, to love, to steward, and to multiply His goodness. And God didn't just create mankind—He *blessed* them. His first act after forming them was to speak blessing: "Be fruitful and multiply; fill the earth and subdue it..." (Genesis 1:28). Humanity was born into blessing, identity, and purpose. We were made to walk in close relationship with our Creator, to live in harmony with one another, and to represent Heaven on earth.

In the garden of Eden, there was beauty, abundance, and perfect communion. Adam and Eve lacked nothing. But in the center of the garden, God placed two trees: the Tree of Life and the Tree of the

Knowledge of Good and Evil. God gave them access to everything but warned them not to eat from the second tree, "for when you eat of it, you will surely die" (Genesis 2:17).

This is a dilemma for many people. After all, why did God even create an opportunity to disobey? What seems like God setting humanity up for the possibility of a fall is, in fact, a tremendous and glorious demonstration of God's love. God is love; therefore, the only thing God can do is establish a world where options exist. How does love exist without freedom?

This was not about fruit. It was about love, free will, and trust. Would they express their love for God by trusting Him and relying on Him to define good and evil, or would they exercise their free will and seize the power to define it for themselves? The option for them to choose had to exist.

Enter the serpent. Subtle, cunning, and strategic. He questioned God's word: "Did God really say you must not eat from any tree in the garden?" (Genesis 3:1). It was the first seed of doubt. Then he challenged God's motive: "You will not certainly die... For God knows that when you eat of it your eyes will be opened, and you will be like God..." (Genesis 3:4–5).

That was the bait: *You can be like God*—on your own terms. You can decide for yourself what is true, what is good, and what your life should be. The deception was based on truth. Adam and Eve were already like God. God created them that way.

At that moment, Eve saw that the tree was desirable—not because she was hungry, but because she wanted wisdom apart from God. She took and ate, and Adam, standing with her, did the same. Their eyes were opened—but not to life, not to glory. They became aware of their nakedness. Shame entered the human story. They hid from God. They blamed one another. Fear and disconnection had begun.

The trap of hindsight leads us to believe that we would have known better. How many of us think that had we been in Eve's or Adam's shoes, we wouldn't have been deceived by the serpent? It's easy once we know how satan operates within a situation to think we wouldn't have fallen for it. How, after all, could Eve have chosen the deception when both she and Adam lived the ideal life in close relationship with God? After Eve ate from the fruit, how could Adam do the same when he had explicitly received from God the guidance not to eat from that tree?

Adam had the option to do better. Why didn't he?

This question haunts us because it reflects something we wrestle with daily—*knowing better but not doing better.* The tragedy of the fall is not just in Eve's deception, but in Adam's silence and passivity. He was there. He heard. He saw. And he chose not to intervene. He chose not to stand on what God had spoken directly to him. Instead, he went along.

We are often told that Eve was deceived, but Adam sinned willingly. His failure wasn't ignorance. It was surrendering leadership, failing to protect what had been entrusted to him, and choosing harmony with Eve over obedience to God. And although we have hindsight, these are patterns we still see today. We continue to choose relational peace, societal acceptance, or internal comfort over divine instruction.

God did not abandon humanity even in the garden, in the aftermath of failure. He pursued them. He asked, "Where are you?" not because He didn't know but because He wanted them to know, to reflect, to return. The invitation to choose Him was still open, even after the fall. And it remains open now.

In the next chapter, we'll discuss God's plan for saving and redeeming humanity through the Second Adam—but before we go there, lets explore a crucial question that shapes everything we're facing today: Was the Fall Inevitable?

Was the Fall Inevitable?

It can feel that way reading the Bible and what seems like how quickly Adam and Eve were deceived. But it wasn't. The fall was not destiny—it was a decision. And that's what makes it so sobering, and so relevant to us today.

What would have prevented the fall? It wasn't just saying no to the fruit. It was remembering who they were, what they had been given, and walking in that truth. Adam and Eve had been given authority—to rule, to name, to subdue, and to protect. They weren't powerless. They weren't victims. They had the ability to resist the serpent, to guard the garden, to speak truth, and to silence lies.

But they didn't use the authority God gave them.

And this is the same choice before us every single day: Will we exercise our God-given authority, or will we hand it over to deception?

The fall happens in our lives when we forget who we are and what we've been given. It happens when we stop living from blessing, identity, and trust—and start living from lack, doubt, and fear. It happens when we let the voice of the enemy carry more weight than the voice of our Creator.

Alternative to the Fall

Eve is in the garden, near the tree, admiring the beauty and wonder of what God has made. The serpent slithers up, subtle and smooth, and begins to speak: *"Did God really say...?"*

But instead of entertaining the question, Eve narrows her eyes and replies, *"Yes, He did. And I believe Him."*

She doesn't doubt. She doesn't lean in. She remembers.

She turns and calls out to Adam, who is not far off. "The serpent is twisting God's words," she says. Adam steps forward—not passive, not silent, but present and alert. He's not just Eve's partner; he's her protector. Together, they remember the command they received. They remember the blessing spoken over them. They remember the authority they carry.

Adam doesn't engage in a debate. He doesn't ask the serpent for clarity or explanation. He speaks from conviction: *"You do not belong here."*

He calls the serpent what he is: a deceiver. A liar. A creature beneath them in the order of creation. And with the authority God gave him, he tells the serpent to leave. To go. To never return.

Eve stands with him, hand in his, rooted in the truth of God's word. There is no fear. No confusion. Only clarity and conviction.

And the serpent retreats—not because he wants to, but because he has no power where God's truth is honored and God's authority is upheld.

That would have changed everything.

That's what it could have looked like. That's what Jesus did in the wilderness. After His baptism, Jesus was led by the Spirit into the desert, where He fasted for forty days—and that's when the enemy came to tempt Him (Matthew 4:1–11). Satan waited until Jesus was physically weak and alone, then tried to appeal to His identity, His desires, and His authority.

"If you are the Son of God..." he said, trying to sow doubt—just as he had done with Eve. *"Turn these stones into bread,"* he whispered, tempting Jesus to use His power for Himself. *"Throw yourself down from the temple,"* he dared, twisting Scripture to bait Jesus into testing God. *"Bow down and worship me, and I'll give you all the kingdoms of the world,"* he offered, promising power in exchange for compromise.

But Jesus didn't argue. He didn't entertain the lies. He didn't prove Himself. He responded to each temptation with truth—by quoting the Word of God.

"It is written... " was His reply, every time.

Where Adam and Eve fell, Jesus stood. Where they doubted, He trusted. Where they reached, He submitted. Jesus overcame the enemy not with effort or emotion, but with alignment—with God's Word, God's will, and God's timing. He stood in authority, anchored in identity. And that's what's possible for us—when we remember who we are, walk in our authority, and refuse to entertain the voice of deception.

Adam and Eve's alternative choice isn't locked in a fictional outcome; it's an invitation extended to us every single day. We, too, are approached by the serpent in subtle ways—through doubt, fear, temptation, and pride. And like them, we have the authority to respond. We can stand firm, rooted in who God says we are, and act from that truth. We can choose to love, to trust, and to obey. This is what it means to turn away from the counterfeit life and step into what's real. And it all begins with something we often take for granted: the power of a choice.

The Power of a Choice

"I have set before you life and death, blessings and curses. Now choose life..."—Deuteronomy 30:19

You could say God is at it again. Just like in the garden with the Tree of the Knowledge of Good and Evil, God presents us with two options. He sets before us His perfect love. And just like before, He doesn't force us. He never coerces or manipulates us into following Him. That's not love. Instead, because He is love, He gave us free will—the ability to choose. He lays out the options plainly. He speaks of the blessings that come from choosing Him and the consequences of turning away. And then, He trusts us with the decision.

That's the nature of real love—it gives freedom. God set life and death before us and invited us to choose life, but He did not take away our power to choose otherwise.

From the very beginning, God has made it clear that our choices matter—not just in a practical sense but in a deeply spiritual, eternal way. When God spoke these words through Moses, He wasn't talking about a one-time decision. He was revealing a pattern that would define the human experience. Every choice—at its root—is a choice between life and death, between trusting God or turning away, between walking in truth or falling into deception.

That may sound heavy. But it's not meant to scare you. It's meant to wake you up—to stir something in you. To invite you into a different way of seeing your life.

We often divide our choices into categories: big or small, temporary or permanent, spiritual or secular. But from God's perspective, every choice is sacred. Every decision reflects what we believe, who we trust, and what kingdom we're aligning with. This book exists to help you see your choices more clearly—not only through the lens of convenience or consequence, but through the lens of truth. And by truth, we mean the Word and ways of God—what He has revealed about Himself, about us, and about how we're meant to live. Truth is not just an abstract concept or a moral ideal. Truth is a person—Jesus Christ (John 14:6). It is found in the Scriptures, shaped by God's character, and revealed through His Spirit. It is unchanging, unwavering, and always aligned with life.

The counterfeit life is built on deceptive choices—subtle compromises, prideful motives, and broken beliefs. And sin is always the result of a wrong choice. Every choice begins within us. It starts in our thoughts, our emotions, our motives, and in the lies we've come to believe about God, ourselves, and others. What varies is how those internal choices manifest—sometimes they're loud and visible in our actions, other times they remain hidden, yet still shape the direction of our lives.

What we base our decisions on is shaped by how we've come to understand the world and our place in it. Our choices are influenced by our upbringing, belief systems, past wounds, culture, trauma, fears, desires, unmet needs, and the voices we choose to listen to. And just as importantly, choosing *not* to act or decide is still a decision—it carries weight and consequence just like any other.

But here's the good news: we're not left to do this on our own. In Moses' time, the Israelites were given the Law—commands written on stone. But we now have something far greater: Jesus, who fulfilled the Law, and the Holy Spirit, who writes truth on our hearts and empowers us to live it. In the next chapter, we'll explore how Jesus made it possible for us to choose differently—and how the Holy Spirit helps us walk in obedience, trust, and love, not by striving, but by transformation from within.

But first, let's slow down and take a closer look at the three choices Adam and Eve were presented with in the garden—the same ones we face today. Love. Trust. Obedience. Each one is a choice. Each one is an action. And each one leads either toward the life we were created for—or away from it.

Love Is a Choice and an Action

One of the clearest pictures of love as action is found in John 13. On the night He would be betrayed, Jesus—knowing His time had come, and fully aware of what lay ahead—got up from the meal, wrapped a towel around His waist, and washed His disciples' feet. These were the same feet that would soon run in fear, the same group that would scatter, and one pair that would walk out to betray Him. Still, He knelt before each of them, one by one, and served them.

This wasn't a symbolic gesture. It was love made visible. Tangible. Costly. It was the act of a King who chose humility. A Savior who chose intimacy. God Himself choosing to serve.

Love is not just a feeling. It is not just affection or warmth or chemistry. Love is a decision to move toward someone, to act in their best interest, and to stay committed—even when it costs you something.

Adam and Eve had the opportunity to love God by choosing Him— by honoring His word, respecting His boundaries, and showing loyalty through action. But they chose something else. They chose self over God. In doing so, they rejected love.

Today, we're presented with that same choice. Love is not just something we feel toward God or others—it's what we *do*. When we choose love, we choose humility. We choose service. We choose presence. We choose forgiveness.

Love must be chosen, again and again. It is the foundation of relationship—and the first thing the enemy tries to counterfeit.

Trust Is a Choice and an Action

One of the most powerful examples of trust in Scripture is found in the life of Abraham. God told Abraham to leave everything familiar—his land, his people, his security—and go to a place He would *show* him. Not a detailed plan. Not a mapped-out route. Just a promise.

"So Abram went, as the Lord had told him…" (Genesis 12:4). That's trust.

Abraham chose to believe God's voice over his own understanding. Later, God promised him a son in old age—an impossible promise from a human perspective. And when that son finally came, God asked Abraham to place him on the altar, to offer Isaac back in full surrender. Again, Abraham trusted. Not because it made sense, but because he knew the One who had spoken. And that trust—consistent, costly, and surrendered—is why Abraham is known as the father of faith.

Because trust is the main ingredient of faith.

Faith isn't simply believing that God exists. It's choosing to trust Him—His timing, His nature, His word—when nothing around you confirms it. Faith is trust in action. And every time we trust God, we are exercising faith in who He is and what He has said.

Trust is not automatic. It is given. It is built. It is tested. To trust someone is to lean on them, to believe what they say, and to rely on their character—even when you don't understand everything.

The serpent didn't start by telling Adam and Eve to disobey. He started by getting them to question God's trustworthiness. "Did God really say…?" That question wasn't about rules—it was about relationship. It was an invitation to doubt.

To live the real life—the authored life—we must make the daily decision to trust God: His Word, His timing, His nature, and His plan. Trust isn't passive. It looks like waiting. It looks like surrender. It looks like continuing even when you don't see the full picture.

We choose trust when we silence the voice of fear and listen to the voice of truth.

Obedience Is a Choice and an Action

Perhaps the clearest and most powerful picture of obedience in all of Scripture is found in the Garden of Gethsemane. On the night of His arrest, Jesus knew exactly what was coming—betrayal, abandonment, humiliation, and the agony of the cross. He prayed with sorrow so deep it brought Him to His knees, saying, *"Father, if You are willing, take this cup from Me; yet not My will, but Yours be done"* (Luke 22:42).

That's obedience.

Jesus didn't obey because it was easy. He obeyed because it was right. He aligned His will with the Father's, not out of obligation, but out of love. He knew the cost—and He still chose to surrender. Obedience is not about perfection. It's about submission. It's not about agreeing with the plan—it's about trusting the One who made it.

Obedience is not control. It's not blind compliance or fear-based conformity. It is the intentional decision to align our actions with God's truth. It is the outward expression of love and trust. Without obedience, love is hollow, and trust remains theoretical.

Adam and Eve had a clear command: *Do not eat from this tree.* Obedience would have meant honoring God's instruction even when they didn't fully understand why. But instead, they allowed desire, deception, and doubt to take the lead.

We do the same when we know what God says, but we choose what we want instead.

Obedience is not always easy—but it is always worth it. It protects us. It anchors us. It aligns us with God's covering, God's wisdom, and God's ways.

And like love and trust, obedience is something we must choose— daily, actively, and intentionally.

Every time we obey, we reject the counterfeit and step into what's real.

Love. Trust. Obedience. These were the three choices before Adam and Eve—and they are the same three choices before us today. They are not isolated events. They are ongoing decisions that shape the direction of our lives and reflect the condition of our hearts. When we choose to love God, trust His character, and obey His voice, we resist the pull of the counterfeit life. We walk in the authority we were created for.

The fall was not inevitable, and the counterfeit life is not unavoidable. But neither is the real, authored life automatic. It must be chosen. Again and again. And the good news is: we are not left to do it on our own. In the next chapter, we'll explore how Jesus—the Second Adam—restored what was lost in Eden, and how the Holy Spirit empowers us to live in the truth we were created for.

Practical Application: Choose Real Today

As you reflect on this chapter, take a moment to examine your own life through the lens of love, trust, and obedience. These aren't abstract spiritual ideas—they're the choices that shape your relationships, habits, thoughts, and identity.

1. Love:

- Am I choosing to love God with my time, my priorities, my responses?

- Who in my life is God inviting me to move toward in love— even when it's uncomfortable?

2. Trust:

- What area of my life am I struggling to trust God with?

- Where have I allowed fear, doubt, or past wounds to influence my decisions?

3. Obedience:

- What has God already spoken to me that I haven't acted on?

- Am I hesitating out of confusion, or simply resisting surrender?

4. Reflection:

Pause and consider what it must be like for God—every time we don't choose Him. Every time we walk away, compromise, ignore, or doubt. He sees it all—not with condemnation, but with heartbreak. Because His offer is always love, always truth, always life. Imagine the ache of offering perfect love and being rejected—not once, but over and over.

Now, ask yourself this: *Where am I applying hindsight to the choices of others—like Adam and Eve—while ignoring my own patterns?* We often believe we would have chosen differently in the garden. But how often do we fall for the same deception in our daily lives?

This kind of honest reflection takes courage. It requires slowing down. It requires becoming a person who examines not just actions, but motives, beliefs, and turning points.

Take Action:

Write down one small but intentional action you can take this week to align more fully with God's truth—an act of love, a step of trust, or a choice to obey. Then, take 10–15 minutes to write a personal story from your life where you made a choice that led to regret—or to growth. Ask: What was I believing at the time? What would I choose differently now?

Remember: choosing what's real doesn't require perfection—it requires willingness. The counterfeit loses its power when we choose what is true, even in the smallest moments.

Closing Prayer

Father, thank You for giving me the ability to choose. Thank You for loving me enough not to force me, but instead inviting me—again and again—into what is true, what is right, and what leads to life. I confess the times I've chosen self over You. I confess the moments I've listened to the wrong voice, acted on fear, or ignored Your presence. Today, I choose differently. I choose to love You, to trust You, and to obey You. Help me walk in the authority You've given me. Help me see my choices clearly and live each day aligned with Your truth. I don't want to live a counterfeit life. I want the life You authored for me. In Jesus' name, Amen.

CHAPTER 2

The Second Adam
— The Way Back to Truth

———————•———————

For as by a man came death, by a man has come also the resurrection of the dead. For as in Adam all die, so also in Christ shall all be made alive. 1 Corinthians 15:21–22

What was lost through Adam's disobedience had to be restored through someone greater. Chapter 1 revealed how the fall distorted truth, broke fellowship with God, and handed over authority to the deceiver. But God, in His mercy and perfect justice, already had a plan—a second Adam. Where the first Adam failed, the Second Adam would triumph.

That man is Jesus Christ.

Jesus is the Son of God—eternally one with the Father and the Holy Spirit. He was not created; He *is* God. He was with God in the beginning, through whom all things were made (John 1:1–3). Yet in love and obedience, Jesus left His place in glory and entered our broken world. He humbled Himself, taking on human flesh, born of the virgin Mary by the power of the Holy Spirit. He lived among us—fully God and fully man—experiencing hunger, fatigue, sorrow, and temptation, yet without sin.

Jesus did not come to simply be a teacher, healer, or moral leader—though He was all those things. He came as the Lamb of God, the perfect and sinless sacrifice who would take away the sin of the world (John 1:29). Every moment of His life pointed to the cross, where He would lay it down willingly, not as a victim, but as a Savior. His mission was to reconcile mankind back to the Father, destroy the works of the devil, and restore what was lost in Eden.

Where the first Adam chose disobedience in a garden, Jesus chose obedience in a garden—the Garden of Gethsemane. Where Adam's act brought death to all, Jesus' death brought life to all who believe. This is why He is called the Second Adam. He succeeded where Adam failed. He made a way back to truth, back to God, and back to our original identity and purpose.

Making The Most Important Decision of Your Life

As mentioned in Chapter 1, through the Law given to Moses, God made it clear that we are constantly faced with a choice: life or death, blessing or curse (Deuteronomy 30:19). The Law defined righteousness and revealed God's standard—but it also exposed just how far we had fallen from it. The Law showed us what holiness looked like, but it didn't give us the power to live it out. Instead, it revealed that sin wasn't just something we occasionally stumbled into—it was something rooted deep within us.

The apostle Paul described it this way:

*"What then shall we say? That the law is sin? By no means!
Yet if it had not been for the law, I would not have known*

> *sin. For I would not have known what it is to covet if the law had not said, "You shall not covet."– Romans 7:7*
>
> *"Although I want to do good, evil is right there with me... What a wretched man I am! Who will rescue me from this body that is subject to death? Thanks be to God, who delivers me through Jesus Christ our Lord!"*
> *– Romans 7:21, 24–25*

Paul knew firsthand the struggle of trying to live rightly apart from Christ—and he made it clear that the Law, though good, could not save us.

> *"Therefore no one will be declared righteous in God's sight by the works of the law; rather, through the law we become conscious of our sin." – Romans 3:20 (NIV)*

God never intended the Law to be our permanent solution. It was meant to reveal our need for a Savior. So, in His love and mercy, God sent Jesus to do what the Law could not do.

> *"For what the law was powerless to do because it was weakened by the flesh, God did by sending his own Son in the likeness of sinful flesh to be a sin offering."*
> *– Romans 8:3 (NLT)*
>
> *"For Christ has already accomplished the purpose for which the law was given As a result, all who believe in him are made right with God." – Romans 10:4 (NLT)*

We need Jesus because without Him, we are spiritually dead. We are incapable of consistently choosing life. The flesh will always default to pride, fear, lust, anger, or compromise. Without the Spirit of God within us, we might choose what looks like life—but it's only a better-dressed version of death.

That's why salvation is not optional. Jesus is not a crutch—He is the cure. He didn't just come to forgive sins; He came to free us from the power of sin. He didn't just offer a better version of life—He is the life.

> *"I am the way and the truth and the life. No one comes to the Father except through Me." –* John 14:6

Without Jesus, all we have is the counterfeited. Only through Jesus can we truly choose life—because only through Him are we given a new heart, a new spirit, and the power to walk in truth.

Striving to Live A Good Life On Our Own

Jordan had always tried to do the right thing. Raised in a moral, hardworking family, he grew up believing that being good, fair, and kind was the path to a meaningful life. He volunteered on weekends, avoided the party scene in college, and always made responsible choices. On paper, Jordan's life looked admirable. People often told him, "You're one of the good ones."

But under the surface, Jordan was exhausted.

Every decision felt weighty. Every failure—whether it was losing his temper, thinking a judgmental thought, or letting someone down—left him flooded with guilt. His inner world was a tightrope act of trying to stay upright, and every misstep echoed louder than the last. The more he tried to "be good," the more he noticed how selfish his motives really were. Was he helping people to feel needed? Was he avoiding conflict just to be liked? Was he sacrificing his peace to earn love?

Eventually, the questions became louder than the praise.

One night, after another day of silently battling anxiety and guilt, Jordan whispered, *"What's the point? I'm trying so hard, but I feel like I'm still failing at life. Still falling short."*

That's when the thought surfaced—clear, quiet, undeniable: *You're trying to live the life only Jesus can live in you.*

Jordan had heard the gospel before, but he had never fully surrendered. He believed in God but had never accepted Jesus as Lord. In his heart, he had been relying on his own goodness, not on His grace. He was trying to earn what could only be received.

That night, Jordan made the most important decision of his life. He laid down his striving and received Jesus—not just as an idea, but as a Savior. And for the first time, he tasted peace—not because he had finally "gotten it right," but because he finally let Jesus make him right.

What Is Salvation?

Jordan's story is not unique. Many people are living just like him— trying to be "good enough," trying to earn love, trying to live rightly in their own strength. And though their lives may look put together on the outside, internally, they're weary, burdened, and quietly breaking under the weight of self-made righteousness.

That's because we were never created to carry the pressure of saving ourselves.

Salvation is the divine exchange where Jesus takes our sin and gives us His righteousness.

It is the moment when we stop striving to be our own savior and instead receive the gift of grace that can only come from Him. It's not a reward for good behavior—it's a rescue mission for the lost, the broken, the exhausted, and the guilty. It's the transfer from darkness to light, from death to life, from striving to resting in what has already been accomplished.

Paul describes it clearly:

> *"But God, being rich in mercy, because of the great love with which he loved us, even when we were dead in our trespasses, made us alive together with Christ—by grace you have been saved." – Ephesians 2:4–5*

We were dead—not weak, not confused, not slightly off-track. Dead in our sins. But through Jesus, we are made alive. That's salvation.

It begins with faith—a choice to believe that Jesus is who He says He is: the Son of God who lived a sinless life, died a sacrificial death, and rose in victory so we could be reconciled to God.

It continues with surrender—letting go of control, releasing our own efforts, and making Jesus not only our Savior but our Lord. That means we submit to His leadership, trust His direction, and follow Him into the life we were created to live.

> *"If anyone is in Christ, he is a new creation. The old has passed away; behold, the new has come."*
> *– 2 Corinthians 5:17*

That's the power of salvation. It's not about self-improvement—it's about spiritual rebirth. You are not just forgiven; you are made new.

What It Cost Jesus

Salvation is free to you, but it cost Jesus everything.

He left heaven's glory, took on human flesh, and lived a life of perfect obedience—facing temptation, rejection, suffering, and sorrow. He was mocked, beaten, falsely accused, and nailed to a cross. He bore the full weight of your sin and mine. Every lie, every betrayal, every selfish act, every injustice—we placed it on Him. *"God made Him who had no sin to be sin for us, so that in Him we might become the righteousness of God."* (2 Corinthians 5:21 (NIV))

The cross wasn't just a symbol of suffering—it was a place of substitution. Jesus took our place, died our death, and paid our debt. And then, on the third day, He rose again in victory—conquering sin, death (the grave), and the enemy once and for all. That's the gospel. That's the good news. And that is what salvation is built upon.

How to Make the Decision

Receiving salvation begins with a response to the truth. It's not just about believing *that* Jesus exists—it's about trusting *in* Him personally. It's not about cleaning yourself up first or waiting until you feel worthy. The truth is, you'll never be worthy on your own. Jesus didn't come because you had it together—He came because you didn't.

Salvation is both simple and supernatural. It's simple because the invitation is open to all. It's supernatural because, in one moment, your eternity shifts, your identity changes, and your spirit is made alive.

Paul lays it out clearly:

> *"If you confess with your mouth, 'Jesus is Lord,' and believe in your heart that God raised Him from the dead, you will be saved." – Romans 10:9*

To receive salvation:

1. Admit that you are a sinner in need of forgiveness.
2. Believe that Jesus is the Son of God, who died for your sins and rose again.
3. Confess Him as Lord of your life—surrendering control and trusting His leadership.

You can express that decision in your own words, or you can pray something like this:

> *Jesus, I believe You are the Son of God. I believe You died for my sins and rose again to give me new life. I confess that I need You. I turn from my old ways and choose to follow You. I receive You now as my Lord and Savior. Thank You for forgiving me, saving me, and making me new. Amen.*

This decision is more than a prayer—it's a turning point. Every poor choice, every mistake, every rebellion—wiped clean by the blood of Jesus. Grace steps in where our efforts fall short. But grace is not just a safety net; it's an empowerment to make new decisions. We are no longer bound by the shame of our past.

What Comes With Salvation

Salvation is not just about getting into Heaven one day—it's about Heaven getting into you now. It's not only about being saved *from* sin, but being saved *for* a life of purpose, peace, and power. Through salvation, we are not simply given a new future—we are invited to return to the life God intended from the beginning: walking in unbroken fellowship with Him, reflecting His image, carrying His authority, and living in the fullness of His love and truth.

When we accept Jesus, we become new creations. The old has passed away, and the new has come (2 Corinthians 5:17). However, even though our spirit is made new, our minds often carry the old patterns and beliefs. That's why Scripture calls us to renew our minds (Romans 12:2). Our new life in Christ requires a new way of thinking, deciding, and discerning—this time, rooted in God's Word, Christ's example, and the voice of the Holy Spirit.

Here is what is included in the gift of salvation:

1. Forgiveness of Sins

You are no longer defined by your past. Every failure, every regret, every hidden shame—wiped clean by the blood of Jesus.

> *"He has delivered us from the domain of darkness and transferred us to the kingdom of His beloved Son, in whom we have redemption, the forgiveness of sins."*
> *– Colossians 1:13–14*

2. A New Identity as a Child of God

You are not who the world said you were. You are God's beloved—adopted, accepted, and secure.

*"But to all who did receive Him, who believed in His name,
He gave the right to become children of God."
– John 1:12*

3. Victory Over Sin and Death

You're not just forgiven—you're free. Sin is no longer your master. Death no longer has the final word.

"We know that our old self was crucified with Him… so that we would no longer be enslaved to sin." – Romans 6:6

"Thanks be to God! He gives us the victory through our Lord Jesus Christ." – 1 Corinthians 15:57

4. Peace With God

The war is over. You're no longer under judgment, but under grace. You are reconciled.

"Since we have been justified by faith, we have peace with God through our Lord Jesus Christ." – Romans 5:1

5. Eternal Life

Not just a promise for someday—but a quality of life that starts now and never ends.

"Whoever believes in Him shall not perish but have eternal life."– John 3:16

6. A New Heart and a Renewed Mind

You don't just try harder—you are changed from the inside out.

"I will give you a new heart and put a new spirit in you." – Ezekiel 36:26

> *"Be transformed by the renewing of your mind."*
> – Romans 12:2

7. Access to God's Presence

You can come boldly into God's presence. He hears you. He welcomes you.

> *"Let us then approach God's throne of grace with confidence."* – Hebrews 4:16

8. Purpose, Calling, and Spiritual Gifts

You were saved for a reason. You have divine assignments, spiritual gifts, and a role in God's Kingdom.

> *"For we are His workmanship, created in Christ Jesus for good works."* – Ephesians 2:10

> *"To each is given the manifestation of the Spirit for the common good."* – 1 Corinthians 12:7

9. Divine Healing

Jesus' sacrifice touches your body as well as your soul. Healing is part of His finished work.

> *"By His wounds we are healed."* – Isaiah 53:5

> *"He heals all your diseases."* – Psalm 103:3

10. Divine Protection

You are not alone or unguarded. God surrounds you with His presence and angels.

"The Lord will rescue me from every evil attack."
– 2 Timothy 4:18

"He will cover you with His feathers... His faithfulness will be your shield."
– Psalm 91:4

11. Divine Provision

Your needs are not too great or too small. God is your faithful provider.

"My God will supply every need of yours according to His riches in glory." – Philippians 4:19

"The Lord is my shepherd; I shall not want."
– Psalm 23:1

12. The Indwelling of the Holy Spirit

God doesn't just save you and leave you—He comes to live within you. The Holy Spirit becomes your guide, your comforter, your source of strength.

"When you believed, you were marked in Him with a seal, the promised Holy Spirit." – Ephesians 1:13

This is the life Jesus died to give us—not just forgiveness, but fullness. Not just a clean slate, but a new identity. Everything listed above is part of a greater invitation: to live the authored life.

The authored life is the life God intended and designed for you before you were ever born—the one He wrote into existence with purpose, love, and destiny. It's not shaped by culture, trauma, performance, or pressure, but by the redemptive work of Christ and the will of the Father. This life is recorded in the Lamb's Book of Life (Revelation 21:27), and it reflects God's best—His truth, His timing, His plans, and His glory revealed through your obedience.

To live the authored life is to walk in the reality of everything salvation provides: to make decisions based not on past pain or present pressure, but on eternal truth. It's to live in alignment with God's Word, led by the Holy Spirit, and grounded in the new nature we've received in Christ. It's a life of victory over the enemy—not just at the end, but every day.

And it all begins with knowing who you are, what you've received, and who now lives in you.

Who Is the Holy Spirit?

To live the authored life isn't something we can do in our own strength. We were never meant to figure it out alone or strive to fulfill God's will by sheer effort. That's why one of the greatest gifts of salvation is the indwelling of the Holy Spirit.

The best person to introduce us to the Holy Spirit is Jesus Himself.

On the night before His crucifixion, during the Last Supper, Jesus prepared His disciples for what was coming. He knew His departure would shake them, but He also knew it was necessary for something greater to come. He said:

> *"Very truly I tell you, whoever believes in Me will do the works I have been doing, and they will do even greater things than these, because I am going to the Father."*
> – John 14:12 (NIV)

Jesus wasn't abandoning them—He was making room for the next phase of God's plan: the indwelling of the Holy Spirit.

> *"And I will ask the Father, and he will give you another Helper, to be with you forever, even the Spirit of truth, whom the world cannot receive, because it neither sees him nor knows him. You know him, for he dwells with you and will be in you."* – John 14:16–17

Jesus describes the Holy Spirit as "another Helper"—not a substitute, but an equal—God Himself, sent to dwell in us. Where Jesus walked beside the disciples, the Holy Spirit would now live within them. This wasn't just a change in location—it was a complete transformation in how God would relate to His people.

The Holy Spirit is not a distant power or vague force. He is personal. Relational. Present. He teaches, guides, convicts, comforts, empowers, and transforms us. He is the Spirit of truth, and getting to know Him is getting to know God Himself.

When we receive Jesus, the Holy Spirit takes up residence in our hearts.

> *"In Him you also... having also believed, you were sealed in Him with the Holy Spirit of promise, who is given as a pledge of our inheritance."* – Ephesians 1:13–14

He is the guarantee of what's to come—the seal that marks us as God's own. He is not only our Helper, but the assurance of our future, the down payment of our inheritance, and the power that enables us to live the life Jesus calls us to.

Why We Need the Holy Spirit

Even Jesus, though fully God, chose to live fully as a man while on earth. He laid aside His divine privileges (Philippians 2:6–8) and walked in total dependence on the Holy Spirit. At His baptism, the Holy Spirit descended on Him like a dove (Luke 3:22). From that moment forward, Jesus was led, empowered, and filled with the Spirit—fulfilling His mission through the Spirit's power (Acts 10:38).

If Jesus, the Son of God, chose to live by the Spirit—how much more must we?

Making the right choices between life and death isn't just hard without the Holy Spirit—it's impossible. He doesn't just help us out here and there; He enables us to follow Jesus, resist sin, walk in love, speak truth, and grow into spiritual maturity. Without Him, we remain stuck in cycles of striving and self-effort. With Him, we are empowered to live from a place of grace and truth.

The Role of Faith in Our Choices

The Holy Spirit empowers us to live the life we were created for—but even that life must be received and walked out by faith.

This chapter has centered on one foundational truth: the choices we make between life and death. Just as Adam and Eve chose death by believing a lie, we reclaim life by believing the truth—and that requires faith. Faith is the bridge between what God says and our willingness to trust and act on it. It's how we receive salvation, follow Jesus, and respond to the leading of the Holy Spirit.

What Is Faith?

Faith is not blind optimism or shallow positivity. It's not belief in yourself or a vague hope that things will "just work out." Biblical faith is deep trust in the character, promises, and power of God—especially when you can't see the full picture.

> *"Now faith is the assurance of things hoped for, the conviction of things not seen."* – Hebrews 11:1

Faith is what pleases God—not performance, effort, or outward success.

> *"Without faith it is impossible to please God, because anyone who comes to Him must believe that He exists and that He rewards those who earnestly seek Him."*
> – Hebrews 11:6

The Christian life begins in faith—but it must also be lived in faith.

> *"The righteous will live by faith."* – Romans 1:17

> *"We walk by faith, not by sight."* – 2 Corinthians 5:7

Faith is what enables us to say "yes" to Jesus, to receive the Holy Spirit, to believe in the forgiveness of our sins, and to trust that we are indeed new creations—even when our feelings or circumstances say otherwise. Without faith, the truths of salvation remain theoretical. But by faith, they become the foundation of our daily choices.

Faith Without Works

But faith is more than belief—it's movement. More than agreement—it's obedience. The Bible is clear: faith without works is dead.

> *"What good is it, my brothers and sisters, if someone claims to have faith but has no works? Can such faith save them? ... Faith by itself, if it is not accompanied by works, is dead."*
> –James 2:14,17

We are not saved by works, but we are saved for them. A living faith always produces visible change. It expresses itself through obedience, repentance, love, trust, generosity, surrender, and holiness. It's one thing to say you believe—it's another to live in a way that reflects that belief.

Yes, we are new creations. Yes, everything Jesus accomplished on the cross is available to us. But we've lived in a fallen world, shaped by broken systems, wounded relationships, lies, and patterns of thinking that don't align with God's truth. That's why faith is not a one-time decision—it's a daily return. A daily choosing. A daily transformation.

The work we are called to do is not to earn salvation—it's to partner with it. It's to work with the Holy Spirit to renew our minds, heal our hearts, and live according to the identity and inheritance we've received. It's the lifelong journey of returning to our original design—unbroken relationship with God, unshaken trust in His Word, and unhindered obedience to His will.

That's why each chapter in this book includes a *Faith in Action* section. Because truth must be responded to. Revelation must lead to repentance. Identity must be walked out. And freedom must be guarded.

Faith isn't just something you confess. It's something you live.

Every time we choose to align with God's truth, we are acting in faith. Every time we respond to the Holy Spirit's prompting, we are walking by faith. And every time we reject the counterfeit and cling to what is real, we are choosing life by faith.

But faith is not unopposed. The enemy knows its power, and he works hard to undermine it at every turn.

In the chapters to come, we'll explore how faith is tested and strengthened in everyday decisions—especially as it comes up against the attacks of the enemy. But before we get there, we must first understand this: the battle begins even before someone receives salvation.

Introducing the Enemy and His Tactics

The decision to receive Jesus is the most important choice a person will ever make—and Satan knows it. So he does everything in his power to prevent that decision from happening.

Before we ever make the decision to follow Jesus, the enemy is already at work. His first and most urgent mission is simple: keep people from hearing the Gospel. If he can prevent the truth from reaching our hearts, he can keep us bound in confusion, shame, and self-deception. But to do this, he has to operate on two fronts: he works on those who have yet to hear the truth, and he works on those *carrying* the truth.

He plants seeds of unbelief, busyness, apathy, and fear in those who don't yet know Jesus—and at the same time, he aims to corrupt, distract, discredit, or silence those called to share the Good News. He doesn't need to stop everyone—just enough people, just enough conversations, just enough truth from getting through.

The enemy works hard to keep the truth from ever reaching us—because once it does, everything changes.

Jesus explained this dynamic in the Parable of the Sower (Matthew 13:3–9; 18–23). In this parable, a farmer sows seed, which represents the Word of God. But not all the seed takes root. Some falls along the path, and birds come and eat it before it can penetrate the ground. Jesus later explains:

> *"When anyone hears the message about the kingdom and does not understand it, the evil one comes and snatches away what was sown in their heart."* – Matthew 13:19

That's the first tactic: interception. The enemy steals the word before it can take root—before understanding can lead to faith.

Others hear the Word with joy, but because they have no root, they fall away when trials come. Still others receive the Word, but it's choked out by the cares of this life, the deceitfulness of wealth, and the desire for other things.

This parable isn't just about how we respond to the Gospel—it reveals what is at work against it. The enemy's goal is not just to stop you from hearing truth—it's to keep you living a life that looks good on the outside but is void of the real power and transformation that salvation brings. He wants you living the counterfeit life.

From the moment truth is revealed, the enemy begins his counterattack. He doesn't always come with horns and fury. More often, his weapons are subtle—doubt, delay, fear, pride, shame, confusion, and distraction.

"The god of this world has blinded the minds of the unbelieving, so that they might not see the light of the gospel of the glory of Christ." – 2 Corinthians 4:4

Here are some of the common lies and tactics the enemy uses:

"You're not ready yet."

He'll convince you to wait. To think about it later. But later often never comes.

"You're too far gone."

He'll tell you that what you've done is too dark, too dirty, or too disqualifying for God to forgive.

"You're fine without Jesus."

He'll tempt you to believe that being a good person is enough. That you don't need saving.

"It's all fake anyway."

He'll sow seeds of cynicism and skepticism, causing you to question everything before you ever fully hear the truth.

"You'll have to give up too much."

He'll highlight what you might lose—friends, habits, control—without showing you what you'll gain: real life.

"You've already missed your chance."

He'll try to convince you it's too late. That God has moved on. That your window closed long ago.

All of it is designed to do one thing: keep you from choosing Jesus.

But none of it is true.

The gospel is for everyone. No one is too far gone. No one is too late. And nothing you've done is greater than what Jesus did for you.

> *"Everyone who calls on the name of the Lord will be saved."* – Romans 10:13

> *"Whoever comes to Me I will never drive away."* – John 6:37

And for those who *do* hear and believe, the fight is not over—it simply shifts. The next level of spiritual warfare is aimed at keeping believers from walking fully in everything salvation provides. The enemy works to keep us forgiven, but still bound. Saved, but still stuck. Loved, but still insecure. Redeemed, but still silent. His strategy is to prevent believers from stepping into the fullness of who they are in Christ—from exercising the power and authority they've been given.

Remember the alternative scenario we imagined in Chapter 1—what would have happened if Adam and Eve had stood firm and silenced the serpent? Satan is aware of it, too. He knows what's at stake if the body of Christ begins to stand in truth. He knows he cannot afford for believers to come into the knowledge of their true identity, take action, and walk in their God-given authority. So he fights—not just to keep us out of the Kingdom, but to keep us ineffective within it.

This chapter lays the groundwork and serves as both a refresher and reference point for what we will explore more deeply throughout this book. Because the choices we make are not neutral. They are choices between life and death, between what Jesus died to give us, and what the enemy deceptively offers in its place.

From being saved, salvation, and the daily walk of faith that follows, there is a constant spiritual battle unfolding around us—and often within us. The enemy's aim is clear: to block the Gospel, weaken its messengers, distort its message, and deceive believers into settling for a powerless, compromised version of the truth. But Jesus came to give us life—and life abundantly (John 10:10). And in Him, we've been given everything we need to live in freedom, purpose, and victory.

In the chapters ahead, we will begin to expose the enemy's counterfeits in greater detail—not to dwell on darkness, but to recognize the lies that have shaped our thinking, choices, and circumstances. And more importantly, to reclaim what's been stolen or forfeited and walk in the fullness of salvation Jesus secured for us.

Practical Application: Respond to Truth, Root in Faith

As you reflect on this chapter, consider the depth of the decision you've made—or still need to make—regarding salvation. Faith is not passive. Salvation is not theoretical. These are the most important, most defining realities of your life. So let's make this practical. Let's make it personal.

1. Salvation:

- Have I truly received Jesus as both Savior and Lord?

- Am I still trying to "be good" in my own strength, or have I fully surrendered?

- What part of salvation do I believe intellectually but struggle to receive in my heart (forgiveness, freedom, identity, authority, etc.)?

2. Faith:

- Where is God asking me to walk by faith—but I keep waiting for proof, clarity, or comfort?

- Do I treat faith like a moment in time, or a daily posture of trust and obedience?

- Am I living by what I *believe*, or by what I *see and feel*?

3. Spiritual Resistance:

- Can I identify areas where the enemy has tried to keep me from hearing, understanding, or acting on truth?

- Have I believed any lies like, "It's too late," "I'm too far gone," or "This doesn't apply to me"?

- Who in my life needs to hear the truth—and how have I allowed fear or distraction to keep me silent?

4. Good Ground:

- What is the condition of my heart right now—hard, distracted, shallow, or ready to receive?

- How am I cultivating a heart that is soft to God, rooted in truth, and protected from the enemy's interference?

Take Action:

Write down one truth from this chapter that stood out to you— something about Jesus, about yourself, or about salvation. Then ask: *What do I need to do with this truth?* Does it require repentance? Surrender? A conversation? A step of boldness?

Now, write a short personal story (even just a paragraph or two) about a time when you either resisted God's truth or responded to it. What happened? What was the outcome? What did it reveal about your faith?

Finally, choose one practical act of faith this week—whether it's sharing your testimony, praying for someone, obeying a nudge from the Holy Spirit, or simply meditating on a promise of God and declaring it daily. Faith becomes real when it moves from belief to action.

Remember:

The enemy loses power every time you choose truth.

Faith grows every time you act on what God has said.

And salvation is not the end of your story—it's the beginning of the life you were born to live.

Closing Prayer

Father God,

Thank You for sending Jesus—the Second Adam—to redeem what was lost and restore what was broken. Thank You for making a way back to truth, to life, and to You. I acknowledge today that I cannot save myself, and I no longer want to try. I believe Jesus is the Son of God, that He died for my sins and rose again so that I might live.

I receive Your gift of salvation—not just in word, but in the depths of my heart. Forgive me for where I have delayed, doubted, or believed the lies of the enemy. Open my eyes to every area where I have settled for the counterfeit. Teach me to walk by faith, to trust Your Word, and to follow Your Spirit.

Holy Spirit, fill me. Lead me. Empower me to live the life Jesus made possible. Help me to recognize the enemy's tactics and stand firm in truth. Train my ears to hear Your voice and give me courage to choose life in every decision I make.

I surrender again today—not just to be saved, but to become all You created me to be.

In Jesus' name, Amen.

Section II

Counterfeit Selves
— The Ways We Drift From the Truth

The enemy rarely starts with blatant rebellion. More often, he begins with subtle redirection—small lies that distort our identity, slow compromises that disguise themselves as wisdom, and inner vows made in pain that we begin to call truth. In *Section I*, we saw the origin of the counterfeit life—how the fall of man opened the door to deception, and how Jesus, the Second Adam, restores what was lost. But restoration is not passive. It requires recognition and repentance. And that begins with confronting the ways we've unknowingly drifted.

This section—Section II—is where the counterfeit becomes personal.

Through five chapters, we uncover the most common ways believers gradually step out of truth and into imitation:

- We perform instead of abide.

- We label ourselves by past pain or present accomplishments.

- We seek validation from man instead of intimacy with God.

- We trade bold truth for culturally acceptable messaging.

- And we resist the fire of refinement when it gets uncomfortable.

Each chapter reveals how the enemy doesn't have to destroy your faith to derail your purpose—he just has to convince you to live from a version of yourself that God never authored. These are not just behaviors—they are identities we've embraced, often unknowingly. But God is calling us back to truth. Back to who we really are in Him. This section is about exposure, not condemnation. It's about illuminating the slow drift, so we can return to the steady anchor.

CHAPTER 3

When Righteousness Becomes a Front — Living From a Religious Spirit

———•———

"This people draw near with their mouth and honor me with their lips, while their hearts are far from me, and their fear of me is a commandment taught by men." Isaiah 29:13

I'm starting the teachings in this book with a personal experience—not because I want the spotlight on me, but because I want you to know I'm not speaking *at* you—I'm walking *with* you. This journey is personal for me, too. If I had a real-life example for every choice I plan to explore in this book, I'd share them all. But to cover the full scope of what God has shown me, I also need to use fictional scenarios. When I do have real experiences that speak directly to the truth at hand, I lead with them— because there's power in knowing someone overcame initially making the wrong choice.

I'm also choosing to begin with a personal example of the religious spirit because it's a trap so many believers fall into—including me. It's subtle, convincing, and dressed in all the right behaviors. You can genuinely love God, seek Him, obey Him—and still end up performing, striving, and judging others while thinking you're doing everything right. That's what happened to me. And I didn't even realize it until years later.

44

God reminded me of this experience while I was in the fiery furnace—a season of intense refinement where He was burning away the things in me that didn't reflect Him. He brought this memory back, not to shame me, but to reveal the truth: that was a time in my life when my righteousness had become a front. That I had been living from a place of discipline and image, not from love and surrender. I share it with you to show what's possible when God exposes the counterfeit and begins the work of restoration.

Personal Experience

Before Christ, I lived my life striving in my own strength—chasing success in business and relationships, only to be met with repeated failure. I was proud, self-reliant, and isolated. Results and accomplishments were my only compass, and I was obsessed with outcomes. I had become independent to the point of arrogance, selfish in my ambition, and blind to my need for grace.

I reached the point where I was so broken, hurt, and in pain, I saw my choice as either committing suicide or giving my life to Jesus. I gave my life to Jesus.

God began working in my life and blessing me in incredible ways. I was obedient to God—but not surrendered. I was still holding on to control, and I didn't invest in my side of the relationship with Him like I should have. I appeared to be a "good Christian" on the outside. I shared my testimony and talked about all the amazing things God had and was doing in my life. I was not shy about expressing how much I loved God. I made some positive changes, but unfortunately, I also wore righteousness like a badge and didn't carry the heart of Christ. I was driven more by pride and ego than love.

I was not led by the Holy Spirit; instead, it was through intense self-discipline that I kept myself from outright sinning. And it breaks my heart to say that while God kept blessing me, I was often mad or angry at Him. I wanted my way and my will more than I wanted His.

I had unknowingly left openings in my heart for the enemy to counterfeit who I was in Christ. That became painfully clear during my time living in Colorado.

My landlord was a kind, generous woman. She also struggled with alcoholism. She was a woman of faith, but she battled deeply rooted strongholds. In her moments of weakness, she would turn to me for help—and I said yes. I threw away her alcohol, including all the hidden bottles, spoke words of encouragement, and tried to comfort her. But internally, I judged her. I saw her sin, not her struggle. I saw her as weaker than me, and I believed I was more spiritual because I had overcome in areas she hadn't.

I thought I was helping her, but in truth, I wasn't loving her. I was managing her. I didn't grieve with her. I didn't sit in her pain. I didn't speak life over her or pray with her or for her. I didn't stand firm against the enemy with her. I didn't see her the way Jesus did. I saw myself as the stronger Christian, and in doing so, I missed the heart of Christ entirely.

What I didn't realize then was that the religious spirit mimics spiritual maturity. It dresses up as obedience but keeps the heart cold. It silences sin, but it suffocates love. I looked righteous, but I wasn't living in righteousness.

The religious spirit is dangerous because it doesn't always look like rebellion—it often looks like devotion. It thrives in performance, pride, and external obedience while keeping us disconnected from the heart of

God. It can convince sincere believers that they're walking closely with God, when in reality, they're relying on their own strength, image, or self-discipline. It resists grace, minimizes compassion, and replaces relationship with routine. And like in my story, it's possible to fall under its influence without ever realizing it.

That's why in each chapter, we'll take a closer look at the choices that open the door to deception—and in this case, to the religious spirit. We'll also expose the enemy's tactics that work behind the scenes to make those choices seem reasonable, even righteous. The goal of the next sections is to bring clarity to what was really at play: not just what I did, but what I believed, ignored, or justified in the process.

Key Choices

Every chapter in this book will include a section like this—where we identify the key spiritual choices at the heart of the story or scenario. These are the crossroads we all face, often without realizing it. The purpose of highlighting them is to bring clarity to the decisions that either align us with God's truth or drift us toward the counterfeit life. In my story, the choices weren't obvious at the time. I thought I was doing everything right. But now, looking back with the Holy Spirit's help, I can see where the enemy was influencing my thinking, and where I had the opportunity to choose differently. These are the choices I believe many of us wrestle with—and they deserve a closer look.

1. Choosing to Live by the Spirit vs. Performing Out of Religious Obligation

In that season of my life, I wasn't being led by the Holy Spirit—I was operating from self-discipline, not surrender. I followed rules, showed up, and avoided sin, but I didn't rely on God's power or seek His presence daily. I thought obedience alone was enough, but it had become a performance. I was doing Christian things in my own strength, checking boxes without inviting the Spirit to lead, convict, or guide me.

Living by the Spirit is about relationship, intimacy, and dependence. It's about yielding moment by moment, not just appearing righteous. I chose outward obedience, but I missed the inward transformation that only the Spirit brings. That left me vulnerable to pride, burnout, and a counterfeit version of the Christian life.

2. Choosing Compassion and Humility vs. Pride and Judgment Masked as "Truth"

I told myself I was helping my landlord. And on the surface, I was. But the truth is, I judged her. I saw her weakness and assumed I was stronger. I didn't weep with her, stand beside her in prayer, or fight for her freedom in the Spirit. I didn't ask God how He saw her—I relied on my own assessment and treated her accordingly.

That's what pride does. It hides behind truth. It says, *"I'm right. I'm better. I know what's best."* But truth without love is still disobedience. Compassion says, *"I see your struggle, and I'm here with you. I'm not above you—I'm beside you."* Pride leads to separation. Compassion leads to connection. I chose judgment dressed up as truth, and it cost me the opportunity to love her the way Jesus would.

3. Choosing to Love Like Jesus vs. Managing People with a Superior Attitude

What I did wasn't love—it was management. I responded to her need, but I didn't let her in. I didn't make space for her pain. I didn't pour out the grace and mercy God had poured into me. I saw myself as more spiritual, more disciplined, more free. That made me feel responsible *for* her, instead of present *with* her.

Jesus doesn't manage us—He loves us, walks with us, bears our burdens, and calls us higher through grace. Loving like Jesus requires humility, patience, and the willingness to sit in the mess with people. I missed that. I gave her control without giving her Christ. I missed the heart-to-heart exchange because I was living from head knowledge, not from a Spirit-filled heart.

Enemy Tactics

In each chapter, we'll also take time to expose the enemy's tactics—because deception is most effective when it goes unnoticed. The enemy doesn't just tempt us with obvious sin; he whispers lies, fuels pride, distorts truth, and encourages us to lean on self instead of God. This section is meant to shine a light on how those subtle strategies play out in real life, and how they influence the choices we make.

As you read, ask the Holy Spirit to reveal where these tactics might be at work in your own life. Use this section to grow in discernment—so you can recognize the difference between what looks spiritual and what is actually Spirit-led. The more we understand the enemy's patterns, the better equipped we are to stand in truth and walk in freedom.

Pride and Self-Reliance – "You're strong in faith. You're doing great."

The enemy twisted the visible fruit in my life into a reason to depend on myself. Because I was avoiding sin, obeying God externally, and receiving blessings, I began to think I had arrived—spiritually speaking. That's when pride crept in. Instead of drawing closer to God, I started standing on my own strength. I measured my faith by what I did for God, not how surrendered I was to Him.

This directly fed into the first key choice: performing out of religious obligation instead of living by the Spirit. Pride told me I could hold it all together. It said, *"You're doing great. Others need your help."* And that made me less dependent on God and less compassionate toward others.

Guilt-Driven Goodness – Serving to Prove Spiritual Worth Rather Than Out of Love

Without realizing it, I was trying to prove I was a "real Christian" by helping others. I did the right things, but not always with the right heart. I helped my landlord, not because I was led by love, but because I believed that serving her validated my walk with God. My service wasn't Spirit-fueled—it was driven by a quiet guilt that whispered, *"You need to do more to be worthy."*

This tactic undermined my second key choice. I wasn't choosing compassion and humility; I was masking guilt as goodness and calling it righteousness. It looked like ministry, but it lacked mercy.

False Identity and Labels – Taking Identity From "Being a Good Christian" Instead of Being a Child of God

I began to identify myself by how I appeared to others: obedient, disciplined, strong in faith. That became my label—*the good Christian woman.* But that wasn't my real identity. My identity is found in being a daughter of God, loved and secure, regardless of what I do. The enemy used this false identity to justify a superior attitude.

I wasn't loving people—I was managing them. I wasn't walking in sonship—I was performing in religion. This distorted identity fed into my third key choice, where I saw myself as "better" and started managing my landlord instead of walking with her in love.

Shame and Condemnation – Hidden Self-Judgment Projected as Judgment Toward Others

Deep down, I still carried shame from my failures and brokenness. But rather than confront that pain, I buried it beneath spiritual activity. That unresolved shame became judgment—not just toward myself, but projected onto others. I judged my landlord's struggle because I hadn't fully dealt with my own.

This tactic reinforced all the key choices. It kept me from the Spirit (because shame silences intimacy). It made compassion feel unsafe (because it exposed my own wounds). And it distorted love into control (because managing others felt safer than seeing myself clearly).

Division and Offense – Seeing Others as "Lesser" or Unworthy Creates Distance and Contempt

This tactic was subtle, but deadly. I didn't hate her. I wasn't cruel. But in my heart, I created distance. I saw her as the one who needed help—and me as the one who had it all together. That's not unity. That's division masked in responsibility. The enemy doesn't need us to hate each other to divide us—he just needs us to believe we're better.

This broke the flow of love and blocked true connection. It's how the religious spirit operates—by creating spiritual hierarchies that make us feel justified while keeping us distant.

Counterfeit Outcome

Every chapter will also include a section highlighting the *Counterfeit Outcomes*—the visible results produced when we make the wrong choices and follow the wrong voice. This section is important because the counterfeit often looks close enough to the real thing that it goes unchecked. But over time, it leads us away from intimacy with God and the power of walking in truth. These outcomes reveal where something is off, even if everything appears fine on the surface.

When we lean on our own strength, judge others through a lens of pride, or manage people instead of loving them—and those choices are fueled by the subtle and strategic tactics of the enemy—the result is a life that appears godly but lacks the heart of God. The outcomes aren't just missteps—they're spiritual counterfeits. They look like faith on the outside but lead us away from truth, power, and love on the inside. That's exactly what happened in my story. My life reflected the appearance of righteousness, but these were the fruit it produced:

Pride disguised as holiness

I believed I was strong in faith, but I was spiritually proud—measuring my walk with God by discipline instead of dependence. My confidence wasn't in Christ; it was in how well I could keep it together. That's not holiness—it's ego wrapped in religion.

Distance from the heart of God and blindness to the pain of others

Without realizing it, I drifted further from God's heart. I didn't grieve with those who grieved. I didn't feel their pain. I saw struggles as spiritual weakness instead of spiritual warfare. And in doing so, I missed countless opportunities to be His hands and feet.

Superficial service without love

I helped others, but not from a place of compassion. I served out of duty, image, and performance. It looked like ministry, but it lacked mercy. The people I "helped" didn't feel loved—they felt managed, because that's what I was doing.

Ineffective witness — pushing people away from Christ instead of drawing them near

Instead of drawing people to Jesus, I became a barrier. My spiritual pride, my lack of empathy, and my performative faith made others feel judged, not welcomed. The religious spirit doesn't just affect your relationship with God—it distorts how others experience Him through you.

Areas of Salvation Impacted

Salvation is more than a moment—it's an ongoing work of transformation that touches every part of our lives. In each chapter, we'll look at the specific areas of salvation that are impacted when we fall into the counterfeit life. This section is designed to show how the enemy's tactics and our misaligned choices don't just produce bad outcomes—they also interrupt the full expression of what Jesus paid for. As you read, reflect on whether any of these areas feel distant, stagnant, or strained in your own life. The goal isn't condemnation—it's revelation, so you can invite God to restore what's been hindered.

Indwelling of the Holy Spirit

Though the Spirit was present in me, I wasn't living in communion with Him. I wasn't being led or empowered by Him. I was living the Christian life in my own strength, silencing His voice with my own self-discipline. This grieved the Spirit and kept me from walking in His power and intimacy.

A New Heart and a Renewed Mind

God had given me a new heart, but I hadn't allowed it to be fully softened. Pride hardened what was meant to be tender. I still operated from old thought patterns—judgment, comparison, self-reliance. My mind wasn't being renewed because I wasn't surrendering it daily.

Peace With God

I had access to peace with God, but I often felt frustrated, angry, or distant. That peace was blocked by my own will. I didn't trust God's ways fully because I still wanted mine. I obeyed externally while wrestling internally, forfeiting the peace that comes through true surrender.

Purpose and Spiritual Gifts

Though I was walking in some form of purpose, it was limited. I wasn't fully submitted, and I wasn't asking the Holy Spirit how to use the gifts God had given me. The religious spirit redirected my gifts toward image and productivity instead of service and love. As a result, my impact was restrained, and my purpose became blurred.

Forgiveness of Sin

Pride made it hard to see my own sin. I wasn't out living wild—but I was self-righteous, and that's just as dangerous. When we don't recognize our need for grace daily, we stop repenting, stop softening, and stop growing. I had been forgiven, but I wasn't walking in the daily humility that keeps us aware of that incredible gift.

Faith in Action

Every revelation requires a response. That's why each chapter includes a *Faith in Action* section—a practical look at what it means to walk in truth, partner with the Holy Spirit, and live out the restoration God is offering. This section isn't about trying harder—it's about surrendering deeper. These aren't tasks to check off, but invitations into transformation. Use this space to prayerfully consider what the Holy Spirit may be asking of you. What needs to be repented of, restored, or reoriented in your heart and habits? Faith doesn't just agree with truth—it acts on it.

As I shared earlier, I didn't wake up one day and realize I had fallen into the trap of the religious spirit. At the time, everything looked right on the outside. But as we'll explore more in another chapter, that same spirit eventually wore me down and led me into deeper compromise. I ended up backsliding for a few years. It wasn't until I returned to God and finally came to a place of full submission and surrender that He began revealing the truth of what had really happened during that earlier season. It was only then that I could begin responding—slowly, painfully, honestly.

These are the steps I had to take. And I want to be clear: they didn't happen all at once. It took time. These are not quick fixes—they are part of a long road of restoration. But each one drew me closer to truth, freedom, and the kind of righteousness that actually reflects Christ.

Repenting of Spiritual Pride and Asking God to Reveal Hidden Judgment

I had to confess that I saw myself as better than others. I repented not just for how I viewed my landlord, but for the deeper pattern in my heart—the instinct to judge, compare, and distance. I asked God to show me the places where judgment had taken root, even when it sounded like "truth." And He did. Conviction came gently, but clearly.

Praying for Genuine Love to Replace Duty-Driven Service

I began to pray differently. Not just for God to help me serve, but for Him to help me love. I asked for His heart—for compassion, patience, and empathy. I stopped trying to "be good" and started asking Him to change me from the inside. I didn't want to look like Jesus—I wanted to love like Him.

Inviting the Holy Spirit to Lead, Guide, and Correct

This meant surrendering daily. Letting go of my to-do list and asking the Holy Spirit to order my steps. To show me what He saw in people, in situations, and in me. I began to ask for correction, not just blessing. I stopped treating the Spirit like a silent partner and started treating Him like the one in charge.

Reflecting on Jesus' Interactions With Sinners and the Outcast

I studied how Jesus responded to people—how He touched the leper, defended the woman caught in adultery, dined with tax collectors. He didn't manage people—He met them. He didn't stand at a distance—He stooped low in love. I asked myself: *Do I treat people like Jesus would? Or like someone trying to earn His approval?* That question began to change how I show up in every relationship.

Seeking Reconciliation Where Spiritual Pride Has Caused Harm

Part of walking in humility meant going back. I had to acknowledge the harm my pride caused, even if it wasn't intentional. I asked God to show me who I had hurt—who I had judged, dismissed, or distanced myself from. And when He did, I reached out. I apologized. I took responsibility. Because spiritual pride doesn't just affect your walk with God—it damages others. And real healing requires going back to make things right.

Prayer

Father God,

I come before You today with an open heart. If there is any way I've been living from pride, performance, or spiritual self-reliance—reveal it to me. I don't want to look righteous on the outside while being distant from You on the inside. Show me where I've judged others instead of loving them. Show me where I've obeyed out of fear or image, instead of surrender and trust.

Holy Spirit, I invite You to lead me. Soften my heart. Replace striving with rest, routine with relationship, and duty with love. Help me walk in truth, not appearance. In humility, not superiority. In grace, not guilt. Break every stronghold of the religious spirit in my life, and teach me how to live from Your presence—not my performance.

Jesus, I want to follow You—not just with my words or my works, but with my whole heart. Thank You for Your mercy, for Your patience, and for calling me deeper. I choose surrender today. Finish the good work You've started in me.

In Jesus' Name I pray, Amen.

Areas of Study

Finally, each chapter will end with a section dedicated to *Areas of Study*—to lead you to the Word of God. This is meant to give you a path for going deeper, because growth doesn't end when the chapter does. Use these references to sit with God, search the Word, and build spiritual endurance through study and reflection. Ask the Holy Spirit to guide your time, highlight what's meant for you in this season, and help you walk more fully in the truth.

Scriptures

Luke 18:9–14 — The Pharisee and the tax collector: two postures before God.

1 Corinthians 13 — Love is the true measure of maturity, not knowledge or gifts.

Romans 8:1–14 — Walking by the Spirit, not the flesh or the law.

Matthew 23:25–28 — Jesus' rebuke of outward righteousness with inward decay.

Biblical Figures

The Pharisees — The danger of pride wrapped in religious tradition.

Jesus — The model of compassion, humility, and truth in love.

Paul (Before and After) — A clear example of transformation from religious zealot to Spirit-led servant.

Spiritual Practices

Daily Repentance — Asking God to reveal hidden pride and judgment.

Surrendering Spiritual Pride — Laying down performance and comparison.

Studying the Compassion of Christ — Meditating on how Jesus treated the broken and outcast.

Listening Prayer — Making space for the Holy Spirit to speak, lead, and correct.

Closing Reflection

It's easy to miss the religious spirit because it hides in the places we feel most proud of—our discipline, our convictions, our visible faithfulness. But as my story reveals, outward obedience without inward surrender is not the life Jesus died to give us. The religious spirit offers a counterfeit righteousness—one that focuses on behavior over heart, performance over presence, and pride over compassion. Overtime this completely distorts who we are and limits what we do for the Kingdom.

Looking back, I realize I wasn't just trying to live for God—I was trying to prove myself to Him. And that need to prove is where the enemy gained ground. Pride told me I was doing better than others. Judgment convinced me I was helping when I was really withholding love. Self-reliance masked as maturity kept me from experiencing the intimacy God desired.

But even in my blindness, God was patient. He let me walk through the fire—not to punish me, but to refine me. And in that refining, He revealed what I could not see on my own: that I was managing righteousness without being moved by love. That I was standing tall in spiritual strength, yet hollow inside.

If this chapter stirred something in you—if you've recognized places where you've performed rather than abided, judged rather than loved, or obeyed without intimacy—then let that recognition lead to repentance. Let it bring you back to the feet of Jesus, where true righteousness begins.

Not in our effort, but in His grace. Not in proving anything, but in receiving everything He already paid for.

You don't have to keep living this way. You don't have to wear strength like a mask or use service to earn worth. The heart of God is not reserved for those who perform the best—it's poured out on those who come humbly. Let the Holy Spirit reveal what needs to shift. Let love replace judgment. Let grace undo pride. And let today be the day you stop striving and start truly abiding.

Because righteousness isn't a front. It's a fruit. And it grows best in surrendered soil.

CHAPTER 4

Whose Voice Defines You? — Identity, Worth, and the Labels We Believe

———•———

My sheep hear my voice, and I know them, and they follow me. I give them eternal life, and they will never perish, and no one will snatch them out of my hand." John 10:27–28

Every day, voices are trying to tell us who we are. Some are loud and obvious—the critics, the culture, the comparisons. Others are quiet but persistent—shame, past mistakes, inner vows, and fears. And unless we're intentional, those voices begin to define us more than the One who created us.

This is the trap the enemy sets. He doesn't just want to tempt you— he wants to rename you. Because if he can convince you that your worth is based on your performance, your past, or other people's opinions, then he can keep you from ever walking in your God-given identity.

This chapter is about whose voice you're listening to—and whose voice you believe.

Scenario

Jason always knew he wasn't the "smart one." At least, that's what he told himself. It wasn't just the report cards or the test scores that confirmed it—it was the way his older brother got celebrated for straight A's while he was met with sighs and disappointment. "If you just applied yourself…" "Why can't you be more like—" He heard those phrases more times than he could count.

Over time, Jason stopped trying. What was the point? Every mistake just seemed to prove he wasn't "cut out for much." The labels stuck—lazy, underachiever, irresponsible. He started wearing them like a second skin, not because he liked them, but because he didn't know how to peel them off anymore.

Now in his early twenties, Jason works part-time stocking shelves at a grocery store. It's not that he lacks dreams—sometimes he imagines owning his own business or going back to school. But just as quickly as the dreams appear, so do the doubts. *Who are you kidding? You can't handle that.* He shrugs them off and scrolls his phone instead.

Jason goes to church off and on. He believes in God—or at least the idea of God. He listens politely to sermons but zones out during worship. When people talk about calling or purpose, he mentally checks out. *That's for people who've figured things out. Not me.* He doesn't reject God— but he can't imagine God would really want to use someone like him.

One Sunday, a man from church—James—approaches him after service. James owns a small but growing business and has been watching Jason over the past few months. "I see potential in you," James says. "You've got a good spirit. You're observant. You're teachable. I think you'd be a great fit for a new role I'm hiring for. It's more responsibility, but I'd be willing to train you."

Jason smiles and nods, but everything in him recoils. *What if I fail? What if he's wrong about me?* He thanks James for thinking of him but says he's not really looking for a change right now. "I'm just not ready for that kind of thing."

What Jason doesn't say is that deep down, he doesn't believe he's capable. The words from the past still echo louder than God's truth. The counterfeit identity still feels safer than the risk of stepping into something new. So he walks away from the opportunity—not because he lacks skill, but because he's still in agreement with a lie.

He doesn't realize it, but he just said no to God's invitation to begin discovering who he really is.

Key Choices

Jason's story may seem ordinary, but it's where countless lives quietly derail. Not with rebellion or scandal, but with resignation. We settle for the names we've been called, the failures we've experienced, or the silence we've endured—and begin to build an identity around them. The enemy knows that if he can shape our sense of self, he can steer the direction of our lives. That's why the question isn't just *"Who am I?"*—it's *"Whose voice do I trust to answer that question?"*

This is the battleground of identity. And on it, we face a critical fork in the road.

1. Believe What the World Says About You... or What God Says About You

You can define yourself by your past, your performance, or other people's opinions—or you can choose to believe what Scripture says is already true of you in Christ. One leads to striving and shame; the other to rest and renewal.

2. Agree with Old Labels... or Break Agreement and Receive a New Name

The enemy often doesn't need to invent new lies—he just needs you to keep agreeing with the old ones. Freedom comes when you renounce false labels and receive the name God gives: *Chosen. Beloved. Redeemed. His.*

3. Live from Fear of Failure... or Walk by Faith in Your Identity

When you don't know who you are, every risk feels like a threat. But when you know you're loved, called, and equipped by God, you begin to step out—not because you're confident in yourself, but because you're confident in Him.

4. Stay in the Familiar... or Step Into Who You're Becoming

The false self is familiar, even if it's painful. But transformation begins the moment you say, "I don't want to live by lies anymore." That choice— to leave behind who the world says you are and embrace who God says you are—is how you begin to walk in purpose.

Enemy Tactics

The enemy doesn't need to steal your future if he can convince you you're unworthy of it. Long before he attacks your calling, he goes after your confidence—distorting your identity, twisting your worth, and silencing the truth with lies.

These attacks don't always look like obvious warfare. Often, they show up in the form of a parent's disappointment, a coach's harsh words, a missed opportunity, or an internal script you've repeated for years. But make no mistake—there's strategy behind the shame. These aren't just unfortunate experiences. They're carefully planted lies, meant to hold you hostage.

Here are three of the enemy's most common tactics in this battle over identity:

False Identity and Labels

The enemy is a master of counterfeit naming. He tries to define you by what you've done or what's been done to you—*failure, addict, victim, burden.* He'll even use your personality, struggles, or circumstances to create a warped identity: "That's just who I am." But when identity is based on anything other than what God has declared, it becomes a trap.

These labels may feel familiar, even protective. But they keep you stuck in cycles of self-doubt and limitation. They blind you from seeing the truth that your identity is not earned—it's received. You don't become who you are by fixing yourself. You become who you are by surrendering to the One who made you.

Shame and Condemnation

Shame is the lie that says, not *only did you mess up—but you are a mess.* It doesn't stop at your actions; it attacks your identity. And condemnation is its weapon. While conviction leads to change, condemnation leads to hiding. You pull back from God, from purpose, from community—because deep down, you believe you're unworthy of restoration.

This is how the enemy keeps you from healing. As long as you're wearing shame, you won't receive grace. You'll keep trying to clean yourself up before coming to God, not realizing He's the only one who can make you whole.

Comparison and Envy

Comparison distorts your vision. Instead of seeing who God uniquely created you to be, you fixate on what others have and where you fall short. The enemy uses envy to shift your focus from gratitude to inadequacy. You begin to believe you're always behind, never enough, or disqualified because someone else is "better."

But comparison isn't just discouraging—it's paralyzing. It keeps you from taking steps forward because you're too busy watching someone else's race. And ironically, it often leads to hidden pride—measuring your worth by the people you think you're better or worse than. Either way, your focus is off of Jesus and onto yourself.

Counterfeit Outcome

When the enemy succeeds in naming you, he doesn't need to bind you— you'll live in a prison of your own agreement.

Jason's life might seem uneventful, but spiritually, he's stuck. Not because he's defying God, but because he's avoiding Him. Instead of resisting God's truth with rebellion, he resists it with resignation. He doesn't expect more because he doesn't believe he deserves more. This is where self-pity becomes one of the enemy's most effective weapons.

Self-pity is deceptive because it feels like honesty. *"I'm just being real with myself—I'm not capable." "I've made too many mistakes."* But self-pity is never rooted in truth—it's rooted in agreement with a lie. It convinces you that your weakness is the end of the story, rather than the starting point of God's grace.

Worse, self-pity subtly turns your gaze inward. You start writing the wrong narratives about your life. What you didn't get. How hard life's been. What others have that you don't. It creates a victim mindset where everyone else is responsible for your pain, and God becomes distant or silent, not because He left—but because self-pity drowns out His voice.

And here's the most dangerous part: self-pity masquerades as humility, but it's often driven by hidden pride. It says, *"I know better than God about what I'm capable of. I've already decided what I am and what I'm not."* It refuses to receive grace because grace requires surrender—and self-pity would rather stay in control of the narrative than risk being transformed.

This is the slow suffocation of the counterfeit life:

- You stay in your comfort zone, not because you have peace, but because you fear being disappointed.

- You settle for survival, not because it's holy, but because you've stopped hoping for more.

- You claim you're "just being realistic," but deep down, you're afraid that God's promises won't apply to someone like you.

The result? A life that looks safe, humble, and unproblematic—but is actually marked by fear, bitterness, and spiritual paralysis. A life that never steps into purpose because it refuses to believe God's truth about identity.

Areas of Salvation Impacted

A New Identity as a Child of God

Salvation doesn't just secure your eternity—it redefines your identity. When you place your faith in Jesus, you are no longer defined by your past, your performance, or your pain. You are adopted into God's family (Romans 8:15–17), sealed with His Spirit, and given a new name: child of God.

But many believers continue to live like orphans—unsure of their place, striving for worth, and insecure in their value. When you fail to embrace your new identity, you miss out on the security, authority, and intimacy that come from knowing who you belong to.

Rejecting false labels isn't just a mindset shift—it's spiritual alignment with the truth of your salvation. You don't need to earn a new identity. You need to believe the one that's already been given.

A New Heart and a Renewed Mind

Ezekiel 36:26 promises that God gives us a new heart and puts a new spirit within us. Romans 12:2 calls us to be transformed by the renewing of our minds. These are not poetic ideas—they are essential parts of salvation.

But when we cling to old labels and patterns of thinking, we resist that renewal. We try to follow Jesus with a mind still shaped by fear and a heart still governed by shame. Self-pity, condemnation, and comparison all block the flow of God's transformative power in our thoughts and emotions.

Salvation equips you with everything needed to think differently and live differently—but it requires participation. You must actively reject lies, take thoughts captive, and invite the Holy Spirit to reshape your inner life. Without that surrender, you carry a new name with an old mindset—and stay stuck in the same pain.

Purpose and Spiritual Gifts

You were not just saved *from* sin—you were saved *for* purpose. Ephesians 2:10 tells us we are God's workmanship, created in Christ Jesus for good works prepared in advance for us to do. Every believer has spiritual gifts and a role to play in the Body of Christ.

But if you don't know who you are, you'll never believe you're qualified to do what God has called you to. False identity stifles purpose. Shame silences your gifts. Comparison leads you to envy someone else's calling instead of walking in your own.

The enemy knows that if he can keep you confused about who you are, he can keep you sidelined from what you're meant to do. When you reclaim your God-given identity, you don't just get freedom—you get direction. You step into purpose with clarity and confidence, knowing your worth doesn't come from what you do but from whose you are.

Faith in Action

Jason didn't rebel—he retreated. Like many of us, he didn't reject God outright. He simply kept listening to the wrong voice. And because of that, he turned down a God-given opportunity not because he couldn't do it, but because he believed he wasn't enough.

Maybe you've been there. Maybe you're still there.

The counterfeit life isn't always marked by obvious sin—it's marked by silent surrender to a lesser identity. That's why breaking free starts with recognition and repentance—not just of outward actions, but of inward agreements.

The good news is: you don't have to keep living this way. If you've identified with Jason's story, then the Holy Spirit may be gently uncovering places in your own life where you've believed lies and walked away from the life God is trying to give you.

Jason's Next Step — and Yours

Recognize the Lie

Jason's decision wasn't just fear-based—it was rooted in an identity formed by years of labels and shame. Take time to ask:

- What beliefs are keeping me from saying yes to God's invitations?

- What labels have I accepted that God never gave me?

Repent for Agreement

Repentance isn't just about what we've done wrong—it's about what we've agreed with. Jason didn't just turn down a job—he aligned with a lie. Ask God to forgive you for believing anything about yourself that contradicts His Word.

Renounce and Declare

Speak the opposite of the lie. "I am not a failure. I am God's workmanship, created for good works." "I am not inadequate. I am equipped by the Spirit of God." Declare truth daily until it becomes your internal reality.

Re-engage With Faith

Jason's next step would be to go back to James and say, "I was scared, but I want to try." What about you? What do you need to go back to? A missed opportunity? A dream you gave up on? A calling you've avoided?

Faith doesn't just believe—it acts. Take a step. Start small if you need to. But move.

Prayer

Father, I confess that I have believed lies about who I am. I've worn labels that You never gave me and allowed fear, shame, and comparison to silence my confidence in You. I repent for the ways I've limited myself and rejected Your truth—out of fear, pride, or pain.

Today, I renounce every false identity I've accepted. I break agreement with labels like failure, unworthy, inadequate, and unwanted. I receive the identity You've given me in Christ—I am chosen, beloved, redeemed, and equipped for every good work.

Holy Spirit, lead me in the renewing of my mind and healing of my heart. Help me hear Your voice above every other. Give me boldness to say yes to what You're inviting me into. I choose truth over comfort. I choose faith over fear. I choose to live as who You say I am.

In Jesus' name, Amen.

Areas of Study

If you want to break free from a counterfeit identity, you must replace the lies with truth—and that begins by immersing yourself in what God says about who you are. These passages and biblical examples will help you root your identity in Christ and live with the confidence that comes from knowing whose you are.

Ephesians 1–2

These chapters are a blueprint of who you are in Christ: chosen, adopted, redeemed, forgiven, sealed with the Holy Spirit, and seated with Christ. Read slowly. Highlight every phrase that speaks to your identity and inheritance.

> *"For we are God's handiwork, created in Christ Jesus to do good works, which God prepared in advance for us to do."*
> — Ephesians 2:10

Romans 8:15–17

This passage reminds us that we are not slaves to fear but children of God, adopted into His family with full access to His inheritance and authority.

> *"The Spirit you received brought about your adoption to sonship. And by him we cry, 'Abba, Father.'"*
> — Romans 8:15

Judges 6 – The Life of Gideon

Gideon saw himself as the weakest of the weak, but God called him a "mighty warrior." His story is a powerful reminder that God doesn't speak to your insecurity—He speaks to your God given identity. Like Jason, Gideon had to choose whose voice he would believe.

"Pardon me, my lord," Gideon replied, "but how can I save Israel? My clan is the weakest... and I am the least in my family." The Lord answered, "I will be with you..."
— Judges 6:15–16

Colossians 3:1–17 – Putting On the New Self

This passage offers a practical and spiritual framework for shedding the old identity and putting on the new one. It's a daily, intentional process.

Closing Reflection

The loudest voice in your life will always shape your identity.

For Jason, that voice wasn't God's—it was a mix of past disappointments, spoken labels, and silent agreements. And even though he believed in God, he didn't yet believe what God said about *him*. That's where many of us get stuck. Not in open rebellion, but in quiet resignation. We don't run from God—we just stop listening to Him where it matters most: in how we see ourselves.

But identity is not something we create. It's something we *receive*. And receiving it starts with rejecting the lies we've carried for far too long.

You may not have grown up hearing words of life. You may have made mistakes that still echo in your heart. You may look at others and wonder if God could ever use someone like you. But here's the truth: He already chose you. He already loves you. He already sees you as His own. The invitation isn't to prove yourself worthy—it's to *believe* you already are because of what Jesus did.

If you've been living beneath your calling, second-guessing your worth, or shrinking back from purpose, this is your moment to choose a new voice. The Father's voice. The one that doesn't flatter, but *restores*. The one that doesn't condemn, but *calls*. The one that doesn't shame, but *saves*.

Let today be the day you stop letting the enemy define you by your past—and let God name you according to your future. Because your identity isn't in what you've done. It's in who you belong to. And He is still speaking.

The only question is: *Will you believe Him?*

CHAPTER 5

The Trap of Performing for Love

———————•———————

Are you so foolish? Having begun by the Spirit, are you now being perfected by the flesh? Galatians 3:3

I'm adding my personal experience here to expand the message to include a different and very real counterfeit: building identity on outcomes, performance, and personal strength, and being driven by the enemy rather than intimacy with God and leading from the Holy Spirit.

While Jason's struggle centers around internalizing lack and inadequacy, mine reveals the danger of relying on capability and achievement—both result in misplaced identity, just on opposite ends of the spectrum. I'm hoping to provide a fuller picture of how identity can be distorted, whether through rejection or pride.

Personal Experience

From a young age, I believed I could do anything. When I was nine years old, I found myself face-to-face with my worst fear. That moment taught me something that shaped who I am: An understanding I could either be trapped by fear or freed by facing it. I chose the latter. I didn't just face my fears—I chased them. I became bold, determined, driven.

God was present even then, trying to teach me how to rely on Him—how to seek, submit, surrender, obey, and follow His leading. But the enemy saw the same potential and twisted it. Instead of learning dependence on God, I learned to depend on myself. Instead of being Spirit-led, I became performance-driven. The enemy took what God meant for strength and forged a counterfeit: self-reliance.

Self-reliance, confidence, drive; it's all very appealing, they're qualities and personality traits that are applauded and encouraged. I embraced the accolades and I learned to chase excellence and set high standards. I wanted to be perfect. I wanted to succeed. But underneath it all, the enemy was establishing the wrong mindsets and understanding. I was learning to believe that love is earned through achievement, approval is gained through results, and worth is proven through success.

It was in my nature to be a big thinker, a visionary, an ambitious doer. I pursued my dreams and visions with everything I had. I've failed a lot—because I've risked a lot. And while God, in His mercy, protected me from success that would have destroyed me, the enemy used each failure to deepen my internal strongholds. I became angry, furious, and deeply wounded by my failures. I had sacrificed everything in the pursuit of my hopes and dreams and thought once I made it everything would be okay so failure led me to go deeper into isolation, ashamed, and convinced I wasn't worthy of love unless I produced something of value.

My identity became entangled in what I did, what I accomplished, and how I performed—especially in entrepreneurship. Even after I gave my life to Jesus, the strongholds didn't disappear. They were deeply rooted—formed by years of striving, reinforced by the lies I had come to accept as truth. I still saw my worth through the lens of results. I still felt like I had something to prove—to others, to myself, and even to God. I still believed I needed to earn love. I was saved, but not yet free.

Those strongholds were driving me. They shaped how I approached God, how I worked, how I related to others. I was still measuring everything by the metrics of performance, not intimacy. My value was attached to what I could produce. I was building and creating, but not from rest. I was still led more by pressure than by peace.

And then came the *fiery furnace.*

God allowed everything around me to be stripped away—not to punish me, but to free me. It was in the fire that I stopped trying to outrun my brokenness. I stopped covering my wounds with achievements. I finally began to face the lies, not just the failures. That's where the real healing began.

I opened my Bible and stayed there. I started renewing my mind. Line by line, verse by verse, the Word began to rebuild me. I began to learn what it meant to live loved—not for what I could do, but because of who He is and who I am in Him.

God began to reintroduce me to my true identity—not the one shaped by performance or pain, but the one secured by grace and sealed by the Spirit. I learned how to rest, how to abide, how to stop striving and start trusting. The more I saw Jesus, the more I saw who I truly was. And the more I saw the truth, the more the strongholds crumbled.

I came to understand that the root of everything I had believed—the driving force behind the ambition, the perfectionism, the pressure—was a deep desire to be loved and accepted. The enemy exploited that desire. But God, in His love, exposed it and healed it.

This chapter isn't about abandoning excellence or ambition. It's about exposing the lie that our value comes from them. It's about laying down the need to perform and picking up the invitation to simply be—loved, chosen, secure, and led by the Spirit.

Key Choices

My story may look different from yours, but the trap is often the same: We start with good intentions and godly desires, but somewhere along the way, the enemy distorts our understanding of value, purpose, and identity. What began as a pursuit of excellence becomes a performance for love. What started as ambition turns into striving. And before we know it, we're building a life around what we do, not who we are. These are the choices I made—some unknowingly, others out of fear or pride—but each one moved me further from truth and deeper into the counterfeit. Let's walk through them together.

1. Choosing to see your value as inherent vs. earned through accomplishments

I spent years believing that I had to *earn* love, worth, and identity through performance. If I succeeded, I felt worthy. If I failed, I felt ashamed and unlovable. But God doesn't value us because of what we do—He loves us because of who we are in Him. Learning this truth didn't come from success, but from being stripped of everything I used to define myself.

2. Choosing obedience over ambition

I was driven. Ambitious. Focused. I believed I was chasing purpose, but I was really chasing validation and results. Obedience felt slow and limiting. But God showed me that obedience is where transformation happens. Ambition builds towers in our name; obedience builds altars in His.

3. Choosing rest and Sabbath vs. hustle and burnout

Even after I gave my life to Jesus, I kept pushing. Working. Producing. Hustling. I called it discipline, but it was really fear—fear of being still, of being unworthy if I wasn't doing something. Sabbath exposed the truth: I didn't know how to just *be* with God. Rest required trust, and I had to learn that He loved me even when I stopped performing.

4. Choosing to trust God vs. taking matters into your own hands

I didn't wait on God's timing—I forced things. I thought my breakthrough would come through effort, not surrender. But taking matters into my own hands led to failure after failure. It wasn't until I trusted God to redefine success that I found peace in the process—even when the results didn't look like I imagined.

5. Choosing to pursue God's purpose for your life vs. chasing worldly success

I didn't chase money or fame—but I *did* chase significance. I wanted my life to mean something, to have impact. But even that pursuit can become a trap if God isn't at the center. It wasn't until the fire stripped away the layers of my dreams that I saw what God was really after—my heart, not my platform.

Enemy Tactics

We don't usually recognize we've made these choices until the fruit begins to show—when burnout sets in, when our worth feels unstable, or when God asks us to rest and we panic. The enemy rarely comes at us with obvious lies; instead, he twists truth just enough to keep us driven instead of led, applauded instead of anchored, exhausted instead of free. These were the choices that formed the foundation of my counterfeit life—and behind each one was a tactic designed to pull me away from living as a daughter and keep me hustling like a servant. Let's expose how the enemy operates in this space.

Counterfeiting Purpose with Performance – "Keep going, this is purpose."

The enemy didn't tell me to stop building—he convinced me I was building for God while actually feeding my own identity through performance. I thought I was pursuing purpose, but I was performing for meaning. I equated being busy with being faithful. The more I did, the more valuable I felt. But it was a trap. I wasn't living out my purpose through intimacy—I was trying to prove my worth through productivity. What looked like purpose was actually pressure.

Twisting Ambition into Self-Glorification – "If you don't do it, no one will."

God gave me vision, but the enemy distorted it. He inflated it until it became all-consuming. He told me I was the one who had to make it happen. What began as a desire to serve turned into a desperate need to be seen. I didn't recognize it at first—because everything I was doing looked good. It looked Kingdom-focused. But the focus slowly shifted off of God and onto what I could build. It became about impact, reach, results. The enemy lured me into thinking my significance was tied to the size of what I accomplished.

Attaching Identity to Outcomes – "Your results define your worth."

I didn't realize how deeply my identity was tied to what I could produce. If things went well, I felt affirmed. If they didn't, I spiraled. I began to view myself through the lens of wins and losses. I questioned my value with every setback. The enemy used my entrepreneurial failures to reinforce the lie that I wasn't enough. I wasn't just experiencing disappointment—I was becoming it. I stopped seeing myself as a daughter and started measuring myself by results.

But it didn't stop there. The enemy used those same failures to plant an even more dangerous lie: that God didn't care. That He wasn't with me. That He had abandoned me in the middle of my calling. I looked at the work I had poured myself into, the sacrifices I had made, and the lack of fruit—and I started to believe that God wasn't showing up. I threw myself pity parties, just like Jason, rehearsing all the things I had done, all the obedience I had shown, and how little I had to show for it. The enemy twisted my disappointment into distrust. He convinced me that I was on my own. That God had stepped back. That my pain was proof of His absence. And once I believed that, I no longer just questioned my worth—I started to question God's character.

Making Love Conditional – "You'll be loved when you succeed."

Without realizing it, I believed love was something I had to earn. I believed I had to show up strong, capable, successful in order to be worthy of affection—from people, from myself, and even from God. The enemy made love feel transactional. He made me think I had to reach a certain level of performance before I could rest in belonging. And when I didn't hit the mark, I pulled away—I didn't want anyone to see me "less than." That wasn't love. That was fear wearing a mask.

Over time, the distortion went even deeper. I began to question if *God's* love was conditional too. I knew what Scripture said, but in the silence, the lack of breakthrough, the constant striving with no reward—I began to wonder if I had fallen short of earning even God's affection. The enemy twisted every delay, every closed door, into evidence that God's love was tied to my results. That if I had done better, tried harder, or produced more, maybe then He would bless me, help me, or come through. I didn't just doubt my worth—I doubted whether I was still loved. And that lie didn't just keep me working—it kept me from resting in the truth of who God is.

Promoting Hustle Over Holiness – "Rest is weakness. Keep producing."

I didn't know how to stop. Hustle had become part of my identity. I called it discipline and drive, but deep down, I was afraid of what stillness would expose. The enemy convinced me that rest was lazy and that if I slowed down, I would lose my edge. So I kept pushing—long after God was calling me to be still. I was doing for God, but I wasn't being with God. And over time, my output outpaced my intimacy, and my soul paid the price.

Using Failure to Reinforce Shame and Isolation – "You blew it. Again."

Each failure cut deeper than the last. I didn't just feel disappointment—I felt disqualified. I isolated. I withdrew. The enemy used my failures to reinforce the narrative that I was a burden, that I should've done better, that maybe I had missed my chance. I stopped sharing honestly. I put up a front. And behind that performance was a lot of pain I hadn't faced. The shame didn't just keep me quiet—it kept me from healing.

Counterfeit OutCome

The tactics worked. That's the thing—we don't just hear the lie; we start living it. And over time, the fruit begins to show. When identity is built on performance, and love feels earned, we start to produce outcomes that look like success on the surface but leave us empty underneath. These aren't just personality traits or bad habits—they're the consequences of living from a counterfeit version of truth. I didn't set out to build my life this way, but when I looked around, this is what I found:

Spiritual exhaustion masked as drive

I was always going. Always building. Always reaching for the next thing. On the outside, it looked like motivation and drive. It looked like perseverance and endurance. But inside, I was tired—physically, emotionally, and spiritually. I was pouring out from a place that was never being refilled. I confused hustle with holiness, and I wore burnout like a badge of honor.

Isolation that felt like independence

I convinced myself I didn't need help, I didn't need people, that I was built differently, stronger, and more capable. But the truth is, I was so fooled that I couldn't even feel or identify loneliness. I wouldn't dare admit I was ashamed to be seen in my failure and too proud to admit I was hurting. What looked like confidence was often just self-protection.

A distorted view of love and worth

Love became something I chased, not something I received. I judged myself harshly and kept others at arm's length unless I felt I had something to offer or gain from them. My ability to receive love—especially God's love—was tied to how "worthy" I felt. And most days, I didn't feel worthy at all.

Deep resentment toward God

When you give everything and it still doesn't work, it's easy to start questioning God. That's where I found myself. I resented Him for not rewarding my obedience the way I expected. I felt abandoned. Betrayed. Like I was upholding my end of the deal and He wasn't. But the truth was—I had made a deal He never agreed to.

A fractured identity

I couldn't tell where my calling ended and my worth began. I thought I was pursuing what God asked of me, but I had tied who I was to what I was doing. So when the work failed, I didn't just feel like I had lost a project—I felt like I had lost myself.

Areas of Salvation Impacted

Forgiveness of Sins

Because I tied love and approval to performance, I carried shame even after being forgiven. I believed I had to earn my way back into God's favor when I failed. I knew God forgave me—but I didn't know how to forgive myself. That kept me from receiving the full freedom that comes from knowing Jesus already paid the price.

A New Identity as a Child of God

I knew I was saved, but I didn't know how to live like a daughter. My identity was still shaped by outcomes, performance, and external validation. I hadn't yet rooted my identity in the finished work of Jesus.

Until that shifted, I was still operating like a servant earning favor—not a child already favored.

A New Heart and a Renewed Mind

My heart still held onto old patterns—self-reliance, perfectionism, shame. And my mind wasn't yet renewed with truth. I was still interpreting my value through the lens of success and failure. Instead of letting the Word of God reshape how I thought, I let the world's measurements rule me. Sanctification stalled because I was trying to transform myself rather than allowing God to do it through His Spirit and His Word.

Access to God's Presence

Busyness and performance created distance. I didn't feel like I could approach God when I wasn't doing "well." I'd pull away when I failed or struggled, not realizing that His presence isn't earned—it's given. The enemy used my striving to make me feel disqualified, but Jesus tore the veil. Access was always available—I just didn't believe I was welcome.

Purpose, Calling, and Spiritual Gifts

I confused calling with personal ambition. I chased vision instead of waiting on God's voice. I was gifted, but I misused those gifts to prove myself rather than glorify Him. My purpose became tangled in outcomes and metrics. Until I let go of performance, I couldn't walk fully in the Spirit-led purpose He had assigned to me.

Faith in Action

This wasn't something I recognized overnight, and it definitely wasn't something I fixed quickly. The transformation came slowly—over time, through tears (lots of tears), Scripture, silence, and surrender. The strongholds that had shaped how I saw myself, how I worked, and how I related to God didn't break all at once. They were deeply rooted. And God, in His mercy, didn't just rip them out—He gently revealed them, layer by layer. There was work to do, lots of work, but a completely different kind of work.

Repenting for Making Results My God and For Resenting God When They Didn't Come

I had to face the truth: I had idolized outcomes. I worshipped success without realizing it. I repented for letting results define my value and for believing they proved whether God loved me. I also had to repent for something deeper—for the anger, bitterness, and blame I had aimed at God when things didn't work out. I told Him I was hurt. That I felt abandoned. That I didn't trust Him. And then I asked Him to help me see Him rightly again.

Renewing My Mind in the Word of God, Daily and Diligently

I committed to being in the Word not for information or inspiration—but for transformation. I needed truth to become the foundation of how I thought, how I spoke to myself, how I saw God, and how I lived. This wasn't a one-week devotional—it was a lifestyle change. I wrote Scriptures out. I read them out loud. I replaced lies with verses. I repeated them until they rewired my thinking.

Letting Go of Image and Embracing Honest Introspection

I stopped pretending I was okay. I stopped performing strength. I let myself feel what I had avoided—disappointment, fear, shame. I journaled. I cried. I told God the unedited version of my story. I let Him speak into the parts of me I had kept hidden, even in prayer. That honesty became a turning point.

Asking the Holy Spirit to Redefine Love and Worth

I didn't just need healing—I needed redefinition. I asked the Holy Spirit to teach me what love actually is. What worth looks like when it isn't earned. I prayed for help to receive, not just to give. I stopped trying to "get it together" and started asking Him to put me back together from the inside out.

Choosing Rest Even When It Felt Unproductive

This was one of the hardest steps. Rest felt like failure. But I knew I had to obey. I began practicing Sabbath. I stepped back from tasks and to-do lists. I stopped trying to earn peace and just let myself experience it. Rest was where I finally began to understand grace—not just as a concept, but as a reality I could live in.

Prayer

Father,

I come before You with everything I've been carrying—every burden I've placed on myself, every lie I've believed, every way I've tried to prove my worth. I'm tired of striving. I'm tired of performing. And I don't want to live this way anymore. I repent for making results, success, and recognition more important than knowing You. I repent for building my identity on what I've done, instead of who You say I am.

God, I admit I've doubted Your love. I've questioned Your presence. I've even blamed You when things didn't go the way I thought they should. Forgive me. Help me see You rightly again. Heal the places in my heart that were shaped by lies. Break the strongholds of perfectionism, shame, and self-reliance. I don't want to be defined by what I do—I want to be defined by Your truth.

Holy Spirit, lead me in the renewing of my mind. I desire to establish Your Word in me. Teach me how to rest, how to receive, how to live as a daughter/son who is already loved. Help me stop performing for what I already have in You. I choose to trust You—even when I don't see the results. I choose to be still—even when it feels unfamiliar. I choose to be led, not driven.

Lead me out of the counterfeit. Lead me into truth.

In Jesus' name, Amen.

Areas of Study

Luke 10:38–42 — Mary and Martha

Study the contrast between Martha's doing and Mary's being. What was Jesus affirming? What was He gently correcting? Let this story expose your own tendency to equate service with value and learn what it means to choose "the better portion."

Romans 12:1–2 — Renewing the Mind

Spend time meditating on what it truly means to offer yourself as a living sacrifice—not just in action, but in surrender. Let this passage guide you into a renewed mind that isn't shaped by performance culture, but by the will of God.

John 15:1–8 — Abide and Bear Fruit

This passage is essential for understanding true fruitfulness. It doesn't come from striving—it comes from abiding. Reflect on what it means to remain in Jesus and let His words remain in you. Fruit that lasts always grows from intimacy, not activity.

Matthew 3:17 — Loved Before the Ministry

Jesus was affirmed by the Father *before* He did any miracles or ministry. Let that truth sink in: "This is My beloved Son, in whom I am well pleased." Study this verse to anchor your identity in being, not doing.

Psalm 139 — Fully Known and Deeply Loved

Return to this Psalm often. It affirms that God knows you intimately, loves you completely, and created you intentionally. You are not a project to manage. You are a person to be loved. Let these words wash over every place performance has distorted your view.

Galatians 3:1–3 — Starting by the Spirit, Finishing by the Flesh

Paul's warning to the Galatians still applies. Examine where you may have started in faith, but drifted into self-effort. This is a call back to grace—a call back to the Holy Spirit's leading.

Closing Reflection

You can give your life to Jesus and still live like you're trying to earn His love.

That was my story. And maybe, if you're honest, it's yours too. It doesn't always look like rebellion. Sometimes, it looks like ambition. Perfectionism. Relentless discipline. You may even think you're doing everything right. But deep down, you're exhausted—because you're not building from love, you're performing for it.

The enemy doesn't just attack your weakness—he exploits your strengths. He uses what looks good on the outside to build strongholds on the inside. And before long, your identity becomes entangled with your output. Your rest becomes compromised by your pressure. Your relationship with God becomes transactional instead of transformational.

Jason's story and mine might look different on the surface—his rooted in inadequacy, mine in achievement—but at their core, they reveal the same strategy of the enemy. Whether it's through shame or pride, failure or success, the enemy builds counterfeit lives by establishing lies and strongholds that distort how we see ourselves, how we see God, and how we define love and worth. Both of us fell into false identities—identities built on what we lacked or what we produced—when God was offering us something so much greater: the freedom to live as sons and daughters, rooted in truth, led by the Spirit, and secure in who He says we are. The enemy's goal is always bondage. But Jesus came to bring us back to the life God authored for us—one not earned by performance, but received through grace.

It took me a long time to realize that what I called strength was often just fear in disguise. That my constant doing was rooted in a belief that being wasn't enough. And that the lies I believed about my worth didn't break until I let God tear down the altar I had built to performance—and rebuild me in the quiet place of intimacy.

Maybe you're in that place now. Maybe the pressure is starting to crack you open. Maybe the striving isn't working anymore. If so, don't be afraid of the fire. Sometimes God allows everything else to fall so we can finally fall into Him.

You don't have to prove anything. You don't have to earn love. You are already seen, known, and chosen. God doesn't want what you can produce. He wants *you*—whole, surrendered, and finally at rest.

The invitation isn't to do more. It's to come home. Will you let go of performing… so you can finally be free?

CHAPTER 6

Shaped by Culture or
Transformed by Truth?

———————•———————

*"Do not be conformed to this world, but be transformed by
the renewal of your mind, that by testing you may discern
what is the will of God, what is good and acceptable and
perfect."* Romans 12:2

We live in a world where influence is currency and relevance is
rewarded. The pressure to be accepted, liked, and followed doesn't
just impact what we say—it can start to reshape what we believe. Culture
is loud, persuasive, and always evolving. And if we're not careful, we begin
to adjust truth to fit the moment instead of being transformed by the truth
that never changes. This chapter explores one of the enemy's most subtle
strategies: not pulling believers away from God, but slowly convincing
them to soften, reframe, and eventually compromise the message of the
Gospel. Because if he can dilute the truth, he can disarm its power.

Scenario

Tiana never set out to become an influencer. When she started sharing
her faith journey online, it was raw, passionate, and unapologetically
grounded in Scripture. Her early videos—messy, unfiltered, but full of
conviction—attracted thousands who were hungry for realness. She spoke

openly about repentance, sin, freedom in Christ, and the power of surrender.

But somewhere along the way, the metrics started to matter more. She didn't notice it at first. It was subtle. A friend DM'd her, "You should be careful how you say that—it might turn people off." A few brand collaborations encouraged her to "keep things inclusive" to avoid alienating any audience segments. When she posted a verse about sexual purity, she lost 800 followers overnight.

She told herself it wasn't compromise—it was strategy. "God's still using me," she reasoned, "I'm just learning how to package the message better."

Soon, she stopped saying "sin" and started saying "mistakes." She avoided the word "repentance" altogether. Hard topics like hell, judgment, or spiritual warfare were off-limits. Her posts still mentioned Jesus, but now He was more of a life coach than a Savior. Comments flooded in: "I love how positive and affirming you are!" "Finally, a Christian who gets it."

Tiana told herself this was impact. But behind the screen, she felt increasingly distant from God. Her quiet time had become content planning. The Word used to convict and shape her—now it served as a source of quotes to keep the algorithm happy.

One night, while prepping a reel on "manifesting God's best," she paused. The verse she'd planned to use—Jeremiah 29:11—felt hollow in her mouth. She couldn't shake the sense that something was off. She hadn't really prayed in weeks. Her Bible was dusty. Her fire had faded.

She'd stayed relevant—but at what cost?

Key Choices

Tiana didn't wake up one day and decide to water down the Gospel. Like many, she simply wanted to be liked, to belong, to "reach people." But when staying relevant becomes the goal, truth becomes negotiable. Slowly, subtly, the shift begins—not with denying God, but with softening His Word. Avoiding "hard" Scriptures. Prioritizing inspiration over repentance. Keeping the peace instead of proclaiming the truth.

It's the trap so many fall into: wanting to influence culture without being shaped by it first. But you can't transform a world you're trying to blend into. Tiana thought she was being strategic—but she was slowly becoming silent where it mattered most. And when you stop speaking truth, you're no longer standing in it.

This is the battleground of conviction. And on it, we face a critical fork in the road.

1. Please People… or Please God

Tiana adjusted her message to avoid offense, chasing likes and affirmation instead of truth. But faithfulness has never been about popularity. You either fear man or fear God—you can't do both.

2. Filter Truth to Keep the Peace… or Speak Truth in Love

She believed she was being more loving by avoiding hard truths. But real love doesn't stay silent when souls are at stake. We're not called to be harsh—but we are called to be honest.

3. Build a Platform… or Build God's Kingdom

Tiana began measuring impact by engagement, not obedience. But God doesn't reward influence—He rewards faithfulness. Are you building something that points to you, or something that glorifies Him?

4. Let Culture Shape Your Message… or Let Scripture Shape Your Mind

The more Tiana tried to "resonate," the more she conformed. Romans 12:2 calls us to be transformed by the renewing of our minds—not conformed to the world's narratives, trends, or ideologies.

5. Neglect the Secret Place… or Return to Intimacy with God

Her public voice grew louder while her private walk grew quieter. But no reel, post, or podcast can replace the voice of the Holy Spirit. When the Word becomes content instead of communion, your message may still look good—but your heart is growing cold.

Enemy Tactics

The enemy doesn't always show up with accusation. Sometimes, he comes with affirmation—strategically placed compliments, applause, or open doors that seem like blessings. That's how he got to Tiana. Not through fear, but through flattery. Not through rejection, but through acceptance. He disguised compromise as wisdom, delay as patience, and silence as peace.

These tactics are as old as Eden and just as effective. Here's how they played out in Tiana's life—and how they often show up in ours.

Flattery: "You're Reaching So Many—Don't Ruin It"

The comments, the messages, the collaborations—they all told Tiana she was "making a difference." The enemy used this praise to plant the idea that if she really wanted to keep helping people, she needed to tone it down. Soften the edges. Avoid controversy. After all, wasn't she being effective? Flattery makes compromise feel noble. It feeds the ego while eroding conviction.

Delay: "You'll Speak the Hard Stuff… Later"

Tiana never intended to abandon truth. She just postponed it. "I'll do a series on repentance next month." "I'll address that issue when I have more credibility." But "later" never came. Delay became disobedience in disguise. Delay dulls discernment. What starts as caution becomes chronic avoidance.

False Peace: "No Backlash Means God's Favor"

The more Tiana avoided hard truths, the more praise she received—and the fewer spiritual attacks she encountered. The enemy whispered, "See? This is the fruit of wisdom. Everyone's responding positively. You're walking in favor." But peace that comes from avoiding conflict isn't God's peace—it's the enemy's counterfeit.

Counterfeit Outcome

Tiana didn't realize what was happening until much later. There wasn't a single moment where she rejected truth—just hundreds of small decisions to soften it. And with each choice, something inside her shifted. She became more polished but less powerful. More accepted but less anchored. She still talked about God, but the fire was gone. The clarity, the conviction, the holy reverence—they'd all been replaced by branding, strategy, and self-preservation.

This is the cost of compromise. The enemy doesn't just want to steal your voice—he wants to distort your message until it no longer carries Heaven's authority. You're still speaking... but truth has been traded for tone. You're still sharing... but it no longer confronts sin, calls for surrender, or points to the cross.

Here's what that looks like in real life:

A Diluted Gospel

What once stirred hearts to repentance now only offers vague encouragement. Tiana's message became more about self-empowerment than salvation—sprinkling Scripture onto cultural mantras rather than preaching the truth that sets people free. People applauded her for being "different," but no one was being discipled. The Gospel was no longer offensive... or transformative.

A Fear of Backlash

Tiana used to speak boldly. Now, she second-guessed every word. What if someone misunderstood? What if she got canceled? What if this post cost her a partnership? The fear of man had taken root where the fear of God used to live. Silence became her default. Conviction became discomfort. And the courage she once carried was buried under caution.

A Shallow Faith

Her platform grew, but her faith withered. Scripture became content. Prayer became an afterthought. Ministry became management. She was pouring out more than she was receiving—and the emptiness was growing. Though still "successful" by the world's standards, her soul was restless. She had influence, but no longer intimacy.

A Confused Audience

Without realizing it, Tiana had modeled a version of Christianity that made compromise look acceptable. Her followers couldn't tell where truth ended and personal opinion began. They didn't need to change their lives to follow Jesus—just change their language. Seeds were sown, but not in good soil. The message may have been palatable—but it no longer carried power.

A Divided Heart

The saddest part? Tiana still loved God. She still wanted to honor Him. But she also loved her audience, her reputation, and her comfort. And that divided loyalty—however understandable—made her vulnerable to further deception. She hadn't fully turned away from God, but she wasn't fully surrendered either. And partial surrender is still disobedience.

Areas of Salvation Impacted

Tiana's story may seem extreme to some—but more often, it's the norm. It's what happens when salvation is received, but not stewarded. When the Spirit is present, but slowly grieved. When the mind isn't renewed, but conformed. Her drift didn't mean she wasn't saved—but it revealed just how much of her salvation had gone unlived.

A New Identity as a Child of God

Tiana knew she was a child of God, but she let the world redefine what that looked like. Instead of being set apart, she blended in. Her identity in

Christ was still hers—but it no longer shaped how she showed up. She traded boldness for branding and slowly lost sight of who she was meant to reflect.

Purpose, Calling, and Spiritual Gifts

God had called Tiana to influence others with truth, but her need to be accepted distorted that assignment. She thought she was preserving her purpose by softening her message—but she was actually surrendering her Kingdom impact. Her calling wasn't gone—it was compromised.

The Indwelling of the Holy Spirit

The Holy Spirit is a guide into all truth, but Tiana began ignoring the prompts, dismissing the conviction, and replacing communion with content creation. Her connection to God wasn't severed—but it was silenced. And the more she ignored His voice, the harder it became to hear.

These aren't small things. They're the foundations of a life rooted in Christ. And when the world is allowed to shape what these foundations mean, the result isn't transformation—it's erosion.

Faith in Action

Tiana didn't renounce her faith—she reshaped it. Quietly. Carefully. She let the world edit the edges of truth until her message was no longer a sword, but a soft echo. Her compromise wasn't born of rebellion—it was born of a desire to belong, to help, to stay "accessible." But in the process, she stopped being faithful.

And maybe you see yourself in her story.

Maybe you've shifted your message to stay in the room. Maybe you've softened truth to protect a relationship, maintain a reputation, or keep the peace. Maybe you've convinced yourself that silence is wisdom, that caution is love, that popularity means you're on the right path.

The counterfeit life doesn't always look like sin—it often looks like strategy. But if it costs you obedience, clarity, and conviction, it's not God's way. It's conformity dressed up as influence. And the longer you walk in it, the harder it becomes to tell who you're really following.

If Tiana's drift stirred something in you, don't run from it. Let it lead you back. The same mercy that's calling her into deeper truth is calling you too. This is your invitation to return—not to platform, not to performance—but to presence. To truth. To intimacy with God that restores your courage and renews your mind.

Repent for Compromising Truth and Seeking Approval from Man

Bring before God the ways you've filtered or avoided truth to stay comfortable or liked. Repent for putting your reputation, reach, or relevance above obedience. Ask God to restore the fear of the Lord in your heart.

Return to the Secret Place

Rebuild the altar. Carve out space again for deep prayer, stillness, and Scripture—not to prepare content or check a box, but to reconnect with the One who called you. Ask the Holy Spirit to rekindle your passion for truth and your hunger for His Word.

Audit Your Inputs

What's been shaping how you think? Your feed? Your followers? Your feelings? Take inventory of the voices that influence your beliefs. Write them down. Then ask: *Does this align with Scripture? Does it draw me closer to Jesus or further into compromise?* Let the answers guide your next steps.

Fast from Media or Platforms That Feed Compromise

If you've grown numb to what grieves God and your discernment feels dull, consider a fast—not just from social media, but from the entire system that rewards conformity. Give your soul time to detox from applause and reset around God's presence. It's in the silence that truth becomes loud again.

Return to Unapologetic Truth

Don't settle for surface-level Scripture. Meditate on Romans 12:2. Study Daniel's unwavering stand in Babylon. Reflect on Paul's warning in Colossians 2:8. Let the Word reshape your thinking and strengthen your resolve. Truth isn't just what you speak—it's what you stand on.

Prayer

Father, I repent for the ways I've compromised truth—for fearing man more than You, for softening what You've made clear, and for seeking approval over obedience. Thank You for showing me the drift. I want to return to the place of fire, faith, and fearless truth. Renew my mind. Restore my boldness. Rekindle my love for Your Word. Holy Spirit, help me to live from conviction, not comfort. I want to be a voice You can trust in this generation.

In Jesus' name, amen.

Areas of Study

If you've identified with Tiana's drift—whether in part or in full—the way forward is through the renewing of your mind. That's not a one-time moment; it's a lifelong discipline. To resist the pull of culture and stand firm in truth, you need more than inspiration—you need formation. These passages and principles are meant to help you unlearn the world's messages, relearn God's truth, and reestablish a mind shaped by Scripture.

Romans 12:2 — Transformed, Not Conformed

"Do not be conformed to this world, but be transformed by the renewal of your mind..."

Study what it truly means to renew your mind. What are the patterns of this world you may have unknowingly conformed to? What does transformation look like practically?

Colossians 2:8 — Don't Be Taken Captive

"See to it that no one takes you captive by philosophy and empty deceit, according to human tradition..."

Explore how worldly ideas—especially the ones that sound kind, inclusive, or empowering—can actually pull you away from Christ. Pay attention to what kinds of "empty philosophies" you may have accepted.

Daniel 1 & 3 — Standing in Babylon

Daniel didn't just survive in Babylon—he remained uncompromised. From refusing the king's food to refusing to bow to idols, Daniel shows what it looks like to live faithfully in a culture hostile to truth. Study his life to understand what courage, consistency, and godly influence really require.

Galatians 1:10 — Whose Approval Are You Seeking?

"For am I now seeking the approval of man, or of God? Or am I trying to please man? If I were still trying to please man, I would not be a servant of Christ."

This verse is a piercing reminder that servanthood to Christ and people-pleasing cannot coexist. Reflect on what motivates your words, your tone, and your silence.

Key Word Study: "Renew" (Greek: anakainōsis)

Look into the original meaning of "renewal" in Romans 12:2. It's not just a fresh coat of paint—it's a complete renovation. Let this deepen your understanding of what it means to allow God to reshape your mind from the inside out.

Closing Reflection

Tiana didn't reject truth—she reshaped it. And that's what makes her story so sobering.

She didn't walk away from the faith. She didn't renounce Jesus. She simply softened her message—until it no longer carried the weight of conviction or the call to repentance. Her drift wasn't born of rebellion— it was born of slow, strategic compromise, dressed up as relevance, kindness, and caution.

That's the danger for all of us. Because the enemy doesn't always come with opposition—sometimes he comes with opportunities. Applause. Open doors. A growing audience. And if our identity isn't rooted in truth, we'll begin to shape our message to keep the platform instead of speaking from the secret place. And once truth gets edited, obedience starts eroding.

Tiana still loved God—but she also loved the approval of people. She loved peace—but not always the kind that truth brings. And in the name of impact, she forfeited intimacy. She lost the fire—not because she turned her back on God, but because she turned down the volume on conviction.

And maybe, if you're honest, you've done the same.

You've hesitated to speak up. You've avoided hard truths. You've chosen tone over truth, strategy over Scripture. Not because you hate God—but because you've tried to blend in, to be accepted, to not lose what you've built. But here's the truth: anything we're afraid to lose by speaking truth is something we've already surrendered to in silence.

The enemy's goal is always bondage. He will use culture, comfort, and compromise to dilute your witness and drain your boldness. But Jesus is still calling you to live set apart—to speak truth, to stand firm, and to remain faithful no matter the cost.

So here's the invitation: Come back to the secret place. Come back to boldness. Come back to truth that transforms—even when it offends. God doesn't need polished messengers—He needs surrendered ones. Your voice isn't powerful because of your strategy—it's powerful when it carries Heaven's authority.

Let that authority be restored. Let your courage be rekindled. Let your loyalty belong to One alone.

Because the Gospel is still good. It's still offensive. And it's still the only message worth standing for.

CHAPTER 7

When the Fire Feels Too Hot: Tapping Out of Refinement

———————•———————

"In all this you greatly rejoice, though now for a little while you may have had to suffer grief in all kinds of trials. These have come so that the proven genuineness of your faith... may result in praise, glory and honor when Jesus Christ is revealed." 1 Peter 1:6–7 (NIV)

At the opening of this section, I shared how I unknowingly partnered with a religious spirit—how I settled for the appearance of submission rather than the pursuit of intimacy with God. But that wasn't the end of the story. That choice—choosing religion over relationship— set me on a path that eventually led to something even more dangerous: disobedience and retreat. I'm sharing this next part because it's where the enemy ultimately wants us to end up. He doesn't just want to distract us— he wants to derail us. And one of his most effective tactics is to get us to avoid the fire of refinement. Because if we avoid the fire, we forfeit the transformation. And if we forfeit the transformation, we remain bound to old patterns, mindsets, and behaviors—and miss the life God authored for us. That's what happened to me.

Personal Experience

After giving my life to Jesus, one of the first things He asked me to lay at His feet was the title of entrepreneur. That wasn't easy. I would wake up at night asking, *"If I'm not an entrepreneur, who am I?"* And each time, He'd answer, *"You're a child of God."* I didn't fully understand what that meant back then. It took two years of reluctantly obeying His leading—returning to the Marine Corps, surrendering the identity I had built around my ambitions—before I truly let go.

But I never stopped seeking Him about what else He had for me.

A few years later, while living in Colorado, I sensed Him prompting me to start Brave Action Ministry. I was ready—all in. But there was a problem: I didn't know the Word well enough to teach it, and I didn't know how to build biblically grounded content or courses. So, I thought the solution was to partner with a pastor who did.

But I didn't know any pastors. I wasn't connected to a church. I tried cold-calling and emailing pastors—no one responded. I did get one meeting, through a Marine Corps connection—the brother of a friend. I pitched him my vision. He said he'd help. I followed up, sent my course, reached out again… nothing.

It started to feel like every other entrepreneurial venture I had tried—and failed—before. The enemy knew exactly how to attack. Old scripts returned: *God's not for you. He's not helping you fulfill your calling. He's not making a way.* The strongholds built through years of disappointment resurfaced, and old wounds reopened. That spiral gave way to self-pity, fear, and doubt.

I told God I wouldn't go through this again. Money was getting tight, and hope was fading. So when I received orders to Okinawa to serve as the III MEF Deputy G-6, I accepted. By then, I was a Lieutenant Colonel.

But something shifted in Okinawa—and even more so after I returned. I kept telling people, *"Something broke in me."* I couldn't explain it, but I felt it. I no longer had the desire to fight sin or live the Christian life in my own strength. I wasn't praying. I wasn't talking about God. Eventually, I stopped thinking about Him altogether.

I had backslid.

Not in an open rebellion. Not in a loud declaration. But in quiet, gradual retreat. I turned my back. I distanced myself. I walked into the trap the enemy had set.

It wasn't until a few years later—after I finally accepted God's invitation to step into the fire with Him—that I saw it for what it was. He showed me that it was back in Colorado where He first called me into the fire. That was the moment He invited me into a deeper walk. But I tapped out. I turned away. I chose what was easier—what didn't require me to face my pain, my past, or the refining fire.

I'm sharing this story because it's not just a chapter from my life—it's a warning and a witness. This is what happens when we say "no" to the fire, but it's also a testament to God's mercy.

He wasn't done with me then. He's not done with me now.

God leaves the ninety-nine to pursue the one. And while I had left Him—He never left me. A few years later, a car accident on the autobahn designed by the enemy to take my life would be the beginning of Him reminding me… "*I'm still here.*"

Key Choices

My journey may not mirror yours, detail for detail, but the pattern is painfully familiar to many of us. God invites us into deeper transformation, but that invitation often comes through fire, tests, trials, and time in the wilderness. And when the heat rises, the ground dries up. The wilderness strips away comfort. The valley quiets every other voice. Prayers feel unanswered, emotions go numb, and old wounds resurface. When the process takes longer than expected or feels more painful than we imagined, we start making small decisions that carry eternal weight.

I didn't wake up one day and decide to backslide. I made quiet choices—some rooted in fear, others in what I saw in my circumstances—that slowly pulled me away from God's refining work.

Scripture tells us, *"My people perish for lack of knowledge"* (Hosea 4:6), and I was living proof of that. I had experienced six years of blessing and favor from God. I was entering a new season with Him, but didn't know it. I didn't recognize the shift, didn't understand the invitation, because I wasn't in the Word. I hadn't joined a Bible-teaching church. I lacked the spiritual foundation to discern what was happening. So, when the discomfort came, I assumed something was wrong, not realizing it was God doing a deeper work in me.

These are the decisions that shaped my drift—and the same ones the enemy still uses to bait believers out of transformation and into retreat. Let's look at them together.

1. Choosing to stay in the fire of refinement vs. choosing comfort and escape

When God called me deeper, I wanted to say yes with my whole heart. But when the testing intensified and the discomfort grew, I began looking for a way out. The fire exposed old pain and required more trust than I was ready or able to give. Escaping felt easier than enduring. But the truth is—every time we step out of the fire, trial, or the wilderness prematurely, we step back into bondage disguised as relief.

When God calls us into a season of growth, transformation, and maturing, it's never to destroy us—it's to purify and strengthen us. But the fire hurts. It reveals what's hidden and burns away what can't remain. In those moments, we must choose whether to stay in the discomfort of sanctification or run back to familiar comforts that stunt our growth.

2. Choosing to trust God's sanctifying work vs. retreating in fear, pain, or weariness

Refinement isn't just a spiritual process—it's an emotional and mental one, too. I didn't realize how much unresolved pain I was still carrying. When things didn't work out the way I hoped, when I felt spiritually abandoned, I chose to retreat. Not because I didn't love God, but because I didn't trust that He was still good in the middle of my pain.

I didn't know that every step we take with God through the fire and wilderness is a step deeper into freedom. Choosing to trust that His work in us is good—even when it doesn't feel good—is essential to becoming who He created us to be.

3. Choosing obedience despite confusion or delay vs. interpreting resistance as rejection

When my efforts to launch the ministry failed, I assumed I had misheard God. I thought His silence meant "no" rather than "wait." Instead of holding onto the last word He spoke, I let disappointment become disobedience. When the path God calls us to doesn't unfold easily—or when doors seem closed—it's tempting to believe He's withholding or punishing us. But obedience isn't always met with instant reward. It's often met with silence, resistance, or testing. We must choose to obey anyway.

4. Choosing to seek intimacy with God vs. settling for spiritual performance

Looking back, I see how easy it was to equate activity for connection. I was doing things for God, but I wasn't spending time with Him. When that performance fell apart, I realized how little intimacy I had built. I didn't know how to be still with God in the fire—I only knew how to serve Him when things were working.

True transformation requires intimacy, not just activity. Choosing to press in, even when emotions are dry or prayers seem unanswered, guards our hearts against religious striving and burnout.

5. Choosing to confront lies and strongholds vs. letting them define your direction

The lies I believed—about God, about myself, about my calling—had been planted years earlier. But when disappointment hit, those lies found fertile ground. I didn't stop to challenge them. I let them take root again. I let them steer me. And as long as those lies remained unchallenged, they became louder than God's voice.

Enemy Tactics

The enemy capitalized on the cracks in my foundation to tempt me into backsliding. He knew exactly where I was vulnerable: my unhealed wounds, my lack of biblical knowledge, my deep longing for purpose and significance. He didn't launch a frontal assault—he used subtle lies, quiet accusations, and discouragement dressed as logic. That's how he works. He watches, waits, and whispers at just the right moment. And if we're not rooted in truth, those whispers start to sound like reason. What began as an invitation from God became, in my mind, a burden I wasn't equipped to carry. And the enemy made sure I believed that walking away was the only option. Let's look at the tactics he used.

Using delay and resistance to create discouragement and doubt

When my ministry efforts stalled, the enemy used the silence as proof that I had misheard God. He twisted the delay into a personal failure and convinced me that resistance meant rejection. His goal wasn't just to discourage me—it was to get me to abandon the assignment altogether.

Exploiting spiritual immaturity and biblical ignorance

I didn't know what a refining season was. I didn't understand the wilderness, the fire, or God's pruning process. The enemy took full advantage of my lack of biblical foundation. Without truth to anchor me, I had no framework to interpret what was happening—so I believed the lies instead.

Reopening old wounds and triggering unresolved pain

Rather than attacking me with something new, the enemy dug up what was already there. He reopened old entrepreneurial disappointments, feelings of rejection, and questions about my worth. By stirring up what I hadn't yet healed from, he kept me stuck in familiar cycles of fear and self-protection.

Feeding spiritual fatigue and emotional weariness

The longer I waited for a breakthrough, the more exhausted I became. The enemy knows that weariness weakens resistance. He doesn't always push us into rebellion—sometimes, he just lets us get tired enough to give up. And that's what I did. I gave up—not with a loud declaration, but with quiet withdrawal.

Distorting God's character through unmet expectations

The enemy kept whispering that God wasn't helping me, wasn't for me, wasn't showing up. He took my unanswered prayers and interpreted them for me: *God has forgotten you. You're on your own.* By twisting my view of God, he drove a wedge between us—and made it feel like distance was my only option.

Counterfeit Outcome

When I backslid, it wasn't just a retreat from refinement—it was the collapse of the religious spirit I had been operating under. It marked the end of striving, the end of pretending, the end of trying to *look* like a Christian while silently struggling inside. I stopped showing up in appearance and in effort. I didn't care about keeping up spiritual performances anymore. I laid it all down—not in surrender to God, but in surrender to weariness and unbelief. And with that surrender came a quiet shift. I began living according to the enemy's lies, no longer convicted, no longer conflicted. That's the tragedy of the counterfeit life—it doesn't demand rebellion. It just invites resignation.

Living According to Lies Rather Than Truth

Once I stepped away from the refining work of God, I began living out the very lies the enemy had planted. I believed I was on my own. I believed God wasn't helping me. I believed nothing was going to change. And since I had accepted those lies, I stopped trying to resist them. I didn't just agree with deception—I adapted to it.

No Longer Feeling Convicted

The more time passed, the less conviction I felt. Not because I was justified, but because my heart had grown cold. Sin no longer troubled me. Disobedience no longer disturbed me. I knew I wasn't living the way God called me to live, but I stopped caring. That's what the counterfeit life produces—apathy dressed up as peace. I was miserable, but I covered it by sinning more. I pursued sexual pleasure and gratification, hoping it would give me back the joy I had lost. It didn't. It only deepened the ache.

False Identity Becomes Normalized

The more I lived disconnected from God's truth, the more I began to see myself through the lens of autonomy, self-reliance, and striving. I wasn't anchored in my identity as a child of God—I was floating in the false identity the enemy had assigned to me. I became comfortable in a version of myself God never authored, convincing myself that this was just who I was now.

Functioning Without Faith

I didn't lose my faith—I just stopped using it. I stopped depending on God. I stopped seeking Him. I operated in my own strength, guided by what seemed logical or necessary, not by what was holy or obedient. I wasn't fighting God—I just wasn't following Him. And that's exactly where the enemy wants us: not openly rebellious, just quietly removed.

Areas of Salvation Impacted

Salvation is more than a ticket to heaven—it's the gateway to a life of transformation, intimacy, and Kingdom purpose. But when we choose to retreat from refinement, we don't lose our salvation—we lose access to its power and impact in our daily lives. That's what happened to me. I was still saved, but I wasn't living like someone who had been set free. I had accepted the title of Christian but was no longer walking in the truth and freedom of my salvation. Here's what was impacted:

A New Identity as a Child of God

I wasn't living from the truth of who I was—I was living from a broken version of who I used to be. The identity Christ gave me was still mine, but I no longer embraced it. I operated as if I had to fend for myself, earn my worth, and prove my value. I lost sight of the intimacy and security that comes with being a daughter of God.

Victory Over Sin and Death

One of the greatest gifts of salvation is the power to overcome sin—not in our own strength, but through Christ in us. But when I stopped walking in step with the Spirit, sin regained its hold. I willingly gave myself over to old patterns, especially in the area of sexual sin. I stopped resisting and started justifying. Victory was still available—but I stopped reaching for it.

A New Heart and a Renewed Mind

God had already begun renewing my mind and healing my heart—but when I tapped out of refinement, I also pulled away from transformation. I allowed old strongholds to take root again. My thinking grew dark, cynical, and self-focused. My heart grew cold. I stopped surrendering my thoughts to Christ and started letting my emotions and pain dictate my decisions.

Access to God's Presence

God never withdrew His presence from me—but I stopped drawing near. I wasn't praying. I wasn't listening. I wasn't seeking. I lived like someone shut out from God, even though the veil had been torn. The access was still there, but I didn't use it. And in that distance, I grew more numb, more lost, more disconnected.

Purpose, Calling, and Spiritual Gifts

God had given me a clear assignment—but when I allowed disappointment and discouragement to speak louder than truth, I stepped away from that call. I let fear and failure silence my gifts. I was still called. The purpose hadn't changed. But I wasn't walking in it. I traded forward movement for spiritual stagnation.

Peace With God

I wasn't at war with God—but I wasn't at peace either. I carried unresolved frustration, silent disappointment, and internal resistance. I didn't talk to Him about it—I just kept my distance. The peace that surpasses understanding was still available, but I chose isolation instead of intimacy. And without that peace, I wandered in anxiety, striving, and self-protection.

The Indwelling of the Holy Spirit

The Holy Spirit never left me—but the truth is, I hadn't been walking in relationship with Him to begin with. I had been doing everything in my own strength and willpower. I didn't fully know Him yet. I hadn't learned to recognize His voice or rely on His power. And in my backsliding, I went even further into grieving Him. He was still present in me—indwelling me—yet having to witness my sin, my rebellion, and my refusal to listen. I wasn't just ignoring His guidance—I was wounding His heart. I didn't understand it then, but the deeper I went into sin, the more I was shutting out the very One who had been sent to help me walk in freedom.

Faith in Action

When we're backsliding, we're not walking in faith—we're walking in the flesh, guided by pain, disappointment, or desire. Faith isn't just belief—it's trust. It's obedience. It's surrender. And in my backsliding, I had laid all of that down. I wasn't depending on God. I wasn't seeking His will. I wasn't even asking for His help. I was functioning entirely on my own, and faith had been replaced by self-reliance and silent resentment.

I didn't return to faith on my own. I didn't wake up one day with conviction or courage. I kept drifting until God made Himself known again—in mercy and power. He protected me from a car accident on the autobahn that should have taken my life. In that moment, I knew: *He was still with me. He hadn't let go.* That encounter didn't just shake me—it softened me. It reminded me that even when I've turned away, God still pursues. Even when I've stopped calling on Him, He hasn't stopped watching over me.

Maybe you're reading this and realizing you've been in that same place. Maybe you've retreated from refinement. Maybe you've stopped praying, stopped hoping, stopped resisting the sin that once broke your heart. If that's where you are, know this: it's not too late. Your story doesn't have to end in retreat. Faith can begin again—right here, right now.

Prayer

Father,

I confess that I've drifted. I've pulled away from Your refining fire, and I've chosen comfort over transformation. I've believed lies, given in to sin, and tried to live in my own strength. I've grieved Your Spirit, ignored Your voice, and turned my back on Your presence. But today—I stop running.

I repent. I repent for retreating from You, for surrendering to fear, for adapting to the counterfeit life. I don't want to live numb anymore. I don't want to keep pretending, performing, or managing life apart from You. I surrender again.

Jesus, thank You for never letting go. Holy Spirit, thank You for staying with me even when I shut You out. Father, thank You for Your mercy that pursues, protects, and restores. I invite You to begin again in me. Break what needs to be broken. Heal what needs to be healed. Restore what I've forfeited. I trust You to finish the work You started.

In Jesus' name, Amen.

Areas of Study

If you've ever wondered how God responds to our wandering, there is no clearer picture than what Jesus gives us in Luke 15. He tells three parables—back to back—to drive the point home: God doesn't abandon the lost. He searches for them. He waits for them. He rejoices when they return.

The Lost Sheep (Luke 15:1–7)

A shepherd leaves ninety-nine sheep to go after the one that's lost. This isn't just about reckless pursuit—it's about personal value. The sheep wasn't forgotten in a crowd. It was sought after *individually*. That's how God sees you when you wander.

The Lost Coin (Luke 15:8–10)

A woman turns her house upside down to find one lost coin. She lights a lamp and sweeps the floor until she finds it. The coin couldn't call out—but its value never changed. God will illuminate every dark corner to find you—even when you don't know how to cry for help.

The Prodigal Son (Luke 15:11–32)

A son takes what he believes he's owed and squanders it. When he returns—not out of love, but out of desperation—his father runs to him, embraces him, and restores him fully. The story isn't about the son's repentance as much as it's about the father's readiness to receive him. That's the heart of our God.

Take time to study these parables not just for what they reveal about the lost, but for what they reveal about the Father. He doesn't shame the wandering. He seeks them. And when they return, He doesn't make them crawl back—He runs to meet them.

Other recommended passages for deeper reflection:

- Hosea 6:1–3 – "Come, let us return to the Lord…"

- Psalm 51 – David's prayer of repentance and renewal

- John 15:1–8 – Abiding in the vine and bearing fruit through pruning

- 2 Corinthians 7:10 – Godly sorrow leads to repentance

- Romans 12:1–2 – A renewed mind and a living sacrifice

- Hebrews 12:5–11 – The discipline of the Lord for those He loves

Closing Reflection

The refining fire of God isn't meant to destroy us—it's meant to transform us. But transformation requires surrender. And when the heat intensifies, when the pressure mounts, when old wounds resurface and prayers seem to go unanswered, it's tempting to step out of the fire and retreat into whatever feels safer, easier, or more familiar.

That's what I did. I didn't rebel loudly—I drifted quietly. I retreated not because I hated God, but because I didn't understand what He was doing. I interpreted His silence as absence. I saw resistance as rejection. I thought the fire meant something had gone wrong—when in reality, it was the very place God had invited me to be refined, healed, and matured.

The enemy doesn't need to convince us to turn our backs on God with defiance. He just needs to convince us to tap out early—to choose comfort over sanctification, logic over faith, and self-protection over surrender. And when we do, we start to live according to lies, numb to conviction, distanced from intimacy, and disconnected from purpose.

But here's the truth: God doesn't abandon us in our retreat. He waits. He watches. He pursues. His mercy never runs out, and His invitation never expires. If you've been drifting, if you've stepped out of the fire, if you've settled for a version of life that no longer requires faith—this is your call to return.

You don't have to climb your way back. Just turn. Just open your heart. Just say, "Here I am, Lord. Begin again."

Section II Conclusion

Drifting Is Subtle—But So Is the Call to Return

If the counterfeit life begins with deception, it is sustained by agreement. Every false identity—whether shaped by religion, rejection, achievement, or culture—thrives in the absence of truth. But once truth enters the room, the illusion begins to break. That's the invitation of Section II: to allow the Holy Spirit to confront not just what we've done, but who we've become—and who we've believed ourselves to be.

Jason's quiet resignation, Tiana's subtle compromise, and my own stories of spiritual striving and retreat weren't loud acts of rebellion. They were slow fades. But just as the drift happened one choice at a time, the return happens the same way.

This section ends not with shame, but with clarity:

You are not the false identity you've performed.

You are not the label you were given.

You are not the product of your hustle, your failure, or your fear.

You are God's—called, chosen, loved, and invited into truth.

The road to restoration continues—but it begins with remembering who you are and refusing to let the enemy define you any longer.

Section III

———•———

The War Within:
Spiritual Pressure and Personal Pain

Not every battle leaves visible scars. Some wars are waged in the private corners of our minds and the deepest crevices of our hearts. These are the battles no one else sees—the ones we fight behind the smile, beneath the surface, and beyond the reach of easy answers. But God sees them. And more importantly, He meets us there.

This section confronts the hidden war: the conflict that wages within our thoughts, emotions, memories, and inner convictions. It's not that this war is more spiritual—it's that it's more *subtle* and more *relentless.* The enemy doesn't just aim to influence what we do—he aims to reshape who we believe we are. And his favorite battleground is the terrain of unresolved pain, unhealed wounds, and unrenewed thinking.

Here, the counterfeit life becomes even more dangerous because it no longer feels like a lie—it starts to feel like truth. Trauma is reinterpreted as identity. Coping mechanisms replace godly healing. And pain becomes the lens through which we view ourselves, God, and others.

In these next four chapters, we'll expose some of the most entrenched strongholds believers carry: depression, doubt and worry, bitterness and anger, and condemnation. These aren't fleeting emotions. They are spiritual attacks against our past, our pain, and our identity—designed to distort truth, divide the heart, and derail the believer from walking in freedom.

But there is hope.

This is not just about recognizing spiritual warfare—it's about confronting the personal pain that makes us vulnerable to it. These chapters invite you to name the lies, examine the roots, and learn to fight back with the weapons of truth, repentance, the renewing of your mind, the healing power of community, and Spirit-led obedience.

This is where the battle intensifies. Because this is where the enemy aims to keep you bound—not by chains, but by shame, silence, and self-doubt.

But this is also where freedom begins.

Because you weren't just saved to be forgiven—you were saved to be whole. You were saved to be free.

CHAPTER 8

When the Darkness Lingers: Depression and the Lie That You're Alone

———•———

So Jesus said to the Jews who had believed him, "If you abide in my word, you are truly my disciples, and you will know the truth, and the truth will set you free."John 8:31–32

I'm starting Section III with one of my personal experiences because this is extremely close and personal to me. The enemy tried to led me to commit suicide since I was 11 years old. I want to make the enemy pay for how much he tortured, pained, and hurt me. I'm so grateful and joyful to remind Satan that he's defeated and he's a loser because Jesus defeated him but I also want every opportunity to encourage, support, and rally behind other believers to drop kick the enemy, take ground from him, and take souls back to the Kingdom of light.

Personal Experience

This happened after my time in the fiery furnace. I was about seven months into a continued deep healing, renewing, and transforming process with God. I was fully submitted and surrendered to God, and He was peeling layers and helping me face and heal past pains and hurt. I was receiving revelations, but the enemy was also busy attacking and working to steal and destroy the work God was doing in me.

I didn't yet know how to stand firm in faith or how to war effectively in the Spirit. The strongholds were still there, and the enemy knew exactly how to engage them.

It was the start of a new year—January 2023—and I was in the depths of depression. Suicidal thoughts were coming in waves. I was struggling financially, not seeing any breakthrough in my business, and my mind had become a battlefield. The enemy hijacked my thoughts and ran familiar scripts—old lies wrapped in new disappointments. I was torn between the person I used to be and the transformation I was fighting for.

I surrendered, I was obedient, and I was committed. I kept going to church, praising and worshipping God. I was holding on—barely—but holding on.

That Sunday, I walked into church with a brave face, like I had done so many times before. But I was falling apart inside. As I was leaving, a friend stopped me and asked, "How are you doing?"

It was a moment of grace. A chance to reach out for help.

But I lied.

I smiled and said, "I'm doing good," then quickly walked away and ran to my car, where I broke down in tears.

Inside, I was completely broken. But I couldn't bring myself to say the truth—whether it was pride, shame, fear, or the lie that no one would care. I carried that weight back to my car, and the enemy used that moment to reinforce one of his most vicious lies: *You're alone. No one can help you. No one really sees you.*

Then God asked me something that stopped me in my tracks: "Why did you lie?"

I couldn't answer. It was just... what I had always done. Pretend. Hide. Push through.

Then He said something that pierced me: "Ann, lying is coming alongside the enemy. He's the father of lies. You could have told her the truth and asked her to pray over you. When you speak the truth, you take away the enemy's power."

I wept even harder.

But I knew what I needed to do.

Key Choices

My experience in that church parking lot wasn't the beginning of the battle—it was the moment I finally saw it clearly. For years, I had been making quiet choices in the midst of pain. I had learned how to hide. How to mask depression with a smile. How to show up in the right places while internally unraveling. The enemy had fed me lie after lie, and I had unknowingly given those lies room to grow by staying silent and trying to survive in my own strength.

I was walking through deep transformation with God, but I didn't yet know how to stand firm. I didn't recognize how much power I still gave the enemy by choosing isolation over truth, shame over vulnerability, and fear over faith. It wasn't the darkness alone that almost took me out—it was the decisions I made in the dark that gave the enemy a stronger grip.

Here are the choices I faced—and the same ones many believers face when the war within gets loud.

1. Choosing to tell the truth vs. hiding behind strength and smiles

That moment in church was a fork in the road. I had a chance to be honest—but I defaulted to survival mode. Hiding felt safer. I'd done it my whole life. But every time we lie about how we're really doing—especially when someone offers to see us—we partner with the father of lies. Truth is risky, but it breaks the enemy's grip. Silence strengthens it.

2. Choosing to cry out to God and others vs. shutting down in silence

Depression silences the soul. And the longer I stayed quiet, the more convinced I became that no one could help me. But that wasn't true. Crying out isn't weakness—it's warfare. It's choosing to believe that connection is still possible and that God still hears.

3. Choosing to stand on God's truth vs. letting the enemy hijack your thoughts

The lies were loud: *You're alone. You're failing. You're never going to make it.* And because I wasn't yet trained to fight those lies with the Word, I let them play on repeat. But God's truth was always available. I just didn't know how to access it in the moment. We have to choose to take every thought captive—not just the dramatic ones, but the daily ones that chip away at our hope.

4. Choosing to persevere in faith vs. letting pain rewrite your theology

I was struggling to see God's goodness through my circumstances. The lack of breakthrough made me question His promises. But pain isn't proof of God's absence—it's an invitation to deeper faith. When we let pain redefine who God is, we lose sight of His unchanging nature.

5. Choosing to reach for connection vs. isolating in spiritual battles

I had people around me—good people who cared. But I still believed I had to handle it on my own. The enemy thrives in isolation. Every time we step into community, share honestly, or ask for prayer, we tear down his strategies and invite the Holy Spirit into the battle.

6. Choosing humility and vulnerability vs. pretending and self-reliance

Pride doesn't always look like arrogance. Sometimes, it looks like self-preservation. I didn't want to be a burden. I didn't want to admit I was still struggling. But pretending kept me bound. Vulnerability is what opens the door for healing. Confessing our need isn't failure—it's faith in action.

Enemy Tactics

The enemy had studied, seeded, and established stronghold in me all my life. He knew how often I had masked depression with a smile. He knew the shame I carried and the scripts I believed. And when I started walking more deeply with God—when I began peeling back the layers and facing what I had always avoided—he launched a targeted assault.

He waited until I was worn down, desperate for breakthrough, and questioning everything I was still waiting for. That's when he moved in—not loudly, but subtly. Not with new lies, but with familiar ones. His goal wasn't just to torment me again but to wear me down, isolate me, and convince me that my suffering disqualified me from help, hope, or healing. He wanted to get me to kill myself.

The enemy doesn't always show up with a roar—sometimes, he whispers in our own voice. He knows how to weaponize our wounds. He studies our patterns, our pain, and our past. And when he sees a place where healing hasn't fully taken root, he moves in with precision.

He hijacked my thoughts with lies I had heard before

The enemy didn't need to come up with something new—he just recycled the old. *"You don't need help. You can get through this on your own. No one can understand you. Accept things as they are, they aren't going to change."* These thoughts didn't scream—they constantly whispered and they spoke to me in a way that caused the most pain and tore me apart. And while I now knew it was the enemy speaking, I didn't yet know how to stand firm against him successfully.

He distorts vulnerability into shame

That moment when my friend asked me how I was doing—I wanted to tell her. But the enemy made me feel like I'd be a burden. Like if I told the truth, I'd be judged, pitied, or rejected. So I smiled. I lied. I left. He made vulnerability feel dangerous, like admitting weakness would lead to rejection or embarrassment. So I stayed silent, thinking I was protecting myself—when in fact, I was staying bound.

The enemy often convinces us that being honest about our pain will cost us more than it heals. But staying silent is the costlier choice.

He turns isolation into a prison

The enemy convinced me I needed space, solitude, and time to "work through things." But what I really needed was prayer, support, and connection. He framed isolation as strength—when really, it was spiritual sabotage.

When we retreat in pain, the enemy whispers louder. Community isn't just helpful—it's protective.

He capitalizes on exhaustion and emotional depletion

I was tired. Emotionally drained. Spiritually stretched. And that's when the pressure intensified. The enemy doesn't usually strike when we're strong—he waits until we're tired. That's when the lies feel most believable and our resistance feels weakest. He wanted me to tap out–one way or another.

Weariness is fertile ground for deception. The enemy counts on our fatigue to keep us from fighting.

He confuses spiritual attack with personal failure

I was under spiritual pressure, but I interpreted it as proof that I was failing God. He wanted me to think the battle was me. That I was the problem. That if I were really transformed, I wouldn't be thinking these things. That I must not really be free. By blurring the line between attack and identity, I would blame myself instead of fighting back.

One of the enemy's deadliest tactics is to make you mistake his attack for your identity.

He praised my silence and disguised it as strength

Every time I stayed quiet, the enemy applauded. He wanted me to believe that speaking up would make things worse, that no one would care, or that it was too late. Because the moment I chose truth, I would begin to break free.

The enemy knows that silence keeps secrets—and secrets keep strongholds alive.

He used pride to disguise pain

Pride isn't always loud. Sometimes it shows up as, *"I've got this."* The enemy twisted my desire to be strong into a refusal to be helped. He made strength synonymous with self-sufficiency—and that's where he gained ground.

Counterfeit Outcome

The counterfeit life doesn't always look like rebellion—it often looks like *quiet survival.* I wasn't out running from God. I was in church. I was praying. I was worshipping. But underneath the obedience was a soul still entangled in strongholds. The enemy had convinced me that I had to keep it together, even as I was falling apart. That's how subtle his counterfeits are. He doesn't just aim to take your life—he aims to redefine how you live it.

Here's what the counterfeit looked like in that season of my life:

Isolation disguised as strength

I looked strong on the outside because I didn't break down in front of others. I kept showing up, kept smiling, kept pressing on. But none of that was faith in action—it was still just self-preservation. I was still living a life that looked brave on the outside but was rooted in fear of being seen.

Suffering in silence as a sign of maturity

I believed the lie that "mature Christians don't suffer from depression." That if I really trusted God, I wouldn't feel this way. So I kept quiet. But all that silence did was deepen the enemy's hold. Real maturity isn't silent suffering—it's bringing our pain into the light and letting God minister through others.

Endurance without healing and faith performance without power

I pushed through. I persevered. But I wasn't healed. I was still carrying the same thoughts, same shame, same weight. I could say the right things. I could praise through tears. But I wasn't yet walking in power. I hadn't learned to war in the Spirit. The enemy loves when we settle for *false faith*—a faith that quotes Scripture without believing it, that raises hands in worship but refuses to open up in truth. I desired more than going through the motions, but false faith doesn't heal—it hides. And what's hidden can't be surrendered.

The counterfeit life thrives in the gap between what we profess and what we truly believe. It convinces us that outward obedience is enough, when what God really wants is inner transformation and Spirit-empowered wholeness.

Lying as protection instead of confession as warfare

That one lie—"I'm doing good"—wasn't just a social response. It was agreement with the enemy. And in that moment, I gave him access. Confession would have broken the cycle. It would have invited truth. But I believed the cost was too high.

That's the heart of the counterfeit: it keeps us managing pain instead of healing it, pretending instead of transforming, surviving instead of overcoming.

Areas of Salvation Impacted

A New Heart and a Renewed Mind

Salvation gives us a new spirit and heart and begins the ongoing renewal of our mind. But in this season, I was in an ongoing battle with enemy over my thoughts. I knew I had the authority but he still had influence. I was saved and in the process of learning how to guard my mind with truth. Old lies still lived in the corners of my thinking, and my heart—though surrendered—was still healing from wounds that hadn't yet been exposed.

The mind must be renewed for the new heart to flourish. Otherwise, we keep living under old patterns in a redeemed life.

Peace With God

The cross reconciled me to God, but I wasn't living in peace. I interpreted my circumstances as punishment. I felt distant and unseen—even though God had never left and was clearly actively at work in my life. I was spiritually at peace with Him, but emotionally tormented by lies.

Peace with God isn't just positional—it's experiential. And the enemy works overtime to rob us of that reality through confusion, shame, and despair.

The Indwelling of the Holy Spirit

The Holy Spirit was in me—guiding, grieving, speaking—but I wasn't yet fully walking with Him. I hadn't learned to listen, partner, or war in the Spirit. So I kept fighting spiritual battles in my flesh. That left me exhausted and vulnerable to more enemy attacks.

The Spirit indwells us at salvation, but we must learn to yield to Him if we want to live in power and discernment.

Purpose and Gifts

I knew I had a purpose. I had a calling. But the enemy clouded it with despair and shame. The torment in my mind paralyzed my movement. I couldn't see forward because I was too weighed down by what was broken inside.

You can be called and still feel stuck. Until internal healing comes, your gifts remain dormant—buried beneath the lies that tell you you're not enough.

Faith in Action

God met me in the parking lot.

Not with lightning. Not with breakthrough. But with truth.

After I walked away from the conversation that could've led to prayer and connection, I broke down in tears. And that's where He spoke: *"Why did you lie?"* I couldn't answer—not at first. Then He said something that marked me forever: *"Lying is coming alongside the enemy. He's the father of lies. You could have told her the truth and asked her to pray over you. When you speak the truth, you take away the enemy's power."*

That was the moment everything shifted.

But the shift didn't do the work for me. The truth exposed what needed to be done, but the doing still required vulnerability. It required that I break the silence. That I risk being seen. That I step into healing instead of pretending I was fine.

And that's what faith looks like. It's not just trusting God—it's responding to Him.

Maybe you've been there. Maybe you're still there.

Maybe you've mastered the smile that hides the pain. Maybe you've said "I'm fine" when what you really meant was "I'm drowning." Maybe you've kept showing up at church, singing songs, and quoting Scripture— while silently believing things will never change.

Maybe this chapter is your *parking lot moment.*
Maybe God is meeting you right here, like He met me, and asking you to stop hiding.

If anything in this chapter has stirred something in you, don't brush it off. Jesus doesn't shame us for the lies we've believed—He breaks their power. But He doesn't force His way in. He waits for us to open the door through confession, honesty, and surrender.

Here's what faith looked like for me—and what it can look like for you:

Start with truth. Speak it out loud.

Don't wait for someone to pull it out of you. Go to God. Go to someone you trust. Say the hard thing. *"I'm not okay." "I need help." "I'm struggling."* Speaking truth is the first act of war against the enemy's lies.

Break the silence. Ask for prayer.

You don't need a perfect explanation—just a willing heart. When I chose to confess my struggle, the power of shame began to crumble. God meets honesty with healing.

Get in the Word—and let the Word get in you.

I didn't just need encouragement. I needed truth. Scripture is how we fight back. It's how we learn the voice of God so we can silence the voice of the enemy.

Partner with the Holy Spirit daily.

One of the most important revelations I had during this battle was that I needed more than what I was walking in. I had the indwelling of the Holy Spirit—I was saved—but I wasn't yet walking in power. I hadn't received the *baptism of the Holy Spirit*, and I didn't even fully understand what I was missing. I began to cry out and ask to be baptized in the Holy Spirit. His presence filled me in a way I had never experienced before and I began to speak and pray in tongues. I began to discern the enemy's lies more clearly, and I finally had the strength to fight back with power instead of willpower. That was the turning point.

The baptism of the Holy Spirit is not just a doctrinal concept—it's a deeply personal and necessary part of walking in the victory Jesus paid for. It's the empowerment Jesus promised His disciples in Acts 1:8: *"But you will receive power when the Holy Spirit comes upon you... "*It's not just for pastors or leaders—it's for every believer who wants to live equipped, bold, and free.

If you've never asked God for the baptism of the Holy Spirit, don't wait. Ask Him now. He is faithful to fill you. Surrender your heart fully and invite Him to saturate your life with His presence, power, and gifts.

The Holy Spirit doesn't just comfort you—He empowers you. And you need both to walk in lasting freedom.

Connect to community—even when you don't feel like it.

The enemy will do everything he can to keep you isolated. Don't let him. God often delivers healing through the body of Christ. Let people in. Let them pray. Let them see the real you.

Prayer

Father,

I come to You now, not with perfect words, but with an open heart. I confess that I've been hiding—behind shame, silence, fear, and pain. I renounce every lie I've believed: that I'm alone, that I'm beyond help, that nothing will change. I declare that You are my Healer, my Deliverer, my Defender, and the Lover of my soul. Holy Spirit, I ask You to fill me afresh.

Reveal the lies. Replace them with truth. Break the silence. Break the shame. Break the strongholds. Help me to walk in truth, live in community, and fight with faith.

In Jesus' name, Amen.

Areas of Study

Scriptures to Reflect on

Psalm 34:18 — "The Lord is close to the brokenhearted and saves those who are crushed in spirit."

Reflect on how God draws near in our most fragile moments—not with condemnation, but with comfort and rescue.

John 8:44 — "...He [the devil] was a murderer from the beginning... for there is no truth in him. When he lies, he speaks his native language, for he is a liar and the father of lies."

Study how the enemy's nature is rooted in deception. Consider where you may have unknowingly agreed with his voice instead of God's.

John 8:31–32 — **"Then you will know the truth, and the truth will set you free."**

Explore what it means to know truth—not just intellectually, but experientially—and how living in truth leads to real freedom.

James 5:16 — **"Confess your sins to one another and pray for one another, that you may be healed."**

Examine the role of confession and community in receiving healing. How might your healing be connected to opening up to others?

Romans 12:2 — **"Be transformed by the renewing of your mind."**

Dive into what it means to let God renew your thoughts and dismantle false narratives. Transformation starts in the mind.

Ephesians 6:10–18 — **The Armor of God**

Study the full passage on spiritual warfare. Identify which pieces of the armor you've been neglecting and how to use them in battle against the enemy's attacks.

Biblical Figures to Study

Elijah under the broom tree (1 Kings 19)

Elijah, after a major spiritual victory, fell into despair and asked God to take his life. Study how God responded—with rest, nourishment, presence, and purpose.

Job

A man who lost everything, questioned deeply, and still held onto God. Job's story teaches us that lament is not a lack of faith—it's often what sustains it.

David in the Psalms

Read Psalms where David pours out anguish, depression, fear, and desperation—but always returns to trust. (See Psalms 6, 13, 22, 42, and 143 in particular.)

Practices to Engage

Counseling — Whether Christian or biblically grounded therapy, receiving counsel helps untangle lies and process pain with wisdom and accountability.

Confession — Practice telling the truth about what you're going through to a trusted friend, leader, or prayer partner. This isn't weakness—it's warfare.

Journaling — Record the lies you've believed, what triggered them, and the truth God is revealing. This helps you track transformation and recognize patterns.

Crisis Prayer — Don't wait until you're composed to pray. Cry out to God exactly as you are. Raw, honest prayers move heaven.

Peer Support — Build intentional relationships with people who will check in, pray with you, and speak truth over you when you can't find it for yourself.

Closing Reflection

The lie that almost took me out didn't sound evil—it sounded familiar. That's how the enemy works. He doesn't just try to destroy us from the outside—he wages war within, targeting the unhealed, unspoken places. But God met me there. In a parking lot. In a moment of collapse and confession. And what He offered wasn't shame—it was truth. That same offer is on the table for you right now.

You don't have to carry what you've been carrying. You don't have to keep pretending. If this chapter exposed your pain, it also revealed your path to healing. Don't let the enemy win by staying silent. Don't let shame be the loudest voice in your life. Let this be your turning point. Let this be the moment God meets you in *your* parking lot—and you say yes to truth, yes to healing, and yes to the freedom Jesus already purchased for you.

It took another six months of putting my faith into action—of doing the work outlined in the Areas of Study, engaging in spiritual warfare, and facing yet another wave of intense attack. But I kept pressing in. I kept saying yes. And eventually, breakthrough came after a very intense attack, the enemy's last ditch effort. That day, it broke open completely. It was a beautiful, undeniable moment—light rising in me, the Holy Spirit filling me afresh, and the Word of God alive in every part of my being. I saw it in the Spirit: white sheets falling and I knew that the lies were dismantled and the strongholds destroyed.

The enemy lost his grip.

Now, I walk in freedom. The enemy still tries to come at me—but he finds no strongholds, no unresolved pain, no broken mindsets to hide in. He has nowhere to land. I meet him head-on with the Word of God, and he flees—because he has to. He's a defeated foe. A liar. A loser.

And I am living proof that victory is not only possible—it's promised. We have been given authority in Christ to trample on snakes and scorpions and to overcome all the power of the enemy; nothing will harm us (Luke 10:19). I don't just walk in that promise—I stand on it. I fight from it. And I invite you to do the same.

CHAPTER 9

The Quiet War in Your Mind: Overcoming Doubt and Worry

———————•———————

"Do not be anxious about anything, but in everything by prayer and supplication with thanksgiving let your requests be made known to God. And the peace of God, which surpasses all understanding, will guard your hearts and your minds in Christ Jesus." Philippians 4:6–7

Doubt and worry rarely announce themselves as enemies. Instead, they pose as wisdom, caution, or "just being realistic." But beneath the surface, they erode faith, steal peace, and keep us from trusting God fully. Left unchecked, they become strongholds—patterns of thinking that shape how we see God, ourselves, and the world around us. And once they take root, they don't just influence our thoughts—they begin to drive our decisions. This chapter exposes how subtle—and serious—the battle of the mind really is. Because what we believe in the quiet determines how we live in the chaos.

Scenario

Amanda never used to be like this.

She grew up in a peaceful, Christ-centered home where security wasn't just physical—it was spiritual. Her parents prayed over her, spoke life into her, and modeled trust in God through every season. As a child, Amanda was carefree and confident. She excelled in school, built strong friendships, and never doubted that her life was in God's hands. Worry wasn't part of her vocabulary.

But everything started to shift in college.

It wasn't one dramatic event—it was slow and subtle. Surrounded by driven peers and high achievers, Amanda began comparing herself to others. She noticed classmates landing internships, launching startups, or traveling the world while she was still figuring out her major. Social media only amplified the pressure. Every scroll became a silent accusation: *You're behind. You're not doing enough. You're not enough.*

The shift was imperceptible at first. Amanda was still reading her Bible. Still praying. Still going to church. But now, she was also replaying conversations in her head, obsessing over timelines, and second-guessing every decision. That once-easy trust in God was slowly being replaced by a need to control and predict the future.

Now, every night, Amanda lies in bed staring at the ceiling. Her day was filled with productivity at work, conversations, even moments of laughter—but as soon as the lights go out, the spiral begins.

What if I'm not making the right career moves?
Am I keeping up with others?

Why isn't God helping me progress faster—for His glory?
Does God care about how I'm doing?

She knows the verses. She leads a Bible study. But when the silence settles in, so does the fear. She tries to pray—but it feels like talking into the dark, and she doesn't feel like any of her prayers are being answered. She tries to redirect her thoughts—but the "what ifs" feel more real than God's promises.

Amanda doesn't realize it yet, but she's not just overthinking—she's under attack. She's never heard her parents or friends talk about spiritual warfare, so she doesn't know what's happening. The enemy isn't trying to break her all at once and make his presence known. He's trying to wear her down thought by thought, until doubt becomes her default and worry becomes her worldview.

Key Choices

Amanda's story is a clear picture of how spiritual battles often take root in our thought life before they ever show up in our actions. What begins as comparison or self-questioning can grow into a mental stronghold if we don't recognize the choices we're making—and the truth we're neglecting. Each of these choices is a spiritual fork in the road. The path we take determines whether we walk in peace or anxiety, faith or fear.

1. Choosing to take thoughts captive vs. letting lies and fear dominate your mind

Amanda didn't knowingly choose to entertain lies—but over time, she allowed them to play on repeat. Choosing to take thoughts captive means actively identifying what doesn't align with God's Word and replacing it with truth.

This is of utmost importance and can only be done when we know the Word of God. If we allow wrong thinking, false mindsets, and worldly influences to take root—or remain—even after being born again, we give the enemy access to rule over areas of our life he has no rightful authority over.

2. Choosing to trust God vs. taking matters into your own hands

Doubt often disguises itself as responsibility. Amanda believed she had to figure everything out, or she'd fall behind. But trying to control what only God can direct is a sign we're no longer trusting Him with our future.

Signs that we've stepped out of trust include losing our peace, forfeiting our joy, and being overtaken by stress, worry, and fear. Trusting God isn't something we can do on autopilot—it's a daily decision that requires repentance, time in His presence, Scripture meditation, and listening for the leading of the Holy Spirit. It's those choices we have to take in our hands.

3. Choosing to renew your mind with truth vs. letting culture shape your worldview

Culture says success is found in hustle, visibility, and self-made achievement. Amanda's worth was never defined by these things—but in college, comparison slowly shifted her beliefs. She needed to return to God's definition of success: faithfulness and obedience.

We are in the world, but not of it. That can be easy to forget, especially when we're just beginning to make our way in the world or when we get swept up in passion and momentum around something we enjoy doing. But if we're not careful, we'll find ourselves letting the world shape us instead of letting the Spirit transform us.

4. Choosing to wait on God's timing vs. forcing outcomes based on fear of missing out

Amanda's anxiety around purpose and career was rooted in a fear of being left behind. The enemy convinced her that if she didn't act quickly, she'd miss out on God's best. But trust waits. Trust believes that what God has for us is not only good—but right on time.

Waiting is hard work. The enemy knows that. He capitalizes on our impatience to lure us into shortcuts and detours. That's why it's vital to know when we're most vulnerable to compromise—and waiting is often when we're most tempted to move without clarity. We step in our own will instead of continuing to seek God's.

5. Choosing prayer and spiritual practices vs. constant distraction or busyness

Though Amanda stayed spiritually active, she was mentally overloaded. True spiritual discipline isn't about performance—it's about presence. Making room for silence, stillness, and personal reflection is what allows us to hear God clearly and follow Him closely.

Sometimes we even need to pause our spiritual activity if it's become just that—activity. If what we're doing "for God" has become a distraction from being with God, it may be time to reset. Our spiritual habits should nourish, not numb. They should anchor us in our identity, not just keep us busy.

Enemy Tactics

The enemy didn't come at Amanda with blatant rebellion—he came with subtle suggestions, disguised as logic, responsibility, and realism. That's how he works in the realm of doubt and worry. He doesn't need to destroy your faith all at once; he just needs you to start questioning it piece by piece. These are the primary tactics he used—and still uses—to win the war in our minds:

Fear and Intimidation

Fear is the enemy's favorite entrance into the mind. Amanda wasn't crippled by terror—but she was quietly ruled by the fear of not measuring up, of being left behind, of missing God's plan. Fear exaggerates what could go wrong and minimizes the power of God to make things right.

The line between what to be concerned about and what to worry over is incredibly thin—and the enemy operates right in that space. He persuades us to cross that line, not with threats, but with lures: making fear feel like wisdom, and control look like stewardship. He even lets us feel good about it at first—offering quick fixes and practical steps that seem helpful, all while drawing us away from trust and into self-reliance, further into his control.

Deception

The enemy twisted Amanda's view of herself, of God, and of success. He whispered lies like: *"God's timing is perfect—maybe He's forgotten you. That's why nothing is going according to plan."* These weren't blatant lies, but half-truths that eroded her confidence in God's faithfulness and blurred her sense of identity.

The enemy takes great pleasure in tarnishing the character of God. It was his original tactic in the garden with Eve—and it remains his most effective strategy. He is patient and calculating. He leverages our God-given desire for purpose and progress to paint God as distant or indifferent. And in doing so, he inserts himself as the voice of reason, the one who "really understands." It's a dark form of manipulation, rooted in his pride and his hatred of mankind.

Shame and Condemnation

As Amanda began to recognize her anxiety and fear, the enemy used it against her. *"You call yourself a spiritual leader, and yet you worry this much?"* He layered shame on top of worry to keep her stuck and silent—afraid to admit she was struggling, even to God.

This is truly evil. The enemy opens the wounds, then pours salt in them. He tempts us to fear, and then mocks us for being afraid. He's not just an accuser—he's a tormentor, skilled at turning conviction into condemnation so we'll retreat instead of repent.

Comparison and Envy

What started as innocent observation of others' accomplishments became a constant inner measuring stick. The enemy leveraged Amanda's environment to fuel feelings of inadequacy and discontent, shifting her focus from God's unique path for her to everyone else's highlight reel.

Confusion

Amanda's once clear discernment became cloudy. With so many voices, timelines, and opinions swirling, she started second-guessing herself—and God. The enemy loves to disorient believers by introducing doubt in small but compounding ways.

Each of these tactics is part of a larger strategy: to erode trust in God's character and convince you that you're alone in figuring life out. Once doubt and worry dominate your inner world, they begin to dictate your outer one.

Counterfeit Outcome

Amanda didn't walk away from God—but slowly, she stopped walking in trust. And that's exactly what the enemy was after. He didn't need her to reject her faith—he just needed her to live like she was on her own.

Instead of peace, Amanda lived with constant low-grade anxiety. Instead of clarity, she felt paralyzed by indecision. Her prayers became rehearsed rather than relational, her worship became performance rather than presence, and her obedience became burdened with fear: *What if I get it wrong? What if I miss it? What if God doesn't show up in time?*

This is the outcome of a mind ruled by doubt and worry.

Anxiety-Driven Living: Her days were shaped not by faith but by fear—constantly reacting to pressure, measuring her pace against others, and trying to avoid failure at all costs.

False Responsibility: She took on the weight of outcomes she was never meant to carry, believing that if she didn't control it, it would fall apart.

Disconnection from God's Peace: Though she still believed in God, she struggled to experience His presence. Worry drowned out intimacy.

Detoured From Her Calling: Ironically, the very fear and doubt that told Amanda she was falling behind became the very force that slowed her down. She feared missing out on God's plan, yet by letting worry guide her, she veered off the path God had prepared for her. Instead of running the race of faith with endurance, she was stuck on the sidelines—driven more by pressure instead of led by purpose.

This is the counterfeit life that masquerades as diligence, ambition, or maturity—but in reality, it's bondage. The enemy's goal is to replace Spirit-led living with fear-driven striving. And unless the root is confronted, the cycle will never break.

Areas of Salvation Impacted

The war within doesn't just affect our thoughts—it weakens our ability to walk in the fullness of what salvation has already secured for us. Amanda's struggle with doubt and worry didn't mean she had lost her salvation, but it did mean she was living far beneath what Jesus died to give her. When our minds are not renewed and our trust is fractured, we forfeit the daily peace and power that are meant to accompany us in our walk with God.

Renewed Mind

One of the first promises of salvation is transformation—starting with the mind (Romans 12:2). Amanda's mental patterns, shaped by comparison and fear, were still rooted in the world's standards rather than God's truth. Without a renewed mind, she couldn't see or receive what God was doing in her life.

Peace

Jesus promised His followers a supernatural peace—not as the world gives, but one that guards our hearts and minds (John 14:27; Philippians 4:7). That peace is part of our inheritance, yet Amanda lived as if it was out of reach. Worry robbed her of rest, even when she was doing all the right "Christian" things.

Intimacy with God

Constant anxiety made Amanda feel distant from God, even though He hadn't moved. Worry isn't neutral—it creates noise that drowns out His voice. Salvation offers us direct access to God, but when doubt dominates our inner world, that intimacy becomes clouded, not because God is silent, but because our fear is louder.

Purpose, Calling, and Spiritual Gifts

Driven by fear and doubt, Amanda lost the ability to live in the fullness of who she is in Christ. She pulled back from risks, opportunities, and Spirit-led promptings—not because she lacked calling, but because she lacked confidence. Salvation equips every believer with purpose and spiritual gifts, but Amanda was stuck in survival mode, too anxious to step into the boldness her calling required.

Faith in Action

You can't always control the thoughts that show up—but you can choose which ones get to stay. Amanda didn't get free by trying harder to stop worrying. She began to experience breakthrough when she learned how to confront the lies, replace them with truth, and build a lifestyle of trust, not fear.

Faith is not passive. It's not just believing in God—it's choosing to believe God especially when the what-ifs scream louder than His promises.

If you've seen yourself in Amanda's story, don't let shame keep you stuck. The enemy wants to isolate you in silence, but your victory starts with a simple admission: *"Lord, I've let fear lead me. I want You to lead me instead."*

Here are steps to help you walk that out:

Identify and Reject the Lie

When worry or doubt rises up, pause and ask: *What lie am I believing right now?* Write it down. Then find a truth from Scripture that confronts it and write that down too. Declare the truth out loud. Do this daily, even hourly if needed.

Declare God's Promises Over Your Life

Create a list of verses that directly speak to your areas of doubt. (Philippians 4:6–7, Isaiah 41:10, Proverbs 3:5–6, Romans 8:28). Begin each morning by declaring these truths before the fear has a chance to speak.

Practice Gratitude and Testimony Journaling

Fear focuses on what might go wrong. Gratitude anchors you in what God has already done. Start a journal where you list daily moments of His provision—both big and small. Include testimonies from your past to remind yourself that God has never failed you.

Choose Stillness and Silence with God

Amanda's anxiety grew louder in the silence because she hadn't yet learned to meet God there. Don't run from stillness—enter it with expectation. Let His peace replace the noise. Even ten minutes a day of silent, surrendered prayer can recalibrate your spirit.

Pray for a Renewed Mind and Spirit

Ask the Holy Spirit to help you see where you've let worry become normal. Invite Him to show you how to renew your thought patterns, to heal your fears, and to reestablish your trust in God's timing and goodness.

Learn to Wait the Right Way

Waiting isn't just about not moving—it's about how you posture your heart while you wait. Waiting in worry is still disobedience. But waiting in worship, in trust, and in expectation builds strength. It re-centers you on who God is, not what hasn't happened yet. Use waiting seasons to deepen your intimacy with God rather than obsess over timelines or compare your pace to others.

Waiting is not wasted time when you're spending it with God. It's a season of preparation, refinement, and redirection. Ask God what He wants to show you in the waiting, what He wants to shape in you, and what needs to be surrendered.

And remember—waiting doesn't mean doing nothing. It's a powerful time to shift your focus from yourself to others. Serving while you wait not only blesses those around you, it repositions your heart to trust God's process. It breaks the grip of self-centered striving and makes room for joy, purpose, and perspective. When you wait well, you don't lose ground—you gain spiritual maturity, clarity, and peace.

A Prayer to Begin Again

Father, I confess that I've allowed fear, doubt, and worry to rule my thoughts. I've agreed with lies that You've forgotten me or that I need to take control. Forgive me. I surrender my thoughts to You. Help me take every lie captive and replace it with Your truth. Help me to renew my mind. Guard my heart. Lead me back into the peace You've promised me. I choose today to trust You, not just with my salvation—but with every unknown and unanswered question.

In Jesus' name, Amen.

Areas of Study

These passages and stories provide biblical grounding for recognizing the war within and learning to fight with truth. As you study, ask the Holy Spirit to highlight what He wants to reveal and renew in your thinking.

2 Corinthians 10:3–5 – *"Take every thought captive..."*

Paul teaches that spiritual warfare starts in the mind. We demolish arguments and lies by identifying them and bringing them under the authority of Christ.

Romans 12:2 – *"Be transformed by the renewing of your mind..."*

Transformation doesn't begin with behavior—it begins with belief. This verse is a call to trade conformity to the world for the clarity that comes through God's truth.

Philippians 4:6–8 – *"Do not be anxious about anything..."*

A powerful blueprint for dealing with anxiety: through prayer, thanksgiving, and intentional focus on what is true, noble, and praiseworthy.

Matthew 6:25–34 – *Jesus' teaching on worry*

Jesus directly confronts the anxiety we carry over the future. His words reveal the heart of the Father—one who sees, knows, and provides.

Isaiah 26:3 – *"You keep him in perfect peace whose mind is stayed on you..."*

A promise of peace that is not circumstantial, but rooted in unwavering focus on God's character and faithfulness.

Proverbs 3:5–6 – *"Trust in the Lord with all your heart..."*

This foundational passage anchors us back in trust. It challenges us to stop leaning on our own understanding and submit to God's direction.

2 Timothy 1:7 – *"For God has not given us a spirit of fear, but of power, love, and a sound mind."*

Fear is not from God. This verse reminds us of what we've been given in Christ: power to overcome, love to anchor us, and a sound mind to walk in clarity and confidence.

Isaiah 40:31 – *"But they who wait for the Lord shall renew their strength..."*

Waiting on the Lord isn't passive—it is spiritually strengthening. This verse reframes waiting as a process of renewal, where trust leads to endurance, worship fuels perseverance, and the result is supernatural strength to keep running the race

1 Kings 19:1–13 – Elijah's despair after Mount Carmel

Even great men of faith experience spiritual exhaustion and fear. Elijah's story is a reminder that God meets us gently in our weakest moments, not with condemnation, but with care and restoration.

Closing Reflection

Amanda's story is more common than we realize—because the enemy prefers to wage war in secret. He whispers doubt where there should be trust, fuels worry where there could be peace, and wears down confidence where bold faith once stood. But the good news is: what the enemy does in darkness, God exposes in light.

If this chapter opened your eyes to the quiet war in your own mind, let that awareness lead you to action—not despair. You are not powerless in this fight. You have been given the mind of Christ (1 Corinthians 2:16), the sword of the Spirit (Ephesians 6:17), and the presence of the Holy Spirit as your guide and comforter. You are not alone. And you are not stuck.

You can choose to break agreement with every lie. You can interrupt the spiral. You can bring your thoughts—one by one—into alignment with God's truth.

And as you do, what once felt like torment will become training.

Amanda hasn't arrived yet. But she's not in bondage anymore. She's learning to discern the difference between her voice, the enemy's, and God's—and she's choosing to follow the One who leads her with peace.

So can you.

You were never meant to be ruled by worry or held captive by doubt. You were meant to run the race of faith with endurance. And the first step forward may just be the next thought you take captive.

CHAPTER 10

The Poison of Bitterness:
When Anger Begins to Take Over

———————•———————

"Be angry and do not sin; do not let the sun go down on your anger, and give no opportunity to the devil."
Ephesians 4:26–27

Bitterness doesn't always begin with offense—sometimes, it begins with disappointment. We pray, serve, give, show up, do what's right... and still feel overlooked. Underneath the surface, something begins to shift. Frustration grows. Expectations calcify. And without realizing it, we begin to keep score—not just with people, but with God. We wonder why others are being rewarded while we're being refined. Why their lives seem to be moving forward while ours remain stuck. What once felt like faithfulness starts to feel like unfairness. This chapter explores what happens when quiet disappointment turns into inward resentment, and how, if left unaddressed, it begins to corrupt how we view God, ourselves, and those around us.

Scenario

Sam never thought he'd feel this way.

He had always been the dependable one. The servant. The guy who showed up early, stayed late, and said yes whenever there was a need. He wasn't after applause—at least that's what he told himself. He just wanted to be faithful. But after years of serving quietly, with little recognition or return, something in Sam began to shift.

At first, it was just a lingering heaviness. A subtle ache when others were publicly acknowledged and he was overlooked. A silent frustration when new people received opportunities he'd been praying for. He told himself not to make a big deal of it—but it started to become one. Little by little, disappointment settled into his heart like dust no one noticed. And without realizing it, bitterness began to take root.

He kept showing up. He kept doing what was right. But something inside was hardening.

He noticed how quickly others were celebrated. How effortlessly they seemed to get ahead. He began comparing effort to reward, and his faithfulness no longer felt fulfilling—it felt ignored. He was too mature to throw a tantrum, too spiritually seasoned to lash out. But his inner dialogue shifted. Instead of *Lord, thank You*, it became *Lord, why them? Why not me?*

What had begun as disappointment and discouragement was now producing something else—anger. It hadn't erupted yet, but it had started to surface. In his tone. In his criticism. In his lack of joy. He wasn't sure if he was mad at people... or at God.

Sam didn't realize it yet, but the enemy had successfully planted a bitter root. And now, slowly, that root was feeding something dangerous. The anger wasn't random—it was spiritual. It was the fruit of an unaddressed lie: *You've been forgotten. You've been cheated. You deserve more than this.*

Key Choices

Sam didn't wake up one day bitter and angry. These things took root slowly—through subtle compromises and silent agreements. The danger with bitterness is that it often grows in the soil of perceived faithfulness. We tell ourselves we're doing all the right things, but deep down, we're tracking what we think we're owed. When the heart starts keeping score, it's no longer operating from grace—it's moved into entitlement.

Here are the key spiritual choices Sam faced—choices we all face when our faithfulness feels forgotten:

1. Choosing surrender over silent scorekeeping

Sam was serving, but not from a place of full surrender. He was starting to expect results, recognition, and reward. The moment we begin to keep a tally, we lose sight of who we're really serving. True surrender means trusting God with both the "what" and the "when."

Silent scorekeeping is subtle—but deadly. It shifts the focus from obedience to outcome.

2. Choosing gratitude over comparison and complaint

At first, Sam's heart was grateful. But comparison slowly replaced gratitude, and complaint took root in its place. This is how bitterness is watered—by constantly measuring our portion against someone else's.

Gratitude protects the heart. Without it, disappointment turns into discontent—and discontent becomes fertile ground for offense.

3. Choosing to speak honestly vs. suppressing hurt

Sam didn't feel permission to express his frustration. So he buried it. But what we bury doesn't die—it grows in secret. Choosing to bring disappointment before God—and safe, trusted people—breaks the enemy's ability to isolate us in silent suffering.

Suppressed pain is still pain. And hidden anger has a way of surfacing when we least expect it.

4. Choosing to celebrate others vs. resenting their blessings

Sam's bitterness deepened when he stopped celebrating others and started resenting them. When someone else's win feels like your loss, it's a sign that bitterness is influencing your perspective.

The Kingdom isn't a competition. But the enemy will make it feel like one if we're not rooted in identity and purpose.

5. Choosing to examine your heart vs. assuming you're justified

One of the enemy's tactics is to make you feel justified in your frustration—especially when you've done "everything right." But godly self-examination is how we stay spiritually healthy. It keeps us from being hardened by disappointment or blinded by pride.

We don't grow by proving we're right—we grow by inviting the Holy Spirit to show us what's not.

Enemy Tactics

The enemy didn't need to push Sam into rebellion—he only needed to persuade him that he'd been wronged. That his effort had gone unnoticed. That his faithfulness had earned him more than what he'd received. That he deserved better.

That's how bitterness begins.

It doesn't start with an explosion—it starts with a whisper: *"You've been overlooked." "They don't value you." "Why are you still doing this?"*

And when those whispers aren't brought into the light, they become strongholds. The enemy uses subtle but potent tactics to feed the root and distort reality:

Comparison and Envy

Sam's internal battle intensified when he began comparing his faithfulness to others' outcomes. The enemy highlighted the success and recognition of others to create resentment. He didn't tempt Sam with rebellion—he tempted him with comparison. *"Look how easy they have it. Look how hard you've worked."* These thoughts weren't random. They were planted. And they led Sam to question not just people, but God's fairness.

Guilt-Driven Goodness

Bitterness quickly breeds entitlement. The enemy whispered that Sam's obedience should have secured blessing. That his service should have earned promotion. He made obedience feel like a transaction instead of an act of love.

Entitlement reframes service as performance and turns God into a taskmaster rather than a loving Father. It creates internal tension when results don't match our expectations—and the enemy thrives in that gap.

Offense and Assumption

Sam began assuming motives—*They must not care... They probably don't see me...* Without conversations, offense festered. The enemy exploited silence and uncertainty to drive emotional distance between Sam and the very people he once served alongside.

Offense unspoken becomes division internalized. And the enemy doesn't just want you hurt—he wants you hardened.

Pride and Self-Righteousness

As the root grew deeper, the enemy shifted Sam's mindset from humility to superiority. *"You're doing more than they are. You're more faithful. You're more committed."* What began as a longing for justice became a spiritual foothold of pride.

When we believe we've done everything "right," the enemy twists that into spiritual arrogance—making us resistant to correction, immune to reflection, and deaf to the Spirit.

Isolation

The enemy convinced Sam no one would understand. That his feelings weren't valid. That he needed to keep quiet to maintain his reputation. And so, Sam withdrew—first emotionally, then spiritually.

Isolation gives the enemy uninterrupted access to reinforce every lie. It robs us of the support, accountability, and perspective that could bring healing.

Each of these tactics is part of a larger plan: to harden the heart, distort the truth, and distance us from God and others. The enemy doesn't need to tear your faith down in one blow—he just needs to poison your perspective enough that you stop walking in love and start living with suspicion.

Counterfeit Outcome

Sam didn't stop serving—but he stopped serving with joy. He didn't walk away from God—but his heart was no longer open before Him. He stayed physically present, but emotionally and spiritually, he was withdrawing. This is the subtle danger of bitterness—it lets you keep up appearances while poisoning the well inside.

At first, it just looked like fatigue. But underneath was frustration, disappointment, and disillusionment that had never been dealt with. And without realizing it, Sam's faithfulness had become performance, his prayers had become complaints, and his worship had become routine.

This is the fruit of a bitter root:

Joyless Obedience

Sam was still doing all the right things, but the delight was gone. Obedience felt burdensome, not beautiful. Faithfulness felt like futility. His service became transactional: *"What's the point, if it doesn't lead to anything?"*

That mindset didn't stay confined to church—it spilled into every part of his life. He started doing the bare minimum at work, checking boxes instead of bringing his full self. He grew short with his wife and disengaged with his friends, going through the motions in relationships the same way he did with God. His tone changed. His presence felt heavy. Joyless obedience wasn't just a ministry issue—it was a mindset that stripped purpose from every part of his life.

Anger Misplaced and Misunderstood

He wasn't sure who he was angry with—others, himself, or God. But the anger was real. It leaked into his conversations, his thoughts, and his attitude. He snapped more easily. He withdrew more quickly. He judged more harshly.

And anger never stays small. It escalates. It clouds judgment. It invites offense. Left unchecked, it damages relationships—at home, at work, and in community. Sam became harder to approach, less willing to listen, and increasingly closed off. His spiritual frustration became emotional volatility. He started pushing people away before they could disappoint him—yet the loneliness that followed only confirmed the lie that no one saw or cared.

Spiritual Stagnation

The intimacy Sam once had with God faded. He stopped expecting God to move. He wasn't asking for fresh direction. He wasn't listening— just doing. His prayers became obligatory, his Bible reading mechanical. He no longer approached God as a Father, but as a boss who never seemed satisfied.

This spiritual dullness bled into his personal life. His vision grew dim. He stopped dreaming. He stopped believing anything new or beautiful could come from his life. He turned inward, slowly disconnecting from people who once sharpened him. Opportunities dried up—not because God stopped opening doors, but because Sam stopped noticing them. He wasn't positioned to hear or receive anything new.

Distorted Identity and Purpose

The longer Sam stayed in silent resentment, the more he forgot why he started serving in the first place. His identity as a beloved son and servant became buried under the weight of doing. His calling felt like a burden, not a blessing.

He began to confuse who he was with what he could produce. And when the "fruit" didn't look like what he expected, he assumed something was wrong with him—or worse, with God. The joy of purpose was replaced by the grind of performance. The heart behind his calling was lost beneath the hurt he never named.

The enemy doesn't need to make you stop following Jesus to derail your purpose. He just needs to drain your joy, distort your identity, and get you to believe that faithfulness doesn't matter. That serving God won't lead to anything. That being unseen means you're unvalued.

Bitterness is the counterfeit reward the enemy offers when faithfulness feels fruitless. But what he offers in the shadows never compares to what God promises in the light. Bitterness is not just an emotion—it's a spiritual stronghold. Left unaddressed, it becomes a foundation for even greater destruction. It distorts how we see God, how we see others, and how we see ourselves. It fuels division, hardens the heart, and poisons perspective. And over time, it opens the door to even deeper strongholds—anger that erupts, depression that paralyzes, cynicism that corrodes, and apathy that convinces us nothing will ever change.

This is why Scripture warns us so clearly: *"See to it that no bitter root grows up to cause trouble and defile many"* (Hebrews 12:15). Because if bitterness takes root, it won't just affect you—it will damage everything connected to you.

Areas of Salvation Impacted

Bitterness doesn't just affect our emotions—it warps our ability to live in the fullness of what salvation has already secured for us. It disrupts our relationship with God, distorts our identity, and disconnects us from the Spirit's leading. Sam didn't lose his salvation, but he lost access to the peace, intimacy, clarity, and power that are meant to flow from it. He was living from a wounded place instead of a redeemed one.

These are the areas of salvation most impacted:

Renewed Mind

Instead of filtering life through God's truth, Sam began filtering life through disappointment. His thinking was no longer Spirit-led—it was emotion-led. The root of bitterness corrupted his perspective, and without active renewal, his thoughts became fertile ground for lies.

Peace

One of the first casualties of bitterness is peace. Sam was restless—internally agitated even when nothing was visibly wrong. His thoughts were loud, his emotions unstable. And though he knew where peace came from, he couldn't access it because his heart was filled with resentment.

Intimacy with God

Bitterness blocks intimacy. Not because God pulls away, but because bitterness hardens the heart. Sam's prayers became surface-level. He stopped expecting God to speak or comfort him. The closeness he once knew was replaced by distance—caused not by sin alone, but by unresolved disappointment.

Purpose, Calling, and Spiritual Gifts

Sam's calling hadn't changed—but his capacity to walk in it had. His gifts were still intact, but his heart was no longer surrendered. When bitterness is the filter, even spiritual gifts feel heavy. Passion fades. Vision blurs. Purpose becomes a task instead of a joy. Sam's bitterness had him functioning, but not flourishing.

Indwelling of the Holy Spirit

The Holy Spirit is our comforter, counselor, and guide—but when bitterness is allowed to remain, His voice becomes harder to hear. Not because He stops speaking, but because we're too consumed by our own inner dialogue. Bitterness grieves the Spirit (Ephesians 4:30). It dulls our sensitivity to conviction, direction, and truth.

As that relationship suffers, so do all others. When we are not aligned with the Spirit within us, we can't walk in love, patience, kindness, or self-control. What overflows from our lives becomes tainted by the very thing we refuse to let go of.

Faith in Action

While Chapter 9 revealed how the enemy wages war in the mind through doubt and worry, Chapter 10 exposes a different front: the heart. Bitterness is not just a mindset—it's a heart condition. But the heart and mind are deeply connected. What we rehearse in our thoughts takes root in our emotions. And what festers in our hearts eventually shows up in our decisions, relationships, and walk with God.

That's why bitterness must be addressed spiritually and relationally. It's not just about correcting thoughts—it's about cleansing wounds, releasing offense, and realigning your affections with God. Sam didn't find healing by ignoring his frustration or doing more for God. He began to experience restoration when he brought his hidden pain into the light and let the Holy Spirit gently uncover the truth.

This is not about pretending you're not hurt. It's about letting God meet you in that hurt before it becomes a hardened heart.

If you recognize any part of Sam's story in yourself, don't brush it off. Bitterness grows best in silence and neglect. But freedom begins with exposure—and healing begins with humility.

Here are steps to help you walk in truth and freedom:

Ask the Holy Spirit to Search Your Heart

Bitterness often hides beneath busyness, self-righteousness, or performance. Pause and pray: *"Lord, have I allowed bitterness or entitlement to take root in me?"* Be still long enough to hear the answer— and be willing to be honest with yourself.

Name the Disappointment You've Buried

What hurt you that you never fully brought before God? What do you feel you've been owed or denied? What prayers went unanswered, or recognition you expected but never received? Write them down. Bring them into the light.

Repent for Bitterness and Agree with Truth

Bitterness feels justified, but it must be repented of. Ask God to forgive you for the attitudes, thoughts, and silent agreements that have taken His place in your heart. Then, declare the truth: *"God is just. God is faithful. God sees me, even when others don't."*

Choose to Forgive Where Offense Took Root

Whether someone hurt you intentionally or not, forgiveness is required for freedom. You can't pull up the root of bitterness without releasing the people and situations that planted it. Speak forgiveness aloud—even if your feelings haven't caught up yet. Forgiveness is a spiritual act of obedience.

Practice Gratitude—Even When It's Hard

Gratitude weakens the grip of bitterness. Start small. Each day, write down at least three things you're thankful for—especially the unseen ways God has sustained, protected, or provided. Gratitude realigns your heart with heaven's perspective.

Serve from Surrender, Not Scorekeeping

Ask God to renew the joy of your calling and reestablish a heart of worship in your service. Don't serve to be seen—serve to be aligned. When we release the need for recognition, we make space for restoration.

Worship Even When You Don't Feel Like It

Bitterness makes worship feel forced or fake. But choosing to worship—even when your emotions don't match—is a declaration of trust. It's saying, "You are still worthy, God, even when I'm hurting." Worship shifts your focus from offense to awe, from self to surrender. It breaks down walls bitterness builds.

A Prayer to Soften the Heart

Father, I've been holding on to pain. I see now that bitterness has taken root in places You want to heal. I confess my resentment, my disappointment, and my attempts to hide it. I don't want to serve You out of duty—I want to love You freely again. Holy Spirit, search my heart. Reveal where I've grown cold, and show me how to return. Help me to forgive. Help me to worship even when I don't feel like it. Renew my joy. Restore my intimacy with You. I lay down every offense and ask You to make my heart soft again.

In Jesus' name, Amen.

Areas of Study

These Scriptures and biblical accounts shine light on how God addresses bitterness, heart wounds, and the restoration of intimacy. As you study, ask the Holy Spirit to reveal if there's any place in your own heart that's been hardened, and invite Him to make it soft again.

Hebrews 12:14–15 – **"See to it…that no bitter root grows up to cause trouble and defile many."**

Bitterness doesn't just affect us—it spreads. This passage warns us to be vigilant, showing how unresolved offense and unhealed pain can grow into strongholds that impact not only our lives, but the lives around us.

Proverbs 4:23 – **"Above all else, guard your heart, for everything you do flows from it."**

The heart is the wellspring of life. What we allow in—resentment, offense, disappointment—will eventually overflow. Guarding your heart isn't about hardening it—it's about being watchful and honest with what's trying to take root there.

Psalm 51 – **David's prayer of repentance**

After sin and spiritual distance, David didn't just ask for forgiveness— he asked for a clean heart and a renewed spirit. This is a model for us when we recognize emotional and spiritual drift: restoration begins in the heart.

Ephesians 4:31–32 – **"Get rid of all bitterness, rage and anger…"**

Paul lists bitterness alongside rage and slander as spiritual toxins. The instruction is clear: get rid of it. This isn't passive—it requires intentional release and forgiveness. But the next verse reveals the key: kindness, compassion, and forgiveness modeled after Christ.

Acts 8:18–23 – **Peter rebukes Simon the Sorcerer**

Peter calls out Simon not just for his actions, but for the condition of his heart: "I see that you are full of bitterness and captive to sin." This moment shows that spiritual bondage can be tied directly to unresolved bitterness—and that healing begins with repentance.

2 Corinthians 1:3–4 – **"The God of all comfort…who comforts us in all our troubles."**

God is not indifferent to our pain. He is the Comforter. Bitterness often masks deeper grief, and comfort is God's invitation to bring those wounds into the open so He can bring healing, not just relief.

Isaiah 57:15 – **"I dwell…with the one who is contrite and lowly in spirit…"**

God is near to the brokenhearted—but bitterness can harden us against Him. This verse is a reminder that God doesn't reject the hurting heart—He draws close to it when it stays soft, humble, and open.

John 4:1–26 – **The Woman at the Well**

A heart weighed down by shame, rejection, and spiritual confusion meets Jesus. Her healing begins not with condemnation, but with honest conversation and revelation. Jesus addresses her deepest wounds with truth and invitation.

Luke 15:25–32 – **The Older Brother in the Prodigal Son Parable**

The older brother is often overlooked—but his story reveals the quiet danger of bitterness. Though he never left the Father's house, he had grown resentful, self-righteous, and joyless. He didn't understand the heart of the Father because he had allowed offense to harden his own.

Closing Reflection

Bitterness doesn't always announce itself. Sometimes, it's tucked beneath fatigue. Sometimes, it hides behind busyness, responsibility, or spiritual performance. But eventually, it reveals itself—in the cynicism that creeps in, in the joy that disappears, in the quiet distance that grows between us and God.

Sam's story is one of many. Maybe it's yours too.

The enemy rarely tries to make you stop serving—he just wants to make you miserable while you do. He wants you to forget why you started. He wants you to believe that your obedience doesn't matter. That your offering isn't seen. That your faithfulness isn't worth it.

But those are lies.

Bitterness is not a harmless feeling—it's a spiritual infection. Left unchecked, it spreads. What begins as quiet resentment soon hardens into entitlement, then morphs into anger, cynicism, and apathy. It doesn't just poison our worship—it spills into how we see others, how we carry ourselves, and how open we are to God's voice. It can rob years of spiritual growth and destroy relationships before we realize it's even taken hold.

That's why the urgency is real.

Your heart matters to God. Your joy matters. Your intimacy with Him matters more than anything you can do for Him. And if you've lost that connection—if resentment, disappointment, or spiritual fatigue have taken hold—you don't have to stay stuck.

You don't have to keep going through the motions with a heavy heart. You don't have to pretend everything's fine when it's not. You can stop. You can repent. You can invite God back into the places that have gone numb or grown hard.

Bitterness is dangerous—but it's not permanent. The Holy Spirit is able to do heart surgery. He can soften what's become calloused. He can restore what's been dried up. He can breathe life into places where joy once lived—and will live again.

This may be your turning point.

What the enemy meant for destruction, God can use for transformation. If you'll let Him, He will pull up every bitter root, cleanse every contaminated thought, and pour fresh oil over your weary spirit.

You don't have to keep performing.
You don't have to keep pretending.
You don't have to serve God with a closed heart.

Let this be the moment you say what Sam finally said:
"God, I miss You. Not just Your work— *You.*"

And that's when restoration begins.

CHAPTER 11

Condemned and Called: Wrestling with Guilt, Shame, and the Flesh

———•———

"There is therefore now no condemnation for those who are in Christ Jesus. For the law of the Spirit of life has set you free in Christ Jesus from the law of sin and death."
Romans 8:1–2

Condemnation doesn't shout—it whispers. It sounds like your own voice replaying what you've done and questioning who you are. It wraps itself around your past like chains, convincing you that you haven't really changed and that grace doesn't apply to you. Unlike conviction, which comes from the Holy Spirit and leads to repentance and restoration, condemnation comes from the enemy. It leads to hiding, isolation, self-hatred, and spiritual paralysis. It makes you feel unworthy of God's love, even after you've repented. And for many believers, it becomes a familiar but destructive background noise that keeps them from walking fully in the freedom Jesus died to give. This chapter exposes the spiritual trap of condemnation and shows how to silence shame with truth.

Scenario

Brianna gave her life to Christ in her early thirties—after years of chasing love, worth, and fulfillment through promiscuity, partying, and sexual experimentation. She followed her desires wherever they led, believing her sexual freedom was empowerment. But now, looking back through the lens of truth, she can see it for what it really was: bondage disguised as liberation.

Brianna doesn't question whether God has forgiven her. She believes the blood of Jesus is powerful. But deep down, she struggles to believe it's powerful enough to wash *her* clean. Not just forgiven—but pure. Not just accepted—but redeemed. Not just new—but worthy.

She's read the Scriptures. She's led devotionals. She knows what grace *says*—but grace feels like a theory, not a reality. Because what she did still clings to her. Flashbacks. Regret. Shame. The weight of her past doesn't seem to have lifted—it's simply shifted into silence.

When she sees other women getting married, she wonders if her history has made her unfit for that kind of love. When she worships, the songs feel hollow. When asked to serve, she smiles and agrees, but the thought always returns: *If they knew what you've done, they'd never let you seve.*

And then it happened.

An old flame reached out. Familiar voice. Familiar pull. The same charm, the same script. He didn't even have to try hard—just reminded her of who she used to be. And somewhere in that moment, her resistance gave out. It didn't feel like temptation—it felt inevitable.

That one night set off a storm in her soul.

Now she's trapped in the aftermath: disgusted with herself, tormented by guilt, buried under shame. She can't stop replaying it. *How could you? After everything God's done...*

The enemy has returned, louder than ever. Not tempting her now—tormenting her.

You were never really changed. You're a fraud. You're damaged goods. Why would God use you?

It's not just a battle of the mind—it's a war in her spirit. Her flesh has spoken. The accuser is shouting. And her heart feels torn between running back to God... and running away in shame.

She's not just wrestling with what she did. She's questioning who she is.

She's forgiven—but she feels more lost than ever.

Key Choices

Brianna's story is a vivid picture of what happens when we don't fully receive the righteousness and identity we've been given in Christ. The enemy knows that if he can't keep us from salvation, he'll try to keep us from living in the fullness of it. And that battle is often fought through the lingering residue of past sins—especially sexual sin, which cuts deeply into our sense of worth, purity, and belonging. These are the spiritual crossroads Brianna is facing:

1. Choosing to Walk in Grace vs. Living Under the Law

Brianna has heard about grace, but she's still measuring her worth by her past behavior. She's trying to earn her way into purity instead of receiving it as a gift through Christ.

Every time she punishes herself for her past, she's agreeing with the accuser, not the Advocate. Choosing grace means releasing the need to "make up for it" and resting in what Jesus already paid for.

2. Choosing to Live from a New Identity vs. Letting the Past Define You

The enemy keeps dragging Brianna back to who she was, hoping she'll forget who she is now in Christ. But she's a new creation—not because she's gotten everything right, but because she's been made new (2 Corinthians 5:17).

This is more than a mindset shift—it's a spiritual stance. Will she keep agreeing with the labels of her past, or will she step into the identity the cross secured for her?

3. Choosing to Confess and Return vs. Hiding in Shame

After giving in to temptation, Brianna's instinct is to hide. She wants to disappear, isolate, and stay silent. But true repentance doesn't run away from God—it runs toward Him.

Hiding in shame only strengthens the stronghold of condemnation. Confession breaks its power. Choosing to come clean—to God and to trusted community—is how healing begins.

4. Choosing to Fight in the Spirit vs. Giving in to the Flesh

The weakness Brianna feels isn't just emotional—it's spiritual. She's exhausted because she's been trying to battle flesh with flesh. But we are called to crucify the flesh and walk by the Spirit (Galatians 5:16–17).

This choice is daily and often moment by moment. Will she feed the Spirit through worship, the Word, and accountability—or continue to feed the flesh through secrecy, regret, and self-condemnation?

5. Choosing to Believe God's Voice vs. Listening to the Accuser

The voice of the enemy is relentless: *You're dirty. You're unworthy. You've blown it.*

But God's voice says: *You are mine. You are clean. Come home.*

Brianna must choose which voice she will believe. This is not about ignoring conviction—it's about refusing condemnation. The Holy Spirit convicts to restore. The enemy condemns to destroy.

Enemy Tactics

The enemy knows how powerful a believer becomes when they walk in the full freedom of who they are in Christ. That's why he targets the wounded places—especially those connected to our past, our identity, and our worth. For Brianna, the battlefield is in her memories, her emotions, and her thoughts. These are the primary tactics the enemy is using against her:

Shame and Condemnation

Rather than letting Brianna rest in God's mercy, the enemy keeps rehearsing her sin. He tells her she's unclean, unworthy, and disqualified. He doesn't just remind her of what she's done—he convinces her that it defines who she is.

This tactic turns past sin into present identity, making her question the legitimacy of her forgiveness and the reality of her transformation.

False Identity and Labels

The enemy constantly tempts Brianna to wear the labels of her old life: "Used." "Promiscuous." "Damaged." These labels become internal accusations that shape her self-perception. And if she accepts them, she'll struggle to receive or believe anything God says about her: that she's beloved, redeemed, chosen, and pure in His sight.

Reopening Old Wounds (Pain and Trauma)

Sexual sin often leaves emotional, spiritual, and even physical scars. The enemy exploits those wounds. He brings back flashbacks, triggers, and memories to drag Brianna into regret and hopelessness.

Instead of allowing her to walk in healing, he pulls her into cycles of self-blame and sorrow, reinforcing the lie: *"You'll never be free of this."*

Temptation and Compromise

The enemy doesn't just want Brianna to feel guilty—he wants her to give up. He uses exhaustion to make temptation feel inevitable. "You already messed up—might as well give in."

This tactic is rooted in deception: that purity is something she lost forever, and obedience now wouldn't make a difference. He uses this lie to lure her back into sin by normalizing the compromise.

Confusion

Brianna is stuck in a fog of spiritual confusion. She knows she's forgiven but doesn't feel free. She knows the Word but feels powerless to stand on it. The enemy clouds her ability to discern truth by attacking her emotions and amplifying her doubts.

This tactic destabilizes her spiritual footing and makes her feel disconnected from God's presence and promises—even though neither has changed.

Isolation

The enemy tempts her to hide. He tells her no one would understand, that people would judge her, and that she has to figure this out alone. Isolation strengthens condemnation. It keeps her from the very relationships, encouragement, and accountability she needs to break free.

Guilt-Driven Goodness

Though Brianna serves at church, the enemy twists her motives— pushing her to serve out of guilt rather than gratitude. Her spiritual life becomes performance instead of worship.

This tactic makes her feel like she has to earn her worth, exhausting her further and weakening her connection with God.

Fear and Intimidation

The enemy intimidates Brianna with lies about her future: *"No godly man will want you. You'll never be clean enough. You're not cut out for ministry."* This fear keeps her from dreaming, stepping out, or believing that God could use her. It paralyzes her purpose and poisons her hope.

Pride and Ego

This may seem like the opposite of shame—but it's actually closely tied. The belief that *"I can't be forgiven,"* or *"What I did is too big for the cross,"* is not humility—it's pride.

It places Brianna's sin above Jesus' sacrifice. The enemy subtly persuades her to hold onto control, to cling to self-assessment, and to believe she must somehow prove her worth before she can fully receive freedom.

Freedom requires surrender—not just from sin but from self. Pride masks itself as unworthiness, but it still keeps Jesus at arm's length.

Together, these tactics create a powerful stronghold of condemnation, with shame as the foundation, isolation as the shield, and guilt as the motivator. The result is that Brianna, though spiritually alive, lives like she's still in chains.

Counterfeit Outcome

Brianna hasn't turned her back on God—but she's trapped in a life where freedom is a concept, not a reality. Condemnation has become her constant companion. She knows all the right verses and still believes in grace—for others. But for herself? Not fully. Not freely.

The enemy doesn't have to drag her back into her old life to keep her bound—he just has to convince her that her new life isn't really hers to live. That's the power of condemnation. It creates a spiritual paralysis and tormentation that keep you showing up but shuts you down inside.

Here's what it looks like when someone lives under the weight of condemnation:

Partial Freedom, Perpetual Guilt

Brianna believes she's forgiven but feels dirty. She walks through life as if she's on probation with God—grateful He let her in, but unsure if He truly wants her there. Her worship is filtered through unworthiness. Her prayers are muted by shame. Her sense of belonging is shallow and unstable.

She lives forgiven, but not free—because she's still holding herself hostage to a sentence Jesus already served.

Recycled Sin Patterns

Condemnation doesn't just accuse—it exhausts. And exhaustion makes the flesh louder than the Spirit.

Because Brianna feels like she can't ever be fully clean, the temptation to return to old sin becomes harder to resist. After all, the enemy whispers, *"You already ruined it. Why keep pretending?"*

This is how many fall back—not because they're chasing sin, but because they're fleeing from a pain they don't know how to heal.

What began as a longing for forgiveness turns into a cycle of defeat, fueled by hopelessness.

Compromised Calling

God hasn't changed His calling on Brianna's life—but condemnation makes her question if she should still walk in it. She pulls back. She hesitates to lead. She second-guesses her ability to witness, encourage, or minister. Opportunities exist but they generate panic and fear. Her gifts remain—but her confidence in them shrinks under the lie: *"You're not worthy to be His hands and feet."*

Eroded Intimacy with God

Though she prays and reads the Word, Brianna's relationship with God feels more dutiful than delightful. She feels like a tolerated guest instead of a beloved daughter. She expects discipline more than delight. And in that emotional distance, the voice of the enemy grows louder while God's feels faint—even though He's never stopped speaking.

When condemnation clouds our minds, it doesn't just distort how we see ourselves—it distorts how we see God.

Twisted Identity

Condemnation keeps Brianna tethered to the person she used to be. She knows the verse— *"If anyone is in Christ, he is a new creation."* But she struggles to believe it applies to her. Instead of walking in her new identity, she constantly re-lives her old one.

Brianna isn't lost—but she's living like she is. That's what condemnation does. It doesn't remove you from grace—it just makes you feel disqualified from it. And as long as you feel disqualified, you'll never step fully into the promises and authority that are already yours in Christ.

This is the counterfeit life:

- A life that knows the truth but can't embrace it.
- A life that hears "You're free" but keeps returning to the cell (bondage).
- A life where you serve a loving Father while still fearing He's disappointed in you.

And this counterfeit life is not neutral—it's tormenting.

Condemnation doesn't just shame you—it *tears you apart.* It keeps you constantly second-guessing, never secure, never settled. It's designed to erode your joy, rob your confidence, weaken your witness, and leave you wavering—never certain of God's love or your standing.

It's not just painful—it's maddening. Because deep down, you *know* the truth. You know what Jesus did. But condemnation makes you feel like it's not enough…for you.

But Jesus didn't die so we could live with half-healed hearts. He didn't rise so we could walk around ashamed. The cross didn't just pay for your sin—it paid to *remove your shame.*

Condemnation is the enemy's counterfeit conviction—designed to keep you broken where God already made you whole.

Areas of Salvation Impacted

When condemnation takes root, it doesn't just affect how we feel—it distorts what we believe about what salvation actually accomplished. The enemy can't undo the cross, but he can try to keep us from walking in its power. And if we don't recognize the ways condemnation is corrupting our theology and crippling our identity, we will live like spiritual beggars even though we're sons and daughters of the King.

Here's what condemnation erodes:

Justification

At the moment of salvation, we are declared righteous before God—not because of what we've done, but because of what Christ did.

Brianna knows this in theory, but condemnation makes her feel like she's still on trial. Instead of standing in grace, she keeps trying to earn God's approval. She lives like she's only partially justified, needing to prove herself worthy of the forgiveness she's already received.

> *"Therefore, since we have been justified through faith, we have peace with God through our Lord Jesus Christ."*
> – Romans 5:1

New Identity

Salvation makes us new creations. The old has passed away. But condemnation keeps the past alive, loud, and looming.

Brianna doesn't feel new—so she questions whether she really is. And the enemy uses every doubt to drag her identity back to her former self, whispering: *"Nothing's really changed."*

But in Christ, our past is not our name. Our identity isn't what we did—it's whose we are.

Intimacy with God

We've been reconciled to God through Jesus. We have access to His presence. But condemnation creates emotional and spiritual distance.

Brianna approaches God cautiously, as if He's disappointed or reluctant to draw near. Condemnation turns prayer into pleading. Worship into penance. And relationship into performance. But God invites us to come boldly—not fearfully—to His throne of grace (Hebrews 4:16).

Freedom from Sin and Shame

Salvation doesn't just cancel the penalty of sin—it breaks its power. But condemnation tells us we're still chained. That we're just forgiven failures instead of victorious children of God.

Brianna's inability to feel clean isn't about her salvation—it's about strongholds of shame the enemy uses to keep her from walking in freedom. And where there is shame, there will always be secrecy, silence, and self-condemnation.

Purpose and Authority

Every believer is called, equipped, and empowered by the Holy Spirit to serve the Kingdom.

But condemnation makes you feel unqualified and unworthy. Brianna has gifts—but she doesn't use them with boldness. She's been called—but she questions if God still wants her.

This is how the enemy sidelines believers. He can't steal your salvation, so he tries to strip your confidence until you sit out the mission altogether.

Faith in Action

Condemnation is not just a feeling—it's a lie. And like every lie, it must be confronted with truth. If you see yourself in Brianna's story, it doesn't mean you're disqualified. It means the enemy has been targeting your mind and your identity—and it's time to take your place as a fully forgiven, deeply loved child of God.

This isn't about pretending the past didn't happen. It's about believing that the blood of Jesus is greater than anything you've done or anything done to you. Your freedom was paid for in full. You don't need to earn it—you need to receive it and walk in it.

Here are practical ways to do that:

Confess the Root of Condemnation

Don't just deal with the surface emotion—ask the Holy Spirit to show you where the door was opened. Was it a sin you haven't fully repented of? A lie you've agreed with? An identity you haven't let go of? Name it. Bring it into the light.

Confess Your Sins to Mature, Trusted Believers

Condemnation grows in secrecy. Scripture tells us to confess our sins to one another and pray for each other that we may be healed (James 5:16). Find a mature believer or mentor who is rooted in grace and truth. Confession brings freedom, healing, and accountability. Don't fight alone.

Participate in a Grace-Based Community

You need spaces where truth, vulnerability, and grace are not just talked about—they're practiced. Surround yourself with people who walk in humility and who know what it means to be redeemed. Healing accelerates in healthy, Spirit-led community.

Declare Your Justification Daily

Start each day with this declaration:

"I am justified by faith. I am forgiven. I am not under condemnation. I belong to Jesus."

Use Scriptures like Romans 8:1, 2 Corinthians 5:17, and Romans 5:1 to retrain your mind and silence the accuser.

Renounce Pride and Ego in Your Struggle

It may feel counterintuitive, but lingering in unworthiness can actually be a form of pride. It says, "What I've done is too big for God to fully redeem." Surrender your need to punish yourself. Let go of your pride and receive the fullness of grace.

Stop Judging Others Through Your Own Pain

Sometimes, those battling condemnation become condemners. If you find yourself judging others—especially those who struggle with sins like yours—ask the Lord to search your heart. Don't be a hypocrite. We often dish out condemnation to others as a misguided way of coping with our own. Let grace flow both in and through you.

Receive—and Keep Receiving—Grace

Grace isn't a one-time gift—it's a daily portion. Every time you're tempted to spiral into shame or self-hate, stop and say:

"Thank You, Jesus, for Your grace. I receive it again right now." Keep coming back to the cross until grace becomes your reflex, not guilt.

Break Agreement with the Accuser

You are not the sum of your past. Break every agreement you've made—silently or aloud—with the enemy's voice. Say it out loud:

"I break agreement with the lie that I am still unclean. I break agreement with the lie that I am disqualified. I am who God says I am."

Submit Your Body and Desires to the Spirit

This battle isn't just in the mind—it's also in the flesh. The temptation to return to old patterns will rise when condemnation is unchecked. You must actively surrender your body, your desires, and your memories to the authority of the Spirit. Fasting, prayer, and accountability are key tools here.

Worship—Especially When You Feel Unworthy

Condemnation wants to mute your worship. Don't let it. When you feel furthest from God, that's the moment to lift your voice the loudest. Worship until truth breaks the lie. Worship until presence replaces performance. Worship until your shame gives way to awe.

Serve Boldly Again

Don't wait until you *feel* worthy—move in obedience and let your confidence grow through action. The enemy wants you to hide. God invites you to shine. You've been cleansed, called, and commissioned.

Prayer

Father,

I've believed the lie that I'm still dirty, still disqualified, still defined by what I've done. But Your Word says there is no condemnation for those who are in Christ Jesus. Today, I break agreement with shame, guilt, and self-hatred. I renounce every lie that says I'm not worthy of Your love or Your purpose. I receive the finished work of Jesus—the blood that makes me clean, whole, and new. Holy Spirit, led me in the renewal of my mind. Teach me to live in the freedom that's already mine. Help me walk in grace toward others—not from pain, but from healing. And when the enemy tries to whisper lies again, help me stand in truth with boldness.

In Jesus' name, Amen.

Areas of Study

Romans 8:1–2 – "There is therefore now no condemnation…"

This is the foundation of the entire chapter. Those in Christ are not under condemnation. Study this passage slowly and let it sink in. Your past cannot follow you into the life Jesus purchased for you.

2 Corinthians 5:17 – **"If anyone is in Christ, he is a new creation…"**

This verse establishes the identity shift. The old is gone. The new has come. It's not a theory—it's a spiritual reality. Let the Word reshape your self-image.

Romans 5:1 – **"We have been justified by faith…"**

Justified means declared righteous. Not "becoming" righteous—declared so, based on what Jesus has done. Condemnation tries to undo this declaration. Return here often.

1 John 1:9 – **"If we confess our sins, He is faithful and just…"**

Confession is a pathway to restoration, not rejection. This verse is a comfort to those battling lingering guilt. It reinforces God's willingness and faithfulness to cleanse.

Isaiah 1:18 – **"Though your sins are like scarlet…"**

This Old Testament promise points to the cleansing power of God's grace and mercy. It also foreshadows what Christ fulfilled.

Psalm 103:12 – **"As far as the east is from the west…"**

God's forgiveness doesn't just cover—it removes. Meditate on the completeness of His mercy and the permanence of your pardon.

Hebrews 10:14 – **"By one sacrifice He has made perfect forever…"**

This verse addresses the lie that we need to keep "proving" ourselves to God. Jesus' sacrifice was sufficient—forever.

James 5:16 – **"Confess your sins to one another…"**

Condemnation thrives in isolation. God designed community as part of our healing. This verse also teaches the connection between vulnerability and breakthrough.

Galatians 2:21 – **"I do not set aside the grace of God…"**

Dwelling in condemnation often reveals a hidden resistance to grace. This verse is a strong reminder that righteousness cannot come through our efforts.

Titus 3:5 – **"Not because of righteous things we had done…"**

God saved you not because you got it right, but because He is merciful. This is a critical verse for uprooting pride and ego hidden in feelings of unworthiness.

Romans 6:11–14 – **"Consider yourselves dead to sin…"**

The struggle with temptation must be reframed in light of who we are in Christ. We don't resist to earn freedom—we resist because we have been made free.

John 8:1–11 – **The woman caught in adultery**

Jesus didn't ignore her sin—but neither did He condemn her. Study this story for a picture of conviction without shame, and truth delivered through love.

Closing Reflection

Condemnation is more than just a feeling—it's a strategy. The enemy uses it not just to shame you, but to slowly dismantle you from the inside out. It's not enough for him to tempt you—he wants to torment you. And condemnation is one of his most devastating tools. It doesn't just whisper that you've failed—it insists that you *are* a failure. That's the counterfeit life it offers: one marked by defeat, despair, and distance from God.

But that's not the life Jesus died to give you.

If you've seen yourself in Brianna's story—if you've wrestled with your past, questioned your worth, or felt too dirty, too broken, or too far gone—then this chapter is your reminder: the cross was enough. You don't have to keep living under what Jesus already died to lift off you.

Condemnation snowballs. It grows if left unaddressed. It leads to isolation, hypocrisy, and often, relapse. It tears you apart, piece by piece— your confidence, your calling, your intimacy with God. That's why it's urgent to confront it. You don't need to wait until you feel "better" to believe the truth. Freedom isn't a feeling—it's a fact.

Jesus doesn't just forgive you—He restores you. He doesn't just cover your shame—He removes it. His sacrifice wasn't partial. His blood didn't miss a spot. And the only thing standing between you and peace may be the lie that you're still unworthy of it.

You are not who you were.
You are not what you did.
You are who He says you are.
And in Christ, you are already free.

So don't wait for the voice of condemnation to get quieter. Silence it with truth. And walk in the grace that has already been given.

Closing to Section III:
The War Within — Spiritual
Pressure and Personal Pain

You've just walked through some of the most personal, painful, and persistent battles believers face—depression, doubt and worry, bitterness and anger, and condemnation. If you saw yourself in these pages, you are not alone. These chapters weren't meant to shame you. They were written to shine a light on the battles the enemy hopes you'll keep hidden.

Each stronghold exposed in this section is evidence of war—but it's also evidence of your worth. The enemy only attacks what he fears. He fears your healing. He fears your obedience. He fears your freedom. And he knows if he can't destroy your faith, he'll try to distort your thoughts, drain your strength, and disqualify your identity.

But God doesn't leave us to fight these battles alone.

In each chapter, we saw that the path to healing isn't through performance or perfection—it's through truth, repentance, community, renewed thinking, and the empowering grace of the Holy Spirit. The same Jesus who saved you is sanctifying you. He's not intimidated by your struggles. He knows how to walk you through them.

There's something else we need to remember: internal battles don't stay internal. What we allow to fester in our hearts and minds eventually leaks into our decisions, our relationships, our worship, our work, and our witness. That's why these chapters matter. They reveal how private pain becomes public patterns—and how God, in His mercy, wants to interrupt the cycle before it takes over your life.

If there's one truth that echoes through every chapter in this section, it's this:

The war within may be intense—but it is winnable.

Victory doesn't come by pretending you're okay. It comes by letting the light of Christ reach the places the enemy has tried to keep in the dark.

So whether you're just beginning to see the strongholds or you've been fighting for years, let this be your turning point. Not toward managing symptoms—but toward true, Spirit-led healing.

Because freedom isn't a fantasy. It's your inheritance in Christ.

Section IV

Counterfeit Connection:
The Enemy's Attack on Relationships

The enemy hates connection—because true, godly connection reflects the nature of God Himself. From the beginning, God designed us for relationship: with Him, with one another, and within covenant. But since the garden, Satan's strategy has remained consistent—divide and isolate. If he can't pull us away from God directly, he'll fracture the relationships God uses to shape, heal, and strengthen us.

This section exposes how the enemy subtly and aggressively sabotages the connections meant to bring life. His tactics aren't always loud or dramatic. Sometimes, they're quiet compromises: emotional distance, unspoken resentment, gossip dressed as concern, surface-level peace that masks deep wounds. He will settle for marriages that look good but feel hollow, churches that preach love but withhold truth, friendships that never go deep, and small groups filled with empty smiles and unsaid offenses.

Each chapter in this section highlights a relational battleground where many believers get caught in the counterfeit:

- Choosing isolation when healing requires community.

- Holding on to offense instead of pursuing forgiveness.

- Confusing gossip with discernment.

- Presenting image over honesty in marriage.

- Abandoning unity when strife feels justified.

These aren't just interpersonal issues—they're spiritual ones. Because every broken or fake connection has ripple effects in the spirit. When the Body of Christ is divided, distracted, or disconnected, it cannot walk in power. And that is exactly what the enemy wants.

But what the enemy fractures, God can restore. This section is a call to examine the ways we relate, reconcile, and remain rooted in truth. It's not about fixing others—it's about recognizing where we've compromised and inviting the Holy Spirit to lead us back into authentic, Christ-centered connection.

CHAPTER 12

When Disappointment Becomes Division: The Attack After Community

———————•———————

Two are better than one, because they have a good reward for their toil. For if they fall, one will lift up his fellow. But woe to him who is alone when he falls and has not another to lift him up! Ecclesiastes 4:9–10

Community is a gift—but one that rarely comes without resistance. We pray for connection, crave belonging, and even take the first bold step into fellowship. But when it doesn't meet our expectations—when the conversation feels awkward, the people seem different, or the welcome isn't warm—the enemy sees an opening. Disappointment becomes a foothold. Subtle lies begin to surface: "You don't fit in here." "This isn't your place." What began as a spiritual step forward suddenly feels like a mistake. But what if the discomfort isn't a sign to leave, but an invitation to grow? What if the enemy's real goal isn't to make you uncomfortable— but to keep you isolated?

Personal Experience

Up until God intervened and taught me how, I never prioritized relationships. My life was about success, achievement, and results. I wasn't manipulative, but I was transactional. I didn't invest in people—I didn't know how because I didn't care to. Changing that didn't happen overnight. It took over a decade of God softening my heart, challenging my thinking, and eventually leading me to commit to my first local church and the uncomfortable work of building community.

Part of that commitment meant joining a small group. To play it safe, I chose a Saturday morning hiking group. I figured if it didn't go well, I would at least get to do something I enjoyed.

As usual, I arrived early. But the hike didn't start on time. A few members were running late, which already irritated me. I value timeliness—and the enemy knows that. Still, I was determined to press through and honor the commitment I'd made to God. Eventually, we prayed and started. Some of the women already knew each other and paired off naturally. I didn't know anyone, and trying to spark conversation felt awkward. I'm not good at small talk. I wasn't interested in chatting about kids or family—topics I categorized at the time as "regular" life. I wanted to talk about entrepreneurship, adventure, and travel—but that didn't seem to fit.

As we hiked, I struggled not only to connect but also I began to battle the internal dialogue that this was a waste of time. The enemy grabbed the opportunity to play familiar scripts: *"This isn't my thing." "I don't belong here."* On the drive home, those thoughts intensified. I started replaying all the ways the hike would've been better if I'd just gone alone. I would've started on time. Gone farther. Hiked faster. Gotten more out of it. According to the enemy, there was no reason to ever go back.

But I recognized my preferences, comfort zones, and what I had come to believe about myself. I knew my flesh and the enemy wanted to convince me to never go back. I had to battle my comfort zones, preferences, and self-imposed limitations. I needed to change my ways. I had made a commitment—not only to the group, but to God. And I keep my commitments to Him.

I showed up the following week.

Toward the end of that second hike, I had a conversation with a new member—a young woman who confessed she was beginning to feel like she didn't belong. Until we started talking. The enemy had used the same tactic on her. And because I had fought through it the week before, I was able to come alongside her and help her fight, too.

That was a few years ago. Since then, I've been part of many small groups—and I've led several. I've watched this same pattern repeat itself over and over. The number that sign-up is larger than the number of member that show-up. The first meeting has high attendance but member attendance slowly dwindles as the enemy works overtime to convince people they don't belong, that they're too busy, or that it's just not worth the time.

Key Choices

That hike wasn't just a test of endurance—it was a test of commitment. Not to the group, but to God. I had already said yes to Him. Yes to building community. Yes to allowing Him to reshape how I engaged with people. But that yes was challenged the moment the experience didn't match my expectations. And that's where the enemy works best—between what we hoped for and what actually happens.

The thoughts that met me on the drive home weren't random. They were targeted. And if I hadn't recognized them for what they were, I might have never gone back. That's how many people miss what God is trying to grow in their lives—they mislabel disappointment, comfort zones, and preferences as the best way forward. But being faced with what's holding us back is not a reason to buckle—it's a reason to press in.

That hiking group wasn't just a weekend activity—it was spiritual ground I needed to conquer and take back from the enemy.

Here are the choices I had to make—and the same ones many believers face when they step into unfamiliar, imperfect community:

1. Choosing to persevere through discomfort vs. withdrawing into isolation

That first hike—and many after—weren't easy for me. Not physically, but relationally. It would've been so much simpler to retreat into what I knew: solo hikes, solo faith, solo life. But isolation isn't safety—it's surrender to the enemy's plan. Community grows through commitment, not convenience. And every time we walk away from discomfort, we walk away from transformation.

2. Choosing to believe God has a place for you vs. believing you don't belong

The voices in my head weren't just thoughts—they were accusations: *"You don't fit." "You're not like them."* And I had to decide whose voice I was going to believe. Who would define my place in the Body of Christ? Would I trust that God had led me there for a reason—even if I couldn't yet see it?

The enemy had long-established strongholds around what I believed about relationships—my lack of need for them and my inability to build them. It wasn't that he had to tell me new lies. He just needed to remind me of the ones he had already planted. And I had to choose whether to keep nurturing those lies or let God dismantle them.

3. Choosing unity and openness vs. judgment and self-protection

It would've been easy to judge those women—to assume they were cliquish or not my kind of people. But that reaction wasn't righteousness—it was a shield. A cover for self-protection. Unity doesn't happen when everyone clicks instantly. It happens when we stay long enough to see people beyond our first impression. I had to lay down my assumptions, open my heart, and become vulnerable—or I could hold on to the wrong mindsets and remain hardened. One path would form community. The other would fortify walls.

Enemy Tactics

The enemy came against God's plan and getting me settled into fellowship because he knows how damaging that is for him. I had been living an isolated life and that's where the enemy wanted to keep me. He couldn't attack me in the isolation I was already living there–he had to keep me isolated by weaponizing my expectations and confirming my fears.

The thoughts that flooded my mind after that hike weren't casual— they were coordinated. And they weren't just aimed at getting me to skip another Saturday. They were aimed at keeping me disconnected, unrooted, and ineffective in the very place God had called me to grow.

When it comes to community, the enemy doesn't usually build new barriers—he leverages the ones we've already constructed. He builds his attack on the foundation of past wounds, familiar fears, and long-held beliefs we've accepted as truth. If you've lived life without deep connection, he'll do everything in his power to keep it that way. The moment you take a step toward fellowship, he moves fast to weaponize your preferences, inflame your insecurities, and magnify your discomfort. His goal isn't just to discourage you—it's to keep the strongholds in place so you never get free.

Here are the tactics the enemy used—and the same ones he still uses to fracture relationships and fracture the Body of Christ:

Division Through Disappointment

The hike didn't go as I hoped, and the enemy jumped on that. He doesn't need you to be wronged—just let down. He takes minor disappointments and inflates them into major offenses. He whispers, *"You're not like them," "You don't fit here,"* until distance feels justified. What starts as discomfort becomes division if left unchecked.

Comparison and Envy

I started noticing what I lacked. How they had easier conversations. How I didn't fit the mold. The enemy is quick to highlight what separates rather than what connects. Comparison makes you feel smaller, lesser, or superior—but never unified. It puts your focus on yourself instead of others, on differences instead of purpose.

False Identity and Old Labels

"You don't belong here." "You're not the type." Those lies weren't new. The enemy had planted them decades before—about my worth, my social limitations, and my supposed independence. All he had to do was press play. That's what makes these attacks so effective—they don't feel foreign, they feel familiar.

Isolation Disguised as Wisdom

The enemy offered what sounded like logic: *"You'd get more out of this on your own." "You don't need this group to grow." "Just hike alone next time."* It felt reasonable and preferrable. But spiritual attacks rarely show up in obvious forms. They hide behind preferences and practicality—until you've slowly withdrawn and called it peace.

Distraction Through Preferences

Rather than ask what God was forming in me, I started focusing on everything that didn't go how I liked: the late start, the pace, the topics of conversation. The enemy didn't have to lie about any of it—he just had to make it the focus. Distraction is one of his quietest strategies. It keeps your eyes on the natural so you miss the spiritual.

Counterfeit Outcome

I wasn't running from God. I had said yes to Him. I was trying to obey. But underneath the obedience were strongholds I hadn't yet surrendered—beliefs about myself, about people, and about what I was or wasn't capable of relationally. The enemy didn't need to push me out of church—he just needed to keep me spiritually unrooted and relationally unavailable. He wasn't just trying to get me to skip a group hike. He was trying to stop me from ever building godly relationships, from ever experiencing what true spiritual connection could do in my life.

God wanted me to destroy strongholds, receive healing and take new ground in my life through relationships and the enemy wanted to stop that from ever happening. The enemy needed me to refuse the change and work God was continuing to do in my life.

Here's what the counterfeit would have looked like if I hadn't chosen to fight back:

Spiritually isolated, with no local support system

I would've stayed in the same pattern—physically present at church, but spiritually unrooted in community. No real friendships. No one to call when life got hard. No one to speak truth when the lies got loud. No one to pray and come into agreement with me. The enemy knows that isolated believers are easier to deceive, easier to discourage, and easier to defeat.

Increased self-focus and disconnection from the Body

Walking away would've deepened the habit of relying on myself. I would've continued operating independently, filtering everything through my own preferences, perspectives, and limitations. Disconnection doesn't just separate us from people—it slowly cuts us off from the flow of the Body, where encouragement, correction, and calling are meant to function.

Delay in healing, accountability, and growth

I didn't realize at the time how much healing God had planned to bring through community. But healing doesn't happen in hiding. Had I withdrawn, the strongholds I carried about connection, value, and vulnerability would have remained unchallenged. I would've stayed "functional" but spiritually stuck—surviving instead of growing.

Missing the people and experiences God had placed on my path

That young woman I spoke to the following week—she needed someone to tell her she wasn't alone. And I needed that moment to see why the enemy fought so hard to keep me away. If I hadn't gone back, neither of us would've had that encounter. And that's the real tragedy of the counterfeit life: we miss the divine appointments because we give up too soon. The enemy doesn't just want to steal our joy—he wants to rob us of the very people and moments that would've ushered in breakthrough.

Areas of Salvation Impacted

Meaningful Community and Belonging

Salvation isn't just personal—it places us into a Body. I wasn't just being saved from sin; I was being called into connection. The enemy knows that when believers stay disconnected, they also stay discouraged, unaccountable, and underdeveloped. Belonging isn't a bonus—it's part of the blessing.

A New Heart and a Renewed Mind

God was renewing my thinking about people, purpose, and participation. Choosing to return—week after week—began to rewrite the internal narrative that said, *You don't need anyone.* My heart softened, and my thoughts shifted. Community became part of my sanctification, not just my schedule.

Peace With God and Others

Peace isn't just the absence of conflict—it's the presence of right relationship. By staying, I partnered with the Holy Spirit in creating unity, even when it was uncomfortable. Peace with God begins to break open in our lives when we stop resisting the ways He draws us into relationship with others.

The Indwelling of the Holy Spirit

The Spirit of God wasn't just prompting me to go—He was empowering me to stay. And every time I resisted His nudge toward connection, I grieved His presence. Community is one of the places where the Spirit is most active—gifting, correcting, and guiding us through the voices and love of others. Staying connected allowed me to experience His work in ways isolation never could.

Faith in Action

Staying in that small group wasn't easy. It didn't become comfortable overnight. But it became sacred because I chose to obey. That obedience wasn't about the group—it was about God. And it required real faith. Faith to believe He had something for me there. Faith to believe I could change. Faith to believe that awkward beginnings could lead to eternal fruit.

The battle for community is spiritual, and so is the response. Here's how to step into that battle:

Return even when it's uncomfortable

Faith looks like showing up again—even when nothing has changed. Don't wait until you feel connected to return. Go because you've made a commitment to God, not because the experience feels perfect.

Ask God to reveal His purpose in the discomfort

Instead of focusing on what's lacking, ask God what He's building. What is He trying to heal, confront, or grow in you through this group? The friction may be the formation.

Pray for love and openness toward others

Ask the Holy Spirit to give you a soft heart and open spirit—especially toward people who seem different from you. Unity is forged through prayer long before it's felt in conversation.

Serve instead of spectate

Look for one way to contribute, even if it's small. Ask a question. Encourage someone. Help clean up. Faith grows through action, and service builds connection.

Journal after each gathering

Write down what stood out—both spiritually and emotionally. Look for patterns in your thoughts. Identify the lies that try to take root. Confront them with truth and Scripture.

Make your yes to God louder than the enemy's no

This isn't about forcing connection—it's about fighting for it. Don't partner with the enemy's lies by shrinking back. Stand on the truth that you *do* belong, that you *are* being formed, and that God *will* meet you there.

Prayer

Father, I confess that community hasn't come easy for me. I've believed lies about not belonging. I've let fear, past wounds, and disappointment shape how I see others—and how I see myself. But I don't want to live isolated anymore. I don't want to settle for surface-level faith or guarded relationships.

I choose today to trust that You have a place for me in Your Body. I surrender the strongholds that have kept me withdrawn and self-protective. Help me to see others the way You see them. Give me courage to show up even when it's uncomfortable, and strength to stay when everything in me wants to retreat.

Holy Spirit, soften my heart. Make me teachable. Make me bold. Help me to build what I've never seen before—a life of connection rooted in Your love and truth. I choose to believe that my healing is found not just in You—but in the people You've placed around me.

In Jesus' name, Amen.

Areas of Study

Key Scriptures

Hebrews 10:24–25 – "And let us consider how we may spur one another on toward love and good deeds, not giving up meeting together…"

Ephesians 4:2–3 – "Be completely humble and gentle; be patient, bearing with one another in love. Make every effort to keep the unity of the Spirit…"

Romans 12:4–5 – "For just as each of us has one body with many members… so in Christ we, though many, form one body…"

Proverbs 27:17 – "As iron sharpens iron, so one person sharpens another."

Biblical Figures & Examples

Barnabas and Paul – Their partnership, disagreement, and eventual separation show both the challenge and value of relational ministry (Acts 15:36–41).

The Early Church – A model of radical fellowship, shared life, and Spirit-empowered community (Acts 2:42–47).

Ruth and Naomi – A picture of faithful connection and the blessing that comes from staying when it would've been easier to leave.

Spiritual Practices

Gratitude for Community – Begin or end your day by thanking God for one person He's placed in your life.

Confession of Disappointment – Acknowledge any hurt or unmet expectations and surrender them in prayer.

Speaking Life Over Your Group – Declare truth, blessing, and fruitfulness over the community you're part of.

Staying Committed Through Awkwardness – Make a personal decision to stay engaged for a set season—even when it's uncomfortable.

Closing Reflection

The enemy almost succeeded in keeping me from something God was using to change my life. And all it took was a disappointing morning and pressing play on the strongholds he had established. That's how the counterfeit life works—it doesn't start with outright rebellion. It starts with hesitation. Discomfort. A reason not to go back.

But God had called me into community, and I chose to fight for what He was forming in me—even when I didn't see the fruit right away. That choice didn't just bless me; it positioned me to bless others. It gave me eyes to see spiritual warfare in everyday moments. And it reminded me that obedience often feels awkward before it feels sacred.

Maybe you're there right now. Maybe your version of the hike didn't go how you hoped. Maybe you've already started to pull back. Let this be your turning point.

Because the truth is: we don't step into community because it's easy—we step in because it's essential. God shapes us through people. He softens our hearts through connection. And He plants us so that we can grow, not just in Him—but alongside His Body.

Don't give the enemy the final word. Don't let disappointment become division.

Stay rooted. Stay open. Stay in the fight.

CHAPTER 13

The Hidden Cost of Holding on
Forgiveness vs. Offense

———•———

*"A brother offended is more unyielding than a strong city,
and quarreling is like the bars of a castle."*Proverbs 18:19

Strife rarely starts loud. It often begins with something quiet—a wound, a misunderstanding, an unresolved offense. But left unchecked, it becomes a spiritual force that sows discord, poisons trust, and turns every relationship into a battleground. It doesn't just divide people—it divides hearts. Strife feeds off the need to be right, the refusal to release, and the belief that protection lies in separation. The enemy loves strife because it looks justified. It sounds like wisdom. But behind the surface is a spirit sent to stir up chaos where God wants to build peace. If we don't learn to forgive and let go, strife will do more than cost us a relationship—it will cost us clarity, unity, joy, and spiritual authority.

Scenario

Michelle and Danielle weren't just business partners—they were friends. Sisters in Christ. Prayer warriors. They had met in a women's Bible study, bonded over a shared heart for purpose-driven entrepreneurship, and eventually launched a faith-based consulting firm together. Their rhythm felt anointed. Meetings opened with prayer. Decisions were bathed in discernment. They co-led devotionals for their clients and encouraged their employees to grow in both excellence and integrity. At one point, they even vacationed with each other's families. It felt like ministry and business flowing as one.

But over time, small tensions began to surface. Michelle started feeling that Danielle dismissed her ideas too quickly. Danielle, in turn, felt Michelle was becoming inflexible and controlling. Schedules got tighter. Communication shortened. Certain conversations got pushed off. Neither of them wanted to rock the boat, so instead of dealing with the discomfort, they internalized it and kept working.

Then came the shift—subtle but sharp. A key financial decision was made without consensus. Feelings got hurt, but rather than talk it through, they smoothed it over publicly and let it fester privately. Texts were left unanswered. "Let's pray about it" turned into "We'll circle back." Team meetings got tense. What used to be collaboration turned into cautious calculation.

And strife slipped in.

At first, it lived in the silence. The unspoken offense. The polite tension in the room. But soon it started to take up space.

Michelle stopped inviting Danielle to weekly lunch meetings with their top client. Danielle began reassigning projects without Michelle's input. They no longer prayed together. What used to be mutual celebration became quiet competition. Each began using employees as go-betweens to avoid direct confrontation. When something needed to be said, it was said through someone else.

The team felt it. Employees started choosing sides, though no one said that aloud. Productivity dropped. Clients noticed the lack of unity. Meetings dragged. Turnover increased. The once-light atmosphere was now heavy with unspoken pressure.

At home, things changed too. Michelle's husband noticed she was more irritable, more withdrawn. "I'm just tired," she said. Danielle's teenage daughter overheard a phone call and asked, "Are you and Miss Michelle still friends?" Danielle brushed it off—but the question lingered.

Strife doesn't just impact a relationship. It shapes environments.

Neither woman had walked away. They were still working together. Still running the business. Still maintaining the appearance of unity. But underneath it all was a fractured foundation. The friendship had been sacrificed on the altar of silent offense, and what once felt like a spiritual partnership now felt like survival.

They each told themselves they had forgiven. That they were being mature. That they were just in a difficult season. But what had actually happened was that offense had opened a door—and the spirit of strife had taken up residence.

And when strife is allowed to stay, it never stays small.

Key Choices

Strife didn't show up in one big explosion—it crept in through a hundred small choices that seemed justifiable at the time. But the longer it stayed, the more power it had. That's the deception. Strife isn't just a result of conflict—it's a spirit that feeds on our reluctance to forgive, our fear of confrontation, and our pride in being right. Michelle and Danielle didn't wake up one day and decide to tear their friendship apart. They simply didn't stop the drift. And once strife set in, it started shaping how they worked, how they communicated, and who they were becoming. That's why we have to make different choices—sooner, deeper, and more intentionally—if we want to break free from its grip.

Here are the key choices we face when strife begins to take root:

1. Choosing forgiveness over emotional control

It's easy to say, "I forgive," while still holding onto subtle punishments—withdrawal, sarcasm, avoidance. But forgiveness isn't passive. It's a surrender of our right to keep the offense alive. It's choosing healing over having the upper hand.

2. Choosing direct, Spirit-led confrontation over silence and distance

Avoidance feels safer than confrontation, especially when the relationship matters. But silence is a seedbed for strife. If we won't speak the truth in love, we'll end up speaking bitterness behind closed doors—or carrying it in our hearts until it spills out sideways.

3. Choosing unity through humility vs. self-protection through pride

Unity doesn't come from agreement—it comes from surrender. From valuing the relationship more than our position. Pride says, *"I shouldn't have to be the one to reach out."* Humility says, *"If the enemy is benefiting from this, I can't afford not to."*

4. Choosing reconciliation with God's help vs. control in your own strength

We often try to manage conflict ourselves—minimize damage, keep up appearances, avoid deeper messes. But reconciliation is a spiritual work.

It requires grace, wisdom, and the help of the Holy Spirit. Control might keep things functional, but only God can make them fruitful again.

5. Choosing to dismantle strife vs. learning to live with it

Many believers settle into relationships shaped by strife and call it normal. They stay polite, stay passive, and stay spiritually stagnant. But God doesn't call us to coexist with strife—He calls us to cast it out. That begins with the decision: *I will not let this rule here anymore.*

Enemy Tactics

The enemy doesn't need to destroy a godly relationship to defeat its purpose—he just needs to distort it enough that it stops bearing fruit. That's what strife does. It doesn't demand an explosive fallout. It settles for silent tension, slow withdrawal, and passive resistance. It feeds on unspoken offense and uses pride, fear, and self-protection to keep us from taking the hard steps toward healing. By the time we notice what's happening, the damage has already spread—from our hearts, to our homes, to everyone around us.

These are the tactics the enemy used—and the same ones he's still using today to fracture the Body of Christ and undermine Kingdom partnerships:

Reopening Old Wounds

The enemy doesn't always create new pain—he just keeps replaying the old one. Every time you try to let go, he reminds you why you shouldn't. He fuels the loop of rehearsed offense, keeping the wound raw and resistant to healing.

Division Through Strife

Strife thrives in spiritual environments that lack truth, transparency, and humility. It turns every difference into a threat and every disagreement into a reason to pull back. What could've sharpened you instead isolates you.

Offense Justified as Discernment

Instead of acknowledging the hurt, the enemy convinces you that your withdrawal is wisdom. You begin to "see clearly" what's wrong with the other person—when in reality, your vision is being filtered through offense. He wants you to believe that distance equals discernment.

Fear of Betrayal

Where strife grows, trust dies. The enemy uses past disappointments to paralyze future risk. You begin to believe that partnership isn't worth the cost. That vulnerability only leads to pain. This fear becomes a wall that no one can scale.

False Peacekeeping

Rather than address the conflict, the enemy tempts you to maintain appearances. Keep things cordial. Keep the team moving. But under the surface, resentment builds. The longer it's unspoken, the more power it gains.

Identity Distortion

The enemy whispers, *"You're better off alone." "You work better when you're in charge."* What began as a team becomes a solo act. But it's not strength—it's self-protection dressed up as independence. And it keeps you from the interdependence God designed you for.

Counterfeit Outcome

The counterfeit life often keeps working. The meetings continue. The projects move forward. The image is maintained. But underneath it all, the power, blessings and favor are gone. That's what strife does—it doesn't always dismantle a relationship immediately. Sometimes, it just drains it of unity, trust, and spiritual effectiveness, until only the appearance of connection remains.

If Michelle and Danielle had continued in that pattern without repentance and forgiveness, the outcome wouldn't have looked like open rebellion—it would've looked like slow relational erosion, hidden under a veil of productivity and professionalism. That's the subtle danger of strife: it doesn't have to be loud to be lethal.

Here's what the counterfeit would've continued to produce:

Superficial peace with underlying division

Outwardly, the partnership still exists—but the connection is fractured. Conversations are cautious. Meetings are short. Smiles are strained. There's no vulnerability, only functionality.

A hardened heart that blocks love, joy, and collaboration

What once was built on trust is now governed by suspicion. Misunderstandings multiply. Emotional distance becomes the norm. Love is replaced with performance, and collaboration turns into cautious coexistence.

Disconnection from godly community and intimacy with God

Strife doesn't just divide people—it distances us from God. It grieves the Holy Spirit. It clouds discernment. It interrupts the flow of grace, especially when we keep calling dysfunction "wisdom" or "strategy."

Leadership and influence compromised

When unity is lost, clarity follows. What once felt fruitful now feels forced. The atmosphere shifts—from peace to pressure, from collaboration to contention. Clients pick up on the tension. Employees feel it in their day-to-day. Progress slows, not because of incompetence, but because spiritual disunity drains momentum. What once flowed with grace now demands more effort. Problems multiply. Stress mounts. Burnout becomes inevitable.

The slow death of what could have been fruitful

The enemy doesn't need to destroy the business—he just needs to choke the purpose behind it. As strife lingers, the original vision fades. And what started as a Spirit-led partnership becomes a transaction between guarded hearts. The light that touched everything disappears.

That's the cost of living with strife. It may look functional, but it is spiritually fatal. And no matter how "professional" or "mature" we think we are, if we're tolerating strife, we're trading our calling for control and our peace for pretense.

Areas of Salvation Impacted

A New Heart and a Renewed Mind

Strife hardens what God is trying to soften. Instead of walking in compassion, humility, and patience, we begin to think the worst of others, justify emotional distance, and protect ourselves with pride. A renewed mind requires the humility to release offense and invite God's perspective.

Peace With God and Others

Strife destroys peace by turning relationships into battlegrounds. It invites confusion, defensiveness, and emotional instability. When we tolerate strife, we resist the very peace Jesus died to give us—not only between us and God, but between one another.

Access to God's Presence

Unforgiveness and relational division grieve the Holy Spirit. Our prayers feel strained. Worship feels hollow. Scripture feels silent. When we cling to strife, it creates spiritual interference that limits our awareness of God's nearness and dulls our ability to hear His voice.

Purpose, Calling, and Spiritual Gifts

Strife blocks the flow of anointing and clarity. It distorts motives and leads to self-preservation instead of Spirit-led partnership. When strife is present, the gifts God placed within us become harder to access, and the people we're called to serve suffer because our unity has been compromised.

The Indwelling of the Holy Spirit

The Holy Spirit cannot flourish in a heart dominated by contention and resentment. His guidance becomes muffled. His power becomes distant. When we allow strife to remain, we quench the Spirit and unknowingly empower the enemy to influence how we relate, lead, and live.

Strife doesn't leave on its own—it must be confronted, confessed, and cast out. It may have entered through a real wound, but it remains through our reluctance to deal with it God's way. The longer we justify offense or avoid confrontation, the deeper the strife digs in. But healing begins when we step out of pride, drop our guard, and surrender our need to be right.

If you've recognized any signs of strife in your heart, your home, or your work, the Spirit is already at work—inviting you to real freedom. Don't ignore His conviction. Step into the fight.

Faith in Action

Here's how you start:

Forgive the offense, not by feeling—but by faith

You don't need to wait until it feels fair. Forgiveness is a spiritual decision, not an emotional conclusion. Choose today to release the debt, even if the wound still aches.

Ask the Holy Spirit to reveal where strife is hiding

Sometimes it's not loud—it's just low-grade tension, coldness, guardedness, sarcasm, or avoidance. Invite the Holy Spirit to show you where you've made room for strife so you can evict it completely.

Bless instead of curse

Pray blessings—out loud—over the person you're still struggling with. Speak life into their future. Ask God to prosper them. This is how you war against offense and reclaim spiritual ground.

Make peace where possible

Ask God if there's someone you need to talk to, apologize to, or confront in love. Don't act impulsively—but don't delay obedience either. Be Spirit-led, not fear-bound.

Break spiritual agreements with offense and strife

Declare: *I break agreement with the spirit of strife in Jesus' name. I will no longer tolerate division in my heart, my home, or my relationships. I choose peace, unity, and truth. I repent of pride, avoidance, and control. Holy Spirit, cleanse me and lead me in reconciliation and truth.*

Lead differently from this moment on

If you're a leader, the atmosphere you carry matters. Begin praying over your workplace, your team, and your partnerships. Ask God to restore unity and drive out every residue of strife. What you permit will multiply—so permit peace.

Prayer

Father, I come before You recognizing that I have tolerated what You never intended me to live with. I've allowed offense to stay longer than it should. I've protected my pride instead of pursuing Your peace. I've let strife influence how I see people, how I lead, and how I live. Forgive me.

I repent for every agreement I've made—spoken or unspoken—with the spirit of strife. I break those agreements now in the name of Jesus. I release every person I've been holding in judgment. I choose to forgive, even if I never receive an apology. I choose obedience over offense. Peace over pride. Freedom over self-protection.

Holy Spirit, show me where strife still has a foothold in my life. Reveal what I've been avoiding. Expose what I've been excusing. Cleanse my heart. Renew my mind. Restore the relationships that can be healed—and give me grace to release the ones that can't.

I ask You to guard my heart, fill my mouth with truth, and help me walk in humility and courage. Let my presence carry peace. Let my leadership reflect Christ. And let every room I enter be one where strife is disarmed, because You dwell in me.

In Jesus' name, Amen.

Areas of Study

Proverbs 17:14 – "Starting a quarrel is like breaching a dam; so drop the matter before a dispute breaks out."

Matthew 5:23–24 – "If you are offering your gift at the altar and there remember that your brother or sister has something against you... go and be reconciled."

Romans 12:17–21 – "Do not repay anyone evil for evil... If it is possible, as far as it depends on you, live at peace with everyone."

Hebrews 12:14–15 – "Make every effort to live in peace... See to it that no one falls short of the grace of God and that no bitter root grows up..."

Colossians 3:13–15 – "Bear with each other and forgive one another… Let the peace of Christ rule in your hearts."

Biblical Figures & Examples

Paul and Barnabas (Acts 15:36–41) – A real conflict that resulted in separation but not spiritual ruin. Their later reconciliations show that disagreement doesn't have to destroy calling.

Joseph and His Brothers (Genesis 37–50) – Joseph refused to let betrayal produce strife. His forgiveness preserved the promise.

Abraham and Lot (Genesis 13) – Abraham took the initiative to avoid strife, trusting God to provide even when he gave up his right to choose first.

Jesus on the Cross (Luke 23:34) – The ultimate model of forgiveness. He released His offenders while still hanging on the cross.

Spiritual Practices

Journaling Forgiveness Letters – Write a letter to the person you're holding offense against. You don't have to send it—just surrender it.

Blessing in Prayer – Commit to praying blessings over someone who hurt you for 7–10 days. Speak Scripture over their life.

Fasting to Break Strongholds of Strife – Set aside a day or several meals to fast and pray specifically for freedom from strife in your life, relationships, and leadership.

Speaking Peace Over Your Environment – Declare aloud that your home, team, or church will be a place of unity, healing, and spiritual clarity—not confusion or conflict.

Conflict Confession – Confess your part in any unresolved relational strain. Ask God to show you what He wants to restore.

Closing Reflection

Strife is subtle—until it isn't. It starts with a misunderstanding, a hesitation, a moment of hurt. But left unchecked, it grows into something that changes how we see people, how we lead, and how we hear from God. Michelle and Danielle didn't fall apart overnight. They simply let the enemy stay in the room too long, whispering lies and stirring division while they called it "managing tension."

That's the deception many of us live under: we think if the relationship hasn't ended, then the enemy hasn't won. But the goal of strife isn't just to end partnerships—it's to neutralize them. To make sure they stop bearing fruit. To turn powerful alliances into quiet rivalries. To drain the joy, the unity, and the spiritual authority out of something God intended to thrive.

You don't have to let that happen.

Maybe you see yourself in Michelle or Danielle. Maybe a friendship, a ministry, or a partnership has started to feel strained. You've noticed the tension. The shift. The distance. You've tried to stay professional or "mature," but if you're honest, something's broken—and strife is standing in the middle of it.

Let this be your moment to reclaim what the enemy has been trying to steal.

You can forgive. You can confront with love. You can repent for what you've allowed. And you can close the door on strife—not just for yourself, but for the people your obedience will impact.

Because when peace returns, fruitfulness follows.

CHAPTER 14

When Gossip Masquerades as Discernment: Truth in Love vs. the Fear That Keeps Us Silent

———————•———————

"Brothers and sisters, if someone is caught in a sin, you who live by the Spirit should restore that person gently. But watch yourselves, or you also may be tempted."
Galatians 6:1 (NIV)

Discernment is a gift—but when weaponized by offense or cloaked in fear, it becomes a counterfeit. In today's church culture, it's not always slander that divides the Body—it's spiritual-sounding conversations rooted in suspicion, preference, or pride. Gossip rarely announces itself boldly. It hides behind phrases like "I just have a check in my spirit" or "We need to pray for them." It dresses itself in concern but refuses the accountability of confrontation. And the damage it causes isn't limited to those who speak—it quietly wounds those who overhear and stay silent. Because silence, when driven by fear or self-preservation, can become agreement. And when truth is withheld in the name of peace, the enemy finds a foothold.

Scenario

The conversations never started as outright gossip. They were wrapped in scripture, shaped like concern, and laced with just enough truth to sound spiritual. But something about them felt…off.

It wasn't just one person—it was a mix of respected men and women in the church. Leaders. Longtime members. Volunteers. They weren't shouting or slandering. They were "discerning." Sharing thoughts about how the church was changing. Questioning decisions the pastor had made. Wondering if the leadership had lost its "spiritual edge." Each comment was mild. Subtle. But together, they created an undercurrent of doubt and division that ran deeper than anyone openly admitted.

Micah, a twenty-something keyboardist on the worship team, wasn't part of the conversation. He was packing up cords after rehearsal when he overheard the first few comments. He didn't mean to listen—but once he heard, he couldn't unhear. At first, it just made him uneasy. But the more it happened, the more it affected him.

He respected the people talking. He'd seen them serve faithfully for years. Some had mentored him. Their words didn't sound malicious. They sounded mature. Spiritually alert. But they were talking *about* people, not *to* them. Week after week, they brought up issues with no intent to address them—only to rehash them.

Micah felt torn. Part of him wanted to believe it was discernment—that maybe they were right. Another part of him was deeply unsettled. His spirit was grieved, but he didn't feel like he had the authority to say anything. Who was he to speak up? These people were older. Wiser. More involved. So he stayed quiet. Nodded when they looked his way. Laughed nervously at a few comments. Then went home and tried to pray—but couldn't shake the discomfort.

He began to feel tension during worship. His joy dulled. His heart grew guarded. He started pulling back from certain friendships, questioning motives, wondering who else felt what they weren't saying. He had come to church to grow—but now he felt spiritually disoriented.

He wasn't offended by leadership. He was confused by the people who said they were discerning—but acted like critics. And what disturbed him most was that *he* was starting to do the same thing in his own mind.

Key Choices

Micah didn't start with offense. He started with confusion. He wasn't looking to gossip—he was looking for clarity. But in the absence of bold truth, spiritual environments get blurry. And when those we respect speak with subtle criticism wrapped in Scripture, it becomes hard to tell the difference between discernment and division. Micah wasn't the one spreading the gossip—but by staying silent, he was being shaped by it. That's how the enemy works. He doesn't just corrupt the vocal—he paralyzes the convicted. The battle in moments like this is not just about what's being said—it's about what we're choosing to do with what we hear, see, and feel.

Here are the key choices we face when gossip tries to pass as discernment and fear threatens to quiet truth:

1. Choosing to speak truth in love vs. staying silent in fear

Micah felt it—something was off. But fear kept his mouth shut. And that's exactly what the enemy wants. Silence, when led by fear rather than wisdom, becomes agreement. Love doesn't stay quiet when something is spiritually unhealthy. It speaks truth—not to stir conflict, but to restore clarity.

2. Choosing to test the spirit vs. accepting spiritual language at face value

Not every spiritual phrase is Holy Spirit-led. When gossip comes dressed as concern, we have to discern the fruit, not just the tone. Is this leading to intercession or accusation? Is it rooted in love or subtle bitterness? We must choose to weigh words through the Spirit, not just assume they're righteous because they sound familiar.

3. Choosing conviction over comfort

It would've been easier for Micah to keep his head down, nod politely, and disengage emotionally. But the longer he stayed quiet, the more compromised he felt. Conviction is uncomfortable—but it's holy. We must decide whether we care more about peace with people or peace with God.

4. Choosing alignment with the Holy Spirit vs. alignment with community norms

Micah knew something was grieving the Spirit—but he was surrounded by others who didn't seem concerned. When you're the only one disturbed by what others have normalized, it's tempting to assume you're wrong. But truth isn't determined by consensus. It's revealed by the Spirit.

5. Choosing restoration vs. resignation

Micah began pulling back—first emotionally, then spiritually. That's what happens when offense goes unaddressed and fear keeps us passive. The call isn't to quietly withdraw. It's to lovingly confront, humbly clarify, and actively preserve unity.

Enemy Tactics

The enemy doesn't just speak through those who gossip—he manipulates those who hear it. He doesn't need everyone to participate—he just needs enough people to stay silent. In spaces where truth is softened for the sake of comfort and criticism is coated in spiritual language, the enemy thrives. His tactics aren't always loud. In fact, they're often smooth, familiar, and hard to question—because they sound wise, cautious, even protective. But the fruit reveals the source. And wherever fear, confusion, and division are spreading, a counterfeit is present.

Here are the tactics at work when gossip masquerades as discernment and silence becomes agreement:

Offense Masquerading as Discernment

The enemy turns unresolved offense into spiritual "insight." What someone is unwilling to confront directly, they will often spiritualize indirectly. Gossip becomes prophecy. Suspicion becomes warning. But behind the words is a wound—still unhealed, still unspoken.

Fear of Man

For those who overhear, like Micah, the enemy uses fear to keep their mouths closed. *"You'll lose respect." "They won't trust you." "It's not your place."* The fear of being misunderstood or rejected outweighs the fear of grieving God. And so truth stays buried under layers of self-preservation.

Gossip Framed as "Concern"

This tactic is especially deceptive because it uses partial truth to spread whole division. The enemy encourages vague statements, passive accusations, and repeated questions with no intent to resolve—only to erode trust and credibility over time.

False Unity Through Passivity

Satan doesn't just want loud division—he'll settle for fake peace. When people refuse to challenge what's wrong in the name of "keeping the peace," they allow rot to spread underneath the surface. It's not peacemaking. It's peacekeeping with a price.

Compromise Through Spiritual Intimidation

Micah wasn't just afraid—he felt spiritually outclassed. The enemy loves to use seasoned believers with spiritual language to intimidate younger ones into silence. *"They know more than you." "They've been here longer."* This tactic convinces us that discernment belongs to the experienced, even when the Spirit is clearly grieving inside us.

Numbing Through Repetition

The more Micah heard the same critiques, the more normal they sounded. That's how the enemy works—he doesn't need you to agree right away. He just needs you to get used to it. Familiarity breeds tolerance, and what once grieved your spirit eventually stops bothering you at all.

Counterfeit Outcome

The counterfeit life doesn't always erupt in scandal—it often settles in the subtle erosion of spiritual clarity and relational trust. What begins as internal hesitation can grow into external disconnection. What feels like cautious wisdom becomes passive agreement with division. Gossip doesn't just harm the person being talked about—it reshapes the hearts of those who listen without responding, speak without love, or disengage to avoid discomfort. And when fear becomes our filter, we stop being led by the Spirit—and start being shaped by the room.

Here's what the counterfeit looked like for Micah—and what it often looks like for believers in similar situations:

A disengaged heart masked by spiritual language

Micah remained present physically, but emotionally and spiritually, he checked out. He could still sing the songs and play the notes—but his heart grew skeptical and cold. Gossip blurred his clarity, and silence muted his spiritual authority.

Compromise in the name of peace

Rather than lovingly confront or seek clarification, Micah settled for avoidance. He stayed "neutral" to avoid tension—but neutrality in the face of deception isn't wisdom, it's compromise. And it left both the gossip and the division unchallenged.

A warped sense of discernment

Without realizing it, Micah started filtering everything through suspicion. Discernment became hyper-awareness, and he began assuming the worst instead of believing the best. What started as caution became cynicism—and his spiritual discernment was dulled by inner conflict.

Agreement with fear over alignment with the Spirit

Each time Micah stayed silent, the enemy's narrative grew stronger. He stopped asking, "What is God saying?" and started asking, "What will they think?" And with every decision rooted in fear of man, his confidence in hearing from God weakened.

Missed opportunities for healing, unity, and growth

Micah's silence wasn't neutral—it was costly. He missed the chance to lovingly redirect gossip. He missed the opportunity to be a light in a confusing space. And he forfeited growth that only comes through Spirit-led courage.

Areas of Salvation Impacted

A New Heart and a Renewed Mind

Remaining in environments of gossip—whether speaking or silently listening—desensitizes the heart and distorts the mind. Over time, we start thinking the way the group thinks instead of how Christ thinks. Instead of being transformed by the renewing of our minds, we are conformed by the caution and compromise of those around us.

Peace with God

When we choose silence out of fear or self-protection, we distance ourselves from God's prompting. The Spirit may be convicting us to speak up or step away, but ignoring His voice creates dissonance. That lack of peace isn't circumstantial—it's spiritual.

Speaking the Truth in Love (Sanctification and Maturity)

This is a core marker of a mature believer—one who is willing to speak when it's uncomfortable, correct when it's needed, and love while being bold. Fear of man interrupts this growth. If left unaddressed, it stunts spiritual development and weakens the Church.

Purpose and Calling

Fear-based silence is often one of the first compromises that pulls believers out of alignment with their callings. Micah was gifted and called, but offense around him, and silence within him, began to cloud his purpose. You cannot walk confidently in your calling while questioning whether God is pleased with your silence.

Indwelling and Leading of the Holy Spirit

The Spirit's voice is quieted in environments of division, criticism, and fear. When we participate in or tolerate gossip, we grieve the Holy Spirit. His leading becomes harder to follow not because He's distant, but because our agreement with the flesh has grown louder.

Faith in Action

Micah's story is not uncommon. Many believers find themselves caught between discomfort and duty, unsure how to respond when what they hear doesn't align with God's heart—but no one else seems to notice or care. And instead of rising with conviction, we shrink back in fear. But silence, when led by fear, is not wisdom—it's surrender. And if we don't recognize the spiritual dynamics at play, we'll confuse avoidance for humility and tolerance for maturity.

But God calls us to something higher. Not louder, not more aggressive—*truer*. Spirit-led boldness isn't about being right; it's about being willing to love with truth and walk in alignment with His voice, not the crowd's.

Here's how we begin to step into that kind of obedience:

Ask the Holy Spirit to Reveal Hidden Compromises

Micah didn't start out wanting to be silent—he simply felt stuck. If you've ever felt paralyzed by fear or unsure whether to speak up, start with prayer. Ask the Holy Spirit to expose any agreement you've made with fear, people-pleasing, or passivity.

Confess and Renounce Participation in Gossip

Whether you've spoken it, tolerated it, or inwardly judged others without love, bring it before the Lord. Confession breaks the enemy's grip, and renouncing your involvement invites cleansing and restoration.

Practice Boldness in Safe Places

You don't have to confront a room to start walking in truth. Begin by discussing what you observed with a trusted mentor or accountability partner. Practice naming gossip when you see it—and asking the Lord for wisdom and timing to address it directly.

Re-engage With Your Gifts in Humility

Micah's gift of worship suffered when fear silenced his spirit. Whatever your gift is, don't let discomfort or disillusionment cause you to withdraw. Return to your calling with a renewed heart, asking God to use you as a vessel of truth and unity.

Choose to Speak Truth in Love—Even When It's Hard

Don't wait for the perfect moment. If the Spirit prompts you to address a conversation, do it in love. You're not responsible for how it's received—only for being obedient to speak with grace and truth.

Prayer

Father,

I don't want to be a bystander when You've called me to be a builder. Forgive me for the times I stayed silent in the name of peace, when it was really fear. Forgive me for tolerating gossip, for calling judgment discernment, and for shrinking back when I should've stepped up.

I ask You to cleanse my heart, renew my mind, and sharpen my discernment. Fill me with courage, wisdom, and love. Teach me to speak truth with grace and to see others the way You do. Let my silence no longer be agreement with the enemy—but an invitation for Your voice to rise in me.

In Jesus' name, Amen.

Areas of Study

Scriptures

Ephesians 4:15 – *"Instead, speaking the truth in love, we will grow to become in every respect the mature body of him who is the head, that is, Christ."*

Galatians 6:1 – *"Brothers and sisters, if someone is caught in a sin, you who live by the Spirit should restore that person gently."*

Matthew 18:15–17 – *Jesus' instruction for addressing sin in a brother or sister.*

Proverbs 27:6 – *"Faithful are the wounds of a friend; profuse are the kisses of an enemy."*

Proverbs 26:20 (NIV)– *"Without wood a fire goes out; without a gossip a quarrel dies down."*

Biblical Figures

Nathan confronting David – A powerful model of bold, loving confrontation (2 Samuel 12:1–13).

Paul confronting Peter – Calling out hypocrisy not with gossip, but direct, Spirit-led truth (Galatians 2:11–14).

Jesus and the woman at the well – Truth-telling that heals rather than condemns (John 4:1–26).

Practices

Journaling to Expose Hidden Offense or Judgment – Write out recent conversations you've heard or participated in and ask the Holy Spirit to reveal truth and correction.

Prayer for True Discernment and Boldness – Seek God's heart before forming your own judgments or reacting in fear.

Honest Feedback and Accountability Conversations – Regularly practice truth-telling with someone who knows your heart and can call you higher.

Closing Reflection

Gossip is one of the enemy's most subtle and destructive weapons—and one of the easiest traps for believers to fall into. It doesn't always come wrapped in obvious malice. Often, it's coated in concern, cloaked in spiritual language, or disguised as discernment. But at its root, gossip isn't just careless speech—it's cooperation with the accuser. It tears down what

God is building, spreads offense like wildfire, and trains our mouths to speak from pride rather than purity.

Micah didn't set out to gossip. He didn't want to be silent either. He was caught in the middle—torn between what he sensed in his spirit and what he heard around him. That's the danger. Confusion becomes agreement when we don't bring it to God. And fear becomes a foothold when we stay silent, convincing ourselves that peace is the same as passivity.

Gossip thrives in environments where truth is avoided and fear of man overrides fear of God. And if we're not intentional, we'll nod in agreement with slander, laugh at half-truths, and call it harmless conversation. But it's not harmless. It's holy ground being trampled by careless words. And the more we tolerate it, the more we desensitize our hearts to what grieves the Holy Spirit.

Maybe you've been there. Maybe you're there now—hearing what doesn't sound right, feeling uneasy, but unsure how to respond. This isn't condemnation. It's conviction. It's an invitation to repentance, realignment, and renewed boldness.

God is looking for voices that don't echo culture, pride, or passive compromise—but reflect His love, His truth, and His character. You don't need to be the loudest in the room—you just need to be faithful to His voice.

Will you speak up when it's easier to stay silent?

Will you stand for truth when gossip calls for your agreement?

Will you fear God more than man?

The purity of the Church depends on it. And your own freedom may, too.

CHAPTER 15

Designed for Connection
Choosing Godly Community When
Isolation Feels Safer

———————•———————

*"For my people have committed two evils: they have forsaken me, the fountain of living waters, and hewed out cisterns for themselves, broken cisterns that can hold no water."*Jeremiah 2:13

We weren't made to walk alone. From the very beginning, God designed humanity for relationship—with Him and with each other. Yet many believers live disconnected lives, not because they don't believe in community, but because they've been hurt by it. Church wounds, relational letdowns, awkward interactions, and unmet expectations become building blocks for spiritual isolation. And the enemy is all too eager to help stack those bricks into a fortress of self-protection. But independence isn't a spiritual gift. Isolation isn't wisdom. Healing, growth, and purpose are always tied to connection—because God works through His people to restore His people. The question is: will we trust Him enough to let others in?

Scenario

Marcus grew up in church—but somewhere along the way, the place that once felt like home started to feel like a battlefield. During his time at a previous church, he entered a serious relationship with someone on staff. At first, it felt like a gift from God—two people on fire for Jesus, serving together, dreaming together. But when the relationship unraveled, everything else did too.

What should have been a private heartbreak turned into public fallout. Friends and staff took sides. Rumors spread. Instead of finding compassion, support, and godly counsel, Marcus was met with silence and cold shoulders. People he had prayed with, served with, even wept with—suddenly kept their distance or turned their backs on him. He kept attending for a while, hoping things would heal. But they didn't. The place that once held his community became a source of deep pain and shame. So eventually, he left—not just the relationship, but the church entirely.

Now in his thirties and single, Marcus calls his faith "private." But the truth is, he's questioning a lot—about people, about church, and even about God. He watches sermons online. He prays alone. He tells himself he's "just in a different season." But fear is calling the shots: fear of being judged, misunderstood, or let down again. And deeper still, fear that God doesn't love him anymore... that maybe even God has rejected him too.

When he hears messages about community, conviction stirs—but so does anxiety. A coworker recently invited him to a men's group, and he almost said yes. But then came the wave: anxiety about meeting new people, about being vulnerable again, about investing in relationships only to lose them. He thought about how hard it is to know who's really for you. How quickly trust can crumble.

So, he didn't go.

He tells himself it's not necessary. That he and God are good. But in the quiet, he knows better. His prayers feel shallow. His Bible feels silent. And his hunger for God is being slowly numbed by isolation.

Deep down, Marcus knows what he's missing—and that fear and anxiety are winning. It's not just fellowship he's cut off. It's the sharpening, support, and healing that only happen in godly community. He senses God prompting him to try again. But the wall he built to protect himself is now the very thing keeping him from everything he truly needs.

Key Choices

Marcus didn't wake up one day and decide to isolate himself. His withdrawal came one disappointment at a time. A broken relationship. A betrayal of trust. A slow, steady erosion of safety. And like so many others, he called it "boundaries" when it was really just fear. He still loved God. He still wanted truth. But somewhere along the way, he stopped believing that healing could come through people. And that's exactly what the enemy wants—to make us fear the very thing God designed to help us thrive: community.

Here are the choices Marcus had to face—and the ones many believers are faced with when fear, anxiety, and isolation start to feel safer than connection:

1. Choosing connection over self-protection

Every relationship carries risk. Marcus had learned that the hard way. But protecting ourselves from pain also protects us from healing. True connection requires courage—to risk being known, to risk being misunderstood, and to believe that what God has for you is greater than what you lost.

2. Choosing obedience to God's call into community vs. listening to fear

God was prompting Marcus to say yes—to the invitation, to the group, to the uncomfortable step. But fear always has a rebuttal. *"What if it happens again?"* *"What if you don't belong?"* The question wasn't whether Marcus was afraid—it was whether he would obey God despite the fear.

3. Choosing to pursue healing through people vs. trying to heal in isolation

God often uses others to bring the breakthrough we've been praying for. Accountability, encouragement, comfort, sharpening—all of it flows through the Body. Marcus kept asking God for healing, but he was rejecting one of the main ways God wanted to bring it.

4. Choosing vulnerability vs. performing spiritual strength

It was easier to say *"I'm good."* To quote Scripture. To appear spiritually stable. But healing never comes through performance. Vulnerability was Marcus's invitation to freedom—to let someone in, to let someone see, and to trust that being weak didn't disqualify him from being loved.

5. Choosing to trust God's heart over past hurt

Ultimately, this wasn't just about people—it was about Marcus's relationship with God. Was God still for him? Would God really lead him somewhere safe? Every moment of hesitation traced back to a deeper wound in his trust with the Lord. And the only way forward was to trust again—not just in people, but in the God who calls us into community.

Enemy Tactics

The enemy didn't need to drag Marcus into rebellion—he only needed to keep him alone. Isolation wasn't new; it was a stronghold the enemy had already been reinforcing through pain, disappointment, and fear. Marcus wasn't rejecting God—he was avoiding people. But that avoidance wasn't neutral. It was spiritual warfare. Because if the enemy can't get you to stop believing in God, he'll work to separate you from the people who strengthen your belief. The attack wasn't just against Marcus's social life—it was against his spiritual growth, healing, and purpose.

Here are the tactics the enemy used—and still uses to keep many believers disconnected, discouraged, and spiritually dry:

Isolation disguised as independence or maturity

The enemy convinces us that we're just "taking space" or "walking with God alone." But isolation framed as maturity is still isolation. It separates us from the very Body we're meant to be part of—and slowly, it starves our spirit of connection, accountability, and encouragement.

Fear and insecurity rooted in past wounds

The memories of rejection, judgment, and relational breakdown aren't just painful—they're weaponized. The enemy replays them over and over to build a narrative: *"It will happen again." "You're not safe with people."* That fear blocks obedience and keeps believers stuck in cycles of avoidance.

Apathy masked as peace

Spiritual apathy doesn't always look rebellious—it often looks quiet, passive, and indifferent. Marcus told himself he was "good." That watching sermons and praying on his own was enough. But that calm wasn't true peace—it was resignation. A slow fade that dulled his hunger and masked his drift.

Shame whispering unworthiness

"You don't belong." "You're too much." "You'll just mess it up again." These lies sink deep. Shame becomes a muzzle, keeping believers from stepping into godly relationships because they believe they're unworthy of being seen, known, or loved again.

Suspicion and mistrust cloaked as discernment

The enemy twists discernment into distrust. Marcus began reading into conversations, questioning motives, assuming rejection before it happened. But that wasn't wisdom—it was fear posing as insight. Suspicion insulated him from the very healing God was trying to offer through others.

Exaggerated interpretation of past pain

Marcus wasn't just wounded—he was convinced he had been completely abandoned. The enemy distorted what actually happened and magnified the betrayal. Yes, some people mishandled his pain—but others likely cared, didn't know how to help, or were navigating their own confusion. But the enemy painted everyone as a villain, amplifying Marcus's isolation and planting deeper seeds of mistrust and bitterness.

Counterfeit Outcome

The counterfeit life rarely announces itself with rebellion—it comes cloaked in self-protection, framed as wisdom, and justified by past pain. Marcus didn't plan to drift. He just wanted to heal. But healing in isolation often leads to deception. The longer he stayed disconnected, the more vulnerable he became to a quiet spiritual decline. He still believed in God. He still prayed. But the fire was gone, and so was the fruit.

Here's what the counterfeit looked like—and how the enemy used isolation to erode Marcus's faith and draw him into compromise:

Spiritual stagnation masked as peace

What Marcus called "a peaceful season" was actually a paralyzed one. No stretching. No growth. Just survival. His prayers were shallow, and his time in the Word became occasional. Without community to challenge or sharpen him, he drifted into passivity—still believing, but barely pursuing.

Eroding convictions and the loss of accountability

Without brothers in Christ to walk with, there was no one to ask hard questions. No one to notice the red flags. No one to call him back when his standards began to slip. Little by little, Marcus started making decisions that no longer aligned with the faith he once lived boldly.

Compromise in relationships and dating

The loneliness wore him down. And without the covering of community, Marcus began dating women who didn't share his values. He still told himself he was a Christian—but he was no longer dating like one. Emotional intimacy without commitment. Physical compromise. Late-night rationalizations. *"It's not like I'm abandoning God."* *"At least I'm being honest."* The enemy didn't have to convince Marcus to sin—he just needed to wear down his standards.

Disobedience dressed in discernment

Marcus knew God was prompting him to re-engage with the Body, but he kept finding reasons to delay. *"Not the right time."* *"That group's not for me." "I'm not ready."* What looked like patience was actually disobedience. The longer he waited, the more his heart hardened—and the easier it became to mistake fear for wisdom.

Becoming indistinguishable from the world

The most devastating part of the counterfeit life is how it slowly reshapes us into someone God never intended us to be. Marcus didn't hate God—but his life no longer reflected Him. His habits, his relationships, his decisions—none of them pointed to Jesus. He still claimed the faith, but his lifestyle had stopped testifying of it.

The counterfeit life convinces us that safety lies in distance. That isolation will protect us. But what it actually does is sever us from truth, accountability, and the grace God so often delivers through His people. Without community, we drift. And eventually, we start living a version of Christianity that looks nothing like Christ.

Areas of Salvation Impacted

Disconnection from the Body of Christ doesn't just affect our social life—it disrupts the flow of grace, growth, and spiritual authority God designed for us to receive in community. Marcus's isolation didn't look dangerous at first, but over time, it weakened every area of his walk with God. What he thought would protect him actually left him vulnerable—and spiritually dry.

Here are the areas of salvation impacted when believers choose isolation over godly connection:

Access to God's Presence (through the Body)

God inhabits the praises of His people. He moves powerfully when two or more gather in His name. Isolation limits exposure to corporate worship, shared prayer, and the unique presence of God that flows through His unified Body.

Activation of Spiritual Gifts

Our gifts are given not for personal fulfillment but for the edification of others (1 Cor. 12:7). When we withdraw, our gifts remain dormant—and so do the gifts God has placed in others that are meant to strengthen us. The Body suffers when even one part stays hidden.

Identity and Belonging

We discover who we are in relationship—with God and with His people. Community reflects our value, affirms our purpose, and calls us higher. Without it, identity warps. Marcus began defining himself by fear, not by faith—by past wounds, not present calling.

The New Heart (softened through love and vulnerability)

Sanctification requires exposure. Without community, the heart hardens. Marcus's heart grew numb—not because he stopped believing, but because he stopped receiving love in action. Vulnerability is where transformation happens. Walls may protect us from pain, but they also block healing.

Ongoing Renewal of the Mind

Without voices of truth, encouragement, and correction, the lies get louder. Marcus's mind was slowly being renewed—but by fear, shame, and compromise, not by the Word. Isolation impairs discernment and increases the power of deception.

Faith in Action

Faith doesn't grow in isolation—it's strengthened in obedience, vulnerability, and community. For Marcus—and for any believer tempted to hide behind pain—the journey back doesn't begin with perfect trust. It begins with a single step. A willingness to believe that what the enemy distorted, God can restore.

The walls that once protected Marcus had become his prison. And freedom came not through forcing connection, but by following God's promptings with humility and courage—especially in the uncomfortable places.

Attend one group or gathering consistently—even when it feels awkward.

Don't chase the perfect group; respond to God's invitation. Healing happens in consistent presence, not instant connection.

Ask someone to pray with you or for you.

It doesn't have to be a deep reveal. Just let someone in. Every moment of vulnerability cracks the door for the Holy Spirit to move through others.

Name the fears—and challenge the narrative.

Ask God: *"Have I believed something that isn't fully true?"* Write down the memories and the conclusions you've drawn. Invite the Holy

Spirit to sift what happened from what the enemy exaggerated. God brings clarity. The enemy thrives in distortion.

Forgive those who didn't show up or caused pain.

This is essential. Unforgiveness will continue to isolate you, even if you step into new community. Forgiveness isn't saying it was okay—it's surrendering the debt and allowing God to heal the wound. Start by simply saying, *"God, I choose to forgive..."* and let Him walk with you from there.

Pray for courage and show up afraid.

God isn't waiting for confidence—He's waiting for obedience. Boldness often comes *after* the step, not before it.

Serve in a small way.

Find one small way to move from observer to participant. Whether it's helping with setup, joining a prayer team, or welcoming someone new—serving breaks the cycle of passivity.

Prayer

Father,

You created me for connection. You called me into a Body, not to be hidden, but to be healed, sharpened, and sent. I confess the fear, the pain, the disappointment that has kept me in hiding. I've let the past define too much of my present. But I don't want to live behind walls anymore.

Give me the courage to show up. Help me to risk vulnerability. Heal what has been broken. I bring You my fears, my mistrust, and my exaggerated memories—and I ask You to reframe them with Your truth.

Give me courage to forgive those who hurt me. Help me release the offense and make room for grace. Bring the right people into my life—people who reflect Your love, speak Your truth, and remind me who I am in You. I trust You to rebuild what I thought was lost.

In Jesus' name, Amen.

Areas of Study

Scriptures

Ecclesiastes 4:9–12 – "Two are better than one... a cord of three strands is not quickly broken."

Hebrews 10:24–25 – "Let us not give up meeting together... but encouraging one another."

Acts 2:42–47 – The early church thrived through fellowship, shared resources, and corporate worship.

1 Corinthians 12:12–27 – We are many parts of one Body—each needing the others.

Proverbs 18:1 – "Whoever isolates himself seeks his own desire; he breaks out against all sound judgment."

Romans 12:4–5 – "In Christ we, though many, form one body, and each member belongs to all the others."

Biblical Figures

Elijah (1 Kings 19) – After great victory, Elijah isolated himself in fear and despair—God met him gently and reminded him he wasn't alone.

David and Jonathan – A model of covenant friendship rooted in mutual strengthening, loyalty, and God's purpose.

Jesus and the Disciples – Even the Son of God didn't walk alone—He invited others into His journey.

Practices to Implement

Journaling distorted memories vs. God's truth – Write out what happened, how it made you feel, and invite the Holy Spirit to correct exaggerations.

Hospitality over hiding – Invite someone for coffee or a simple meal. Creating space for others weakens the grip of isolation.

Memorize verses about the Body of Christ – Let Scripture reshape your understanding of community.

Pray for "your people" – Ask God to reveal the friendships and communities He wants to build or restore in your life.

Accountability check-ins – Invite a mature believer to ask about your faith habits, thoughts, and obedience.

Closing Reflection

Marcus's story may seem extreme, but the enemy's strategy isn't. Isolation is one of his oldest—and most effective—tools. He uses pain to create distance, disappointment to foster distrust, and fear to keep us silent. And before we know it, we're calling disconnection "peace" and avoidance "wisdom." But something inside still aches. That ache is evidence—we were created for connection.

You may not have experienced what Marcus did, but maybe you've slowly pulled away. Maybe you've allowed busyness, past wounds, or self-preservation to keep you on the fringes. Maybe you've told yourself that "just you and God" is enough, while your heart quietly longs for real community, accountability, and friendship.

The enemy wants to keep you there—in hiding, rehearsing the past, overplaying the betrayal, and underestimating the healing power of God through His people. But you weren't made to do faith alone. The very freedom you've been praying for may be on the other side of obedience and vulnerability.

It doesn't require a leap. Just a step.

Let this be the moment you step out from behind the walls. Let this be the chapter where you say yes—not just to showing up, but to being seen. You don't have to have it all figured out. You just have to be willing to try again.

CHAPTER 16

False Unity vs. True Peace
The Spiritual Cost of Peacekeeping Over
Peacemaking

———•———

"But the wisdom from above is first pure, then peaceable, gentle, open to reason, full of mercy and good fruits, impartial and sincere. And a harvest of righteousness is sown in peace by those who make peace." James 3:17–18

There is no such thing as a perfect marriage, but it is something everyone desires and imagines. It's also what many people want to portray as having—which is costly. Because behind the polished posts, matching outfits, and Sunday morning smiles, real issues are often buried. Instead of addressing the tension, many couples silently agree to "keep the peace" by avoiding hard conversations. But what looks like peace is often just a well-managed performance. The enemy loves this. He doesn't need to tear your marriage apart publicly if he can quietly convince you to live in false unity. As long as you stay silent, stay resentful, and stay in hiding, he's winning. And all the while, what God meant to be a source of sharpening, joy, and covenant growth becomes a shallow performance— two people in agreement not to deal with what truly matters.

Scenario

Taylor and Renee have been married for eight years. To their church friends, they're the couple others look up to—consistent, committed, and always smiling. They serve on the hospitality team, show up for every event, and give the impression of unity. But behind the carefully managed image is a slow drift of disappointment.

Renee didn't get married expecting perfection, but she did expect partnership. She imagined a husband who would lead with strength, initiate family prayer, speak life over their children, and carry the spiritual weight of their home. Instead, what she got was silence. Taylor is kind, faithful, and easygoing—but he avoids leadership. He defers to Renee on nearly every decision. Whether it's discipline, devotions, or direction, the weight falls on her.

At first, Renee filled in the gaps, assuming he'd grow into the role. But the longer things stayed the same, the more frustrated she became. She never said it out loud, but the inner dialogue grew louder: *Why do I have to be the one to bring up everything? Why doesn't he lead? Why do I feel more like his mother than his wife?*

The pressure built quietly. They didn't argue—but they didn't really connect either. Renee stopped initiating meaningful conversations. Taylor stopped asking how she was really doing. They settled into a rhythm of routines and logistics, presenting well in public but slowly unraveling in private.

The church offered marriage classes. Small groups. Mentorship opportunities. But Renee didn't want to go alone, and Taylor didn't see the need. They weren't fighting, after all. And so the pretense remained—

the polished version of a couple everyone admired, while behind closed doors, intimacy faded and resentment grew.

Renee keeps praying, but her prayers have changed. They're no longer hopeful—they're tired. She asks God to fix her husband. To wake him up. To turn him into the man she thought she was marrying. But God keeps nudging her to stop performing and start confronting—in love, not anger. The hard conversations she's been avoiding aren't the problem—they might be the beginning of real peace.

Key Choices

Renee's silence wasn't submission—it was surrender. Not to God, but to the fear of rocking the boat. On the outside, their marriage looked stable. But inwardly, resentment had become a second voice in her head—one she consulted more often than the Holy Spirit. And Taylor, unaware of the weight his wife was carrying, assumed no news meant good news. But the enemy thrives in assumptions. The longer hard conversations are avoided, the deeper the roots of bitterness grow.

Every couple faces gaps—between expectation and reality, intention and perception. But how we respond to those gaps is everything. Do we fill them with grace and truth? Or do we let frustration fester and pretend peace is present when it's not?

Here are the key choices that confront couples like Renee and Taylor—and anyone trying to maintain a "picture-perfect" relationship at the expense of real healing:

1. Choosing peacemaking through truth vs. peacekeeping through avoidance

Peacekeeping says, "As long as we're not fighting, we're fine." But true peace doesn't come from silence—it comes from honesty. Renee had to decide if she would continue stuffing her frustrations or invite her husband into the truth with love and humility. The risk of conflict was real—but so was the reward of intimacy.

2. Choosing vulnerability over resentment

Every time Renee chose not to speak, resentment took up more space in her heart. But vulnerability—the willingness to share disappointment without accusation—was the only path to healing. The enemy wants us to believe that silence protects love. But in truth, it poisons it.

3. Choosing obedience to God vs. control through performance

Renee wanted her husband to lead—but in the absence of that, she took control. Not out of rebellion, but out of fear. The problem wasn't her competence—it was the spiritual cost of trying to hold everything together without trust. God wasn't asking her to fix Taylor—He was inviting her to surrender her expectations and let Him lead.

4. Choosing to shine a light on hidden issues vs. hiding behind appearances

They were the "model couple" to others, but neither was living authentically. Renee didn't want to admit things weren't okay. Taylor didn't want to cause a scene. But marriage is not strengthened through image—it's refined through truth. Attending a marriage class or reaching out for help wouldn't have been failure—it would have been faith in action.

5. Choosing to see your spouse through God's eyes vs. judging them by your unmet needs

The enemy had distorted Renee's vision—turning every gap into a grievance. But God was calling her to see Taylor not as a disappointment, but as a man in process. That shift didn't mean lowering the standard—it meant raising the level of grace.

Enemy Tactics

The distance in Renee and Taylor's marriage didn't begin with a blowout argument—it began with silent agreements. Agreements that said, *"It's better not to bring this up." "This is just the way things are." "He'll never change, so why bother?"* The enemy didn't need to destroy their marriage; he just needed to keep it superficial. He didn't have to incite betrayal—just delay the truth.

That's how he works in relationships, especially in marriage. He exploits emotional gaps, fuels quiet disappointments, and then convinces both people to protect an image instead of pursuing real peace. He keeps Christians busy managing appearances, distracted by roles, and too fearful to confront what's really going on.

Here are the tactics the enemy used—and still uses to erode intimacy, stall spiritual growth, and counterfeit peace:

Counterfeit Unity – Masking silence and suppression as spiritual agreement

It looked like unity from the outside—but it was agreement in appearance only. The enemy wants couples to confuse calm with connection and to label silence as maturity. When hard things go unspoken, unity becomes a performance instead of a partnership.

Fear of Conflict – Making discomfort feel dangerous or unspiritual

Renee feared that addressing the issue would cause tension. Taylor feared that any confrontation would mean failure. The enemy uses that fear to keep couples stuck—convinced that peace equals the absence of conflict, rather than the presence of truth and resolution.

Control and Image Management – Avoiding truth to maintain the appearance of strength

They smiled in public, held hands in church, and played their roles. But the effort it took to look "put together" was draining the energy they could've used to actually get real. The enemy thrives when couples choose managing perceptions over mutual healing.

Resentment and Comparison – Nurturing resentment through unmet expectations

Renee didn't just want a more engaged husband—she wanted him to look like the biblical leader she had imagined. But those expectations, left unspoken and unmet, gave the enemy room to whisper comparison, disappointment, and eventually, resentment.

Passivity Encouraged as Peace – Keeping the husband from leading by dulling conviction

Taylor didn't see a problem because there wasn't open conflict. The enemy fed him comfort in complacency—reassuring him that everything was fine as long as Renee wasn't complaining. That spiritual dullness didn't come from laziness—it came from a spirit of passivity disguised as peace.

Counterfeit Outcome

The counterfeit in Renee and Taylor's marriage didn't look chaotic—it looked calm. But not all calm is godly. Sometimes, the enemy keeps couples smiling in public and silent in private so he can quietly dismantle their covenant from the inside out. The enemy doesn't always start with division or shouting—he often begins with suppression, pretending, and an internal drift that no one talks about. He establishes strongholds of resentment beneath the surface while convincing both spouses that peacekeeping is the same as peace. That emotional suppression is the same as spiritual maturity. And that presenting well is more important than being well.

Here's what the counterfeit looked like for Renee, Taylor, and countless couples like them:

Resentment disguised as grace

Renee told herself she was being patient, understanding—even Christlike. But beneath her silence was a growing resentment. The longer she avoided hard conversations, the more distorted her view of Taylor became. Grace without truth created a breeding ground for disappointment and bitterness, which eventually poisoned even her prayers. She started pulling away emotionally while appearing supportive on the outside. And what felt like endurance became avoidance.

Passivity mistaken for humility

Taylor believed he was honoring Renee by stepping back and letting her lead. But his reluctance to take spiritual ownership of their home didn't bring unity—it deepened the disconnect. His silence wasn't servant-hearted; it was spiritually disengaged. Their young son began to witness a marriage that looked polite but lacked power. The enemy doesn't just attack marriages—he infects legacies. The strongholds that go unbroken in one generation often become the battles of the next.

A marriage that functioned but didn't flourish

They split tasks. They co-parented. They showed up for church. From the outside, things seemed fine. But their connection lacked depth. There was no sharpening, no spiritual alignment, no pursuit of God together. What looked like teamwork was actually toleration. And what they tolerated—disconnection, fear, and unspoken expectations—slowly eroded what God intended to be sacred.

A relationship built on roles instead of relationship

He provided. She nurtured. They fulfilled their duties. But neither felt fully seen or deeply known. The enemy had subtly redefined their covenant as a checklist of responsibilities rather than a union fueled by mutual truth, growth, and intimacy with God. The result wasn't love—it was performance.

Missed healing and spiritual transformation

They had access to help—marriage classes, mentors, even close friends. But fear of being judged kept them from reaching out. What could have been a breakthrough season became another missed opportunity. Their silence didn't just cost them healing; it robbed others of the testimony that could have set them free. The very thing they were hiding was the story someone else desperately needed.

The counterfeit life in marriage isn't always dramatic—it's subtle. It thrives in what's unspoken. It grows in the gap between who we pretend to be and who we really are. It celebrates image over intimacy, silence over honesty, and keeping the peace over making it. But God's design for marriage is not just to survive—it's to be refined. To become a union where truth is spoken, love is fierce, and transformation is ongoing.

Areas of Salvation Impacted

A New Heart (Healed and Softened by Truth)

When we suppress our true thoughts and feelings in relationships, our hearts become calloused. Unspoken resentment hardens us, making it difficult to give or receive love as God intends. But truth—spoken in love—softens and restores the heart.

Peace With God

Peacekeeping rooted in avoidance is not the peace of Christ. When we lie with our silence, we grieve the Holy Spirit and step out of alignment with God's truth. Real peace with God invites us to walk in honesty and trust Him with the results.

Relationships and Covenant (Marriage, Family, Church)

Covenant relationships—especially marriage—are meant to sharpen and sanctify us. When we choose image over intimacy or tolerate dysfunction instead of confronting it, we miss out on the refining power of truth-filled love. Avoiding conflict in the name of comfort robs both individuals of the spiritual transformation that comes through truth, grace, and mutual submission.

The Indwelling Spirit

The Holy Spirit cannot be fully active in spaces where deception— even quiet, well-intentioned deception—reigns. He is the Spirit of Truth.

When couples live in a performance rather than in vulnerability, they quench His voice and power in their home.

Faith in Action

Living in false peace might feel easier in the moment, but it's costly over time. It costs intimacy. It costs spiritual growth. It costs connection with God and with each other. But that cost isn't final—it's an invitation. Every moment of tension, silence, or suppression is a chance to choose differently. To choose truth. To choose healing. To choose real peace. These steps aren't quick fixes—they're acts of faith. And faith doesn't wait until everything is perfect. Faith moves while things are still messy.

Invite God into the silence.

Ask the Holy Spirit to reveal what you've been afraid to say and what your spouse might need to hear. Write it down in prayer before you speak it out in love.

Bring expectations to God first.

Lay down the version of your spouse you've been holding onto—the image, the ideal—and ask God to show you His heart for them. Let Him purify your desires and align your vision.

Break agreement with resentment.

Repent for the resentment you've allowed to grow in silence. Name it. Renounce it. Forgive your spouse for what they haven't seen or done—and ask God to help you see them through grace, not disappointment.

Step out of roles and into relationship.

Set aside time to reconnect not as co-parents, providers, or ministry partners—but as husband and wife, friends, and spiritual companions. Be intentional about rebuilding emotional and spiritual intimacy.

Attend one marriage class, together or alone.

Don't wait for your spouse to be ready. Go first. Healing often begins with obedience before agreement.

Let someone in.

Ask a trusted couple, mentor, or leader to walk with you. Vulnerability invites healing—and your courage may inspire others to stop pretending too.

Speak one truth in love this week.

Whether it's a need, a hurt, or a hope—start the practice of peacemaking through honest, grace-filled conversation.

Pray for your marriage aloud—together.

Even a short, simple prayer breaks spiritual stagnancy. If that's not yet possible, begin by praying daily for your spouse's heart and leadership without trying to control the outcome.

Prayer

Father God,

I bring my marriage before You—not the version we present, but the truth of what it has become. You see every unspoken word, every buried hurt, every place where resentment has taken root. Forgive me for choosing silence over honesty, for mistaking avoidance for peace, and for allowing disappointment to shape how I see my spouse.

Lord, I confess the expectations I've clung to—expectations that have become idols, fueling frustration and judgment. I lay them at Your feet and ask for Your perspective. Show me who You created my spouse to be, and teach me to love them in truth, not just in performance.

Heal the distance we've allowed to grow. Uproot every stronghold of bitterness, pride, and fear that keeps us from true connection. Rekindle our spiritual intimacy and give us the courage to be real—with You, with each other, and with those around us.

Let our marriage reflect Your covenant love. Use our vulnerability as a light to others who are silently struggling. Redeem what's been lost, restore what's been strained, and renew our hearts to pursue each other—and You—with honesty and grace.

In Jesus' name, Amen.

Areas of Study

Scriptures:

Matthew 5:9 – "Blessed are the peacemakers, for they will be called children of God."

James 3:17–18 – Wisdom from above is "first pure, then peaceable… without hypocrisy."

Ephesians 4:25–27 – "Speak truthfully… do not let the sun go down while you are still angry."

Proverbs 27:6 – "Wounds from a friend can be trusted, but an enemy multiplies kisses."

Colossians 3:13–14 – Bear with each other and forgive as the Lord forgave you.

Biblical Figures:

Priscilla and Aquila – A couple who labored in unity, truth, and Kingdom purpose (Acts 18).

Ananias and Sapphira – A married couple whose agreement in deceit brought spiritual destruction (Acts 5).

Sarah and Abraham – Moments of misalignment and silence, yet also faith and growth in covenant.

Practices:

Honest marriage check-ins (weekly or monthly)

Attending a marriage class or retreat together

Confessing unspoken expectations in prayer and dialogue

Seeking pastoral or spiritual counsel for deeper healing

Speaking a blessing over your spouse daily

Closing Reflection

The enemy doesn't always need to destroy your marriage—he just needs to keep it superficial. He doesn't have to stir up chaos if he can convince you to keep pretending. And that's what Renee and Taylor had started doing: pretending. Pretending the silence was peace. Pretending distance was maturity. Pretending image was enough.

But marriage isn't meant to be a performance—it's a covenant. A spiritual partnership that reflects the relationship between Christ and His Church. And that kind of relationship requires truth. It requires vulnerability. It requires the courage to shine a light on what's hurting, not just hide it for the sake of appearances.

Maybe you've been there. Maybe you're there now. Avoiding the conversations that need to happen. Telling yourself it's not that bad. Minimizing the disconnection and calling it peace. But what if the very thing you're trying to avoid is the very thing God wants to use to bring healing?

Renee and Taylor didn't need a perfect marriage—they needed a truthful one. They needed the kind of unity that grows through fire, not the kind that avoids it. And so do you.

Real peace isn't found in silence. It's found in the presence of Jesus— where truth and grace meet, where hard conversations become holy ground, and where the love of God can restore even the places you've given up hope.

If the Holy Spirit is tugging at your heart—don't ignore Him. Start the conversation. Tell the truth. Invite the healing. And remember: God isn't asking you to fix everything—He's asking you to stop hiding.

Section IV Closing

Stay Watchful—Because the Enemy Still Seeks to Divide

Every relationship is spiritual ground. Whether it's your marriage, your church, your friendships, or even how you engage in community—each one has the potential to reflect the love, unity, and truth of God…or to be subtly overtaken by the schemes of the enemy.

This section has shown just how deceptive those schemes can be.

- **Strife** doesn't always announce itself with yelling—it seeps in through unresolved tension.

- **Offense** doesn't always feel sinful—it often disguises itself as discernment or protection.

- **Gossip** isn't always malicious—it can sound spiritual, even wise.

- **Isolation** feels safe at first—but slowly, it starves your spirit.

- **False unity** looks polished—but it's powerless to heal or transform.

The enemy is not always trying to destroy relationships through chaos—he's often trying to *preserve* them in counterfeit peace, shallow connection, and emotional avoidance. And the longer we settle for that, the more we miss out on the refining, sharpening, and spiritual maturity that only come through authentic, truth-based relationship.

Let this section serve as a mirror and a warning:

- Are you suppressing truth to keep the peace?

- Are you harboring unspoken resentment while maintaining an image of unity?

- Are you calling independence spiritual maturity when it's actually a form of self-protection?

- Are you listening to the enemy's whispers instead of confronting brokenness with courage and grace?

These aren't just relational issues—they're invitations. Every counterfeit connection is an opportunity to invite the Holy Spirit in, to be brave, to tell the truth, to forgive, to try again, and to reflect the Kingdom of God in how we love.

Stay alert. Stay humble. Stay connected.

Because relationships are where revival begins—and the enemy knows it. He wants us isolated, offended, performative, and guarded. But God is calling us into something far greater: authentic connection, real peace, deep forgiveness, and transformative unity.

The next section will lead us into the final battleground—the realm of influence, purpose, and impact. But you cannot carry out your calling in power if you're still tethered to counterfeit connection. Let what's been revealed here strengthen your resolve to walk in truth, love, and Spirit-filled relationships.

Section V

Counterfeit Decisions
– Spiritual Consequences

Not every deception looks dangerous. Some arrive dressed as wisdom, wrapped in good intentions, or buried in busyness. In this section, we expose the counterfeit choices that often go unnoticed—not because they're dramatic, but because they're daily.

These are the moments where we rationalize compromise, delay obedience, or chase comfort over calling. But every choice we make forms the direction of our walk with God. And the enemy knows it. That's why he tempts us to believe that small decisions don't matter.

But they do.

Because obedience today shapes destiny tomorrow.

Each chapter in this section is a call to sharpen your spiritual discernment and remember that you are always building something—either in obedience to the Spirit or in agreement with the enemy's subtle distortions.

CHAPTER 17

The Slippery Slope of Small Compromises: Where Little Lies Lead to Big Losses

———•———

"One who is faithful in a very little is also faithful in much, and one who is dishonest in a very little is also dishonest in much." Luke 16:10

It rarely starts with a major fall. It starts with a glance, a rationalization, a "just this once." A Christian business owner tells a small lie to land a contract—after all, it's for a good cause. A leader bends a rule to meet a deadline. A believer stays silent in a moment that called for truth. These may seem like harmless decisions in the moment, but compromise is never neutral—it shapes who you are becoming. The enemy rarely launches a frontal assault on your faith. Instead, he chips away at your convictions one small decision at a time, until what once grieved your spirit no longer even stirs your conscience. This is how the erosion begins—not in rebellion, but in justification. And that's why this chapter matters—because where you make room for "just a little," the enemy builds a foothold.

Scenario

Michael started his business with sincere intentions. He dedicated it to the Lord, prayed over every decision, and committed to stewarding it as a representative of the Kingdom. From day one, he wanted his company to reflect God's character—marked by integrity, excellence, and trust in God as his provider. But as time went on, the challenges piled up. Growth was slow. Bills went unpaid. Payroll became a recurring source of anxiety. And somewhere between the vision he started with and the pressures he now faced, Michael began to drift.

It wasn't immediate—it never is. He still prayed. He still believed. But his decisions were now shaped more by fear than faith.

Then came the opportunity: a high-revenue contract with a national client. It could stabilize the company overnight. Solve the cash flow issues. Ease the stress. There was just one problem—the client's brand and practices didn't fully align with Kingdom values. Nothing illegal. Nothing obviously immoral. Just…off. Their messaging was manipulative. Their product exaggerated benefits. Michael had always drawn a line in the sand when it came to the types of clients he represented—but suddenly, that line didn't feel so firm.

He told himself it was temporary. That God could use this for good. That he was still honoring God by taking care of his employees. But in truth, Michael had stopped consulting God. He was making decisions to survive, not to obey. And what he once saw as non-negotiable had become flexible under pressure.

Key Choices

Michael's compromise didn't begin with a blatant betrayal of his values. It began with stress, survival mode, and the desire to protect what he built. He didn't stop believing in God—he just started trusting money more. And that's the slow drift many of us face. We start strong, we set boundaries, we declare convictions… until those convictions cost us. And in that moment, the enemy whispers, *"It's just business,"* or *"God understands,"* or *"You can't afford to be too rigid."*

But Kingdom living doesn't allow for blurred lines. The standard doesn't change just because the pressure rises. And the choices we make under pressure reveal where our true allegiance lies. Here are the key decisions that often define whether we stay faithful—or slide into counterfeit stewardship.

1. Choosing to trust God as Provider vs. manipulating outcomes for financial security

It's one thing to say *"God will provide"* when things are going well. But real trust is tested when the numbers don't add up and the bills are due. Michael believed God was his source—until fear of lack convinced him to take matters into his own hands. Manipulating the outcome to secure a client may have solved his short-term problem, but it undermined his long-term faith. Trust requires surrender, even when the outcome is uncertain.

2. Choosing to uphold Kingdom standards vs. compromising for "success"

Success isn't always a blessing—it can be a test. Michael once refused to work with companies that violated his values. But now, the line felt negotiable. He told himself it wasn't that bad, that he could use the money for good, that God would understand. But partial obedience is still disobedience. Upholding Kingdom standards in business—or any area of life—means saying "no" when the world expects you to say "yes."

3. Choosing conviction over convenience

Conviction will cost you. That's why the enemy works so hard to wear it down through inconvenience. He doesn't always tempt us with evil—

sometimes he tempts us with ease. Michael was tired. Tired of being on the edge. Tired of always having to choose the harder road. But spiritual authority is cultivated in those hard choices. Convenience may open doors, but conviction determines whether God can trust us with what's behind them.

4. Choosing to remain accountable to God vs. justifying decisions apart from Him

One of the most dangerous shifts in Michael's journey was not the deal itself—it was the silence. He stopped inviting God into the process. He stopped asking, *"Is this pleasing to You?"* and started telling himself, *"It's fine."* Justification is the language of compromise. The more we explain away our choices, the less room we give the Holy Spirit to convict, redirect, and protect us from ourselves.

Enemy Tactics

Michael didn't plan to compromise—he drifted into it. And that's exactly how the enemy works. He's not always looking to make you fall in one giant leap; he's content with a slow erosion of conviction. A slight shift in language. A small concession made under pressure. A redefinition of success that subtly edges God out of the equation. What starts as a moment of survival can quickly become a new standard of operation. The enemy is strategic—and when it comes to those called to lead, build, and steward with integrity, he leverages every weakness and pressure point. Here are some of the tactics he uses to lead believers from obedience into spiritual compromise.

Temptation through rationalization

The enemy rarely tempts with outright sin when he can tempt with "reason." He didn't have to convince Michael to lie—just to loosen his standards. Phrases like *"just this once," "God understands,"* or *"I have to do what's best for my business"* become spiritual anesthetics. Rationalization is how the enemy helps us feel spiritual while walking in disobedience. It softens conviction until we no longer recognize when we've crossed a line.

Financial pressure as spiritual leverage

The enemy thrives in lack—not because God isn't present, but because lack often makes us forget He is. Financial pressure can become a wedge that drives believers out of faith and into fear-based decisions. The bills were real. The payroll stress was real. But the enemy used those realities to reframe Michael's theology: from God as Provider to self as protector. When we stop seeing God as the solution, we start accepting counterfeits.

False peace

Not all peace comes from God. Sometimes, what we call "peace" is just the absence of immediate consequences. After signing the deal, Michael felt relieved—less stress, more cash flow, a sense of stability. But peace that comes from disobedience is counterfeit comfort. The enemy is willing to let things calm down on the surface if it means you're drifting further from your convictions beneath it.

Desensitization through success

One of the enemy's most subtle tactics is to reward compromise with visible success. If the deal had fallen apart or caused a scandal, Michael might have repented. But instead, it worked. Business picked up. His team was thriving. And that's the danger—success without surrender can become a snare. When what "works" becomes more important than what's right, we've already stepped into the counterfeit.

Counterfeit Outcome

At first glance, everything seemed to be going well. The client was pleased. The staff was secure. The numbers were finally in the black. From the outside, Michael's decision looked like a smart business move. He still claimed Kingdom values, but he had partnered with systems that didn't reflect them. And though the company grew, the fruit of his life shriveled. Peace was replaced by pressure. Conviction gave way to convenience. What began as a strategic pivot became a spiritual drift—and by the time he realized it, he was far from the God-honoring foundation he had once laid.

The enemy isn't after our business—he's after our witness, our discernment, and our ability to hear from God.

Here is what happens when we start to compromise:

Spiritual Numbness: Michael no longer felt the tension he used to feel when making questionable decisions. What once pricked his conscience now passed unnoticed. He didn't feel convicted because he had stopped listening.

Weakened Witness: Though his business grew, his spiritual credibility shrank. His team admired his strategy but no longer saw a man led by God. His influence remained—but it lost its eternal weight.

Distorted Dependence: Instead of seeing God as his Provider, Michael began to trust his own hustle. Success became his safety net. And because it worked, he assumed God was still in it. But provision apart from obedience is a trap—not a blessing.

Disconnection From Purpose: He started with a vision to build for the Kingdom. But compromise shifted that purpose. He was still building—but no longer for God's glory. His calling had been traded for contracts, his mission reduced to milestones.

This is the counterfeit life that wears the appearance of success but is hollow underneath. A life where faith is replaced by strategy, conviction by convenience, and calling by compromise. The enemy's goal wasn't just to change Michael's business—it was to dull his spirit until he no longer noticed what he'd surrendered.

Areas of Salvation Impacted

Integrity of Witness

Salvation doesn't just change where we'll spend eternity—it transforms how we live now. Michael's choices dulled the light he was meant to carry. His witness wasn't destroyed in one moment; it was weakened through quiet concessions that blurred the line between Kingdom values and worldly gain. As integrity faded, so did his ability to reflect Christ to others.

Stewardship of Gifts and Calling

Michael was gifted—and he knew it. But instead of stewarding those gifts for the glory of God, he began to manage them for personal and professional survival. He didn't lose his abilities, but he did lose their alignment. Every believer is called to use what they've been given for eternal impact—but when compromise leads, calling gets distorted.

Peace With God

One of the earliest signs of compromise is the erosion of peace. Michael may have achieved external stability, but internally, something shifted. He stopped sensing the nearness of God in decision-making. The subtle but sacred confidence that comes from obedience was replaced by stress management and self-reliance. The peace that surpasses understanding can't coexist with a conscience numbed by compromise.

The Indwelling of the Holy Spirit

When we consistently choose what's expedient over what's righteous, we grieve the Spirit. Michael didn't stop believing—but he did stop communing. The intimacy that once marked his relationship with God was replaced by functional faith. He spoke about God more than he spoke with Him. And eventually, that distance became normal.

Divine Provision

Trusting God as Provider is a core aspect of salvation—it's how we walk by faith and not by sight. But when Michael chose to secure provision through compromise, he shifted his dependency from God to self. He began to believe the outcome rested solely on his efforts, not God's faithfulness. The enemy's strategy wasn't just to meet Michael's financial needs another way—it was to disconnect him from the One who promised to meet them.

Michael's turning point won't come from another contract or strategy session—it will come from repentance and a return to dependence. God's mercy isn't withdrawn when we compromise, but His invitation to course-correct becomes louder. The grace that saved us is also the grace that empowers us to live with integrity. And that means we don't have to stay on the path of justification and self-reliance. We can turn around. We can rebuild on what's true. Faith in action begins with confronting compromise—and choosing obedience again.

Faith in Action

Confess and course correct

It's easy to explain away small compromises, but healing starts with honest confession. Bring your decisions before God without excuse. Ask the Holy Spirit to expose what you've justified or ignored—and be willing to make changes. The path back to integrity always starts with truth.

Reestablish accountability

Compromise thrives in isolation. If you've drifted, you need voices around you who will call you higher. Reconnect with spiritual mentors or community who can speak truth, pray with you, and challenge your decision-making when necessary. Accountability isn't weakness—it's wisdom.

Make restitution if needed

Obedience sometimes requires undoing what disobedience built. If a decision harmed your witness or enabled deceit, ask God how to make it right. Integrity isn't just about not sinning—it's about cleaning up where compromise left a stain. Sometimes that means walking away from a deal, other times it means telling the truth you once hid.

Recommit your business (or area of influence) to the Lord

What you surrendered once, you can surrender again. Whether it's your business, career, or finances—bring it back under God's authority. Pray over your goals. Invite Him into the details. And ask for renewed conviction to build in a way that honors Him fully, not just publicly.

Prayer

Father,

I confess that I've allowed fear, pressure, and self-reliance to guide some of my decisions. I've compromised in places where You called me to stand firm. I've trusted in outcomes more than I've trusted in You. But I don't want to live this way—not another day. I repent for every moment I prioritized success over surrender, results over righteousness, convenience over conviction.

Thank You for Your mercy. Thank You for never walking away, even when I've drifted. Today, I choose to return. I lay my business, my decisions, my reputation—and my future—back at Your feet. Teach me again to hear Your voice. Strengthen my resolve to walk in integrity, even when it costs. Let everything I build point back to You.

In Jesus' name, Amen.

Areas of Study

Daniel 1 – Daniel's Resolve Not to Defile Himself

Daniel's decision to uphold his convictions, even in a foreign land under pressure, is a powerful model for integrity. He didn't bend to the culture around him, even when the consequences could have been severe.

His story reminds us that God honors those who honor Him—especially in the small things.

Proverbs 4:23 – "Above all else, guard your heart..."

Compromise doesn't begin in our actions—it begins in the heart. This verse is a foundational call to watch over the inner life, because what we tolerate in our thoughts and motives eventually shapes our choices and outcomes.

James 4:17 – "If anyone knows the good they ought to do and doesn't do it, it is sin."

This verse clarifies that sin isn't only about doing what's wrong—it's also about avoiding what's right. When we know God's standards but justify doing otherwise, we step into disobedience, even if our actions seem harmless or necessary.

Genesis 22 – Abraham and the Test of Trust

Abraham's willingness to surrender Isaac is one of the clearest biblical pictures of trusting God as Provider. He didn't know how God would come through—he just knew that God would. Studying this passage helps us examine whether we're clinging to control or releasing outcomes in faith.

Matthew 6:33 – "Seek first the Kingdom of God..."

This promise anchors our decisions in proper order. When we prioritize the Kingdom, provision follows. But when we chase provision apart from God's will, we risk stepping out of alignment. This verse serves as both a call and a correction.

Closing Reflection

Compromise rarely feels like rebellion—it feels like relief. A moment of quiet. A quick fix. A problem solved. But relief without righteousness is deception in disguise. The enemy doesn't always tempt you to fall—he just wants you to drift. Slowly. Quietly. Until the convictions that once shaped your life become flexible under pressure.

Maybe that's where you are right now. Maybe your compromise was small, strategic, or even well-intentioned. But deep down, you know something shifted. The peace you once carried has been replaced with tension. The clarity you once walked in has grown dim. You haven't walked away from God—but you've stopped walking in full obedience.

Here's the good news: you don't have to stay there. The God who called you hasn't changed His mind. The foundation you laid can be rebuilt. Repentance isn't punishment—it's the path back to purpose.

So let this be your line in the sand.

No more justifying. No more drifting.

What God builds through you must be built *with* Him.

And He is ready to lead you again—one obedient step at a time.

CHAPTER 18

Discerning His Voice in the Noise
Obedience in the Promptings
We Often Ignore

———————•———————

*"Whether you turn to the right or to the left, your ears will
hear a voice behind you, saying, 'This is the way; walk in it.'"*
Isaiah 30:21 (NIV)

It's not that God isn't speaking—it's that we don't know how to listen
or have stopped listening. In a world buzzing with alerts, opinions, and
obligations, the gentle nudge of the Holy Spirit can feel like background
noise. But delayed obedience is still disobedience, and ignoring His
voice—even unintentionally—comes at a cost. We often expect God to
shout, but He rarely does. He whispers. He prompts. He leads with peace,
not pressure. And in the constant hum of modern life, we've trained
ourselves to move at the pace of urgency instead of the rhythm of the
Spirit. That's how Kingdom assignments get missed—not through
rebellion, but through distraction.

Scenario

Jasmine hadn't always been this busy, but over the past year,
something had been driving her to say "yes" to more—to make a bigger

difference in her community and church. She was a respected professional, involved in ministry, mentoring younger women—her schedule was filled with good things. She prayed regularly, kept a devotional on her nightstand, and genuinely wanted to honor God with her life. But somewhere along the way, *"be still and know"* had become more of a concept than a practice. There simply wasn't time to be still.

One afternoon, while rushing to prepare for a work presentation, Jasmine felt a subtle tug in her spirit: *Call your friend Dana.* It wasn't loud or urgent—just a soft prompting. She paused—but then glanced at the time. *I'll call her later,* she told herself. *Right now, I just can't afford the interruption.* After work, she rushed straight to serve at Youth Group, and—well, later never came.

The next day, Jasmine found out Dana had been hospitalized the night before after a severe panic attack. She had been alone, overwhelmed, and on the edge—and she had thought of Jasmine. Jasmine's heart sank. She hadn't meant to ignore the Holy Spirit. She just didn't realize that nudge was Him.

She had another full day ahead of her, but she told herself she would make time.

Key Choices

Jasmine's story isn't uncommon. Many of us live on mission for God while missing moments with Him. We pack our calendars with purpose, but crowd out the still, small voice that was meant to guide us. And while we may not think of ourselves as disobedient, every time we ignore a prompting, delay a response, or assume it's not that serious—we risk missing a Kingdom assignment. The Holy Spirit isn't loud, but He is faithful. And how we respond to His whisper reveals what we truly prioritize.

1. Choosing to obey the Holy Spirit vs. rationalizing the prompting away

That quiet nudge to call someone, pray, or pause doesn't always feel urgent—but it's always significant. Jasmine didn't reject the Spirit; she postponed Him. But delay is still disobedience. The more we rationalize away the prompting, the more we train ourselves to disregard His voice. And eventually, we stop noticing it at all.

2. Choosing stillness over busyness

Jasmine's calendar was full of service—but not stillness. And that's the trade many believers make: doing for God without being with Him. It's easy to assume God is pleased with our activity, but the Holy Spirit leads us in *availability*, not just productivity. Stillness isn't laziness—it's posture. It says, "Your presence matters more than my pace."

3. Choosing sensitivity to God's voice vs. sensitivity to outcomes

Jasmine cared deeply about showing up for people—but she had become more responsive to visible needs than spiritual promptings. This is a subtle shift that happens when we value what we can measure over what we must discern. But Kingdom impact often begins with unseen obedience.

4. Choosing intimacy with God vs. performance for God

Though Jasmine was sincere, her pace had become performance. She was serving, leading, giving—but in the process, she had started to confuse momentum with intimacy. God doesn't want your output more than your heart. And when performance replaces relationship, promptings feel like interruptions instead of invitations.

Enemy Tactics

The enemy didn't need Jasmine to rebel—he just needed her to stay busy. He didn't have to silence God—he just had to flood her life with enough noise to make His voice harder to hear. That's the danger of distraction: it feels harmless. Helpful, even. Especially when we're doing "good" things. But busyness is one of the enemy's most effective tools, because it keeps us moving without listening, serving without surrender, and doing without discerning. And if we're not careful, we'll confuse our pace with purpose and miss the very moments God has assigned to us.

Distraction disguised as purpose

The enemy isn't always trying to make you sin—sometimes, he just wants you too busy to listen. He'll fill your life with meaningful activity and urgent demands, all while nudging you further from stillness. Jasmine's schedule wasn't filled with rebellion—it was filled with good intentions. But even good things become dangerous when they drown out God's voice.

Delay through rationalization

"I'll do it later." That's one of the enemy's favorite lines. He doesn't always need you to say no—he just needs you to say "not now." Jasmine didn't feel like she was disobeying God—she just thought she was being responsible with her time. But obedience isn't obedience when it's postponed. Delay often leads to disobedience by default.

Confusion through noise

The more voices you listen to—emails, texts, podcasts, people—the harder it becomes to discern the One voice that matters most. The enemy loves to blur the line between urgency and importance. He'll keep your mind so full and your spirit so distracted that the promptings of the Holy Spirit become just another passing thought instead of divine direction.

False assurance through performance

Because Jasmine was doing "Kingdom work," she felt spiritually safe. That's the trap. The enemy will gladly let you stay active—as long as you don't stay attuned. Performance can mask the absence of intimacy. And when we begin to equate doing for God with being with God, the enemy no longer has to deceive us. We're already disconnected.

Counterfeit Outcome

Jasmine didn't fall into some obvious sin. She didn't walk away from church or abandon her faith. But the enemy didn't need her to. All he needed was for her to stay distracted just long enough to miss the moment to answer God's call to serve one of her friends. That's how the counterfeit life creeps in—not through defiance, but through delay. When our lives are filled with motion but lack margin, we become believers who are active but unavailable. And over time, the cost of that unavailability adds up— not just in missed opportunities, but in spiritual dullness, misplaced identity, and growing disconnection from God's presence.

This is what happens when distraction drowns out discernment:

Missed Kingdom Assignments

Dana's crisis wasn't just a missed opportunity to support a friend—it was a divine appointment. Jasmine was meant to be a vessel of comfort, a lifeline in a dark moment. But distraction caused her to overlook a prompting that had eternal weight. And it wasn't the first time. There had been other nudges, other names that came to mind, other moments she dismissed because they didn't fit her schedule.

Spiritual Numbness

The more Jasmine ignored the promptings of the Holy Spirit, the harder it became to recognize them. What used to stir her heart now barely registered. Her ability to discern God's voice began to fade—not because He stopped speaking, but because she stopped slowing down to hear.

Peace Replaced by Pressure

Without realizing it, Jasmine had shifted from Spirit-led to enemy-driven. Her peace was circumstantial, tied to how well she could keep up. The more she tried to be everything for everyone, the more anxious and overwhelmed she became. And though she still quoted verses about rest and trust, she no longer lived from that place.

Dependence on Performance Over Presence

In her heart, Jasmine still wanted to honor God—but she had begun to believe that showing up, producing results, and staying involved was the measure of faithfulness. Her identity became entangled with her output. And the more she performed, the more distant God began to feel—not because He moved, but because she did.

Areas of Salvation Impacted

Fellowship with the Holy Spirit

The Holy Spirit doesn't compete for our attention—He waits for our attention. As Jasmine ignored the promptings of His voice, she unknowingly created distance in their relationship. The prompting to call

Dana wasn't just about Dana—it was an invitation into deeper partnership with God. The more Jasmine delayed, the more that sense of closeness began to fade. When we live distracted, we stop recognizing the voice that was meant to lead us.

Intimacy with God

Jasmine stayed active in ministry, but her intimacy with God became shallow. Her prayers were quick, her quiet time fragmented. She wasn't in rebellion—but she wasn't fully connected either. True intimacy with God requires margin. When we consistently prioritize activity over abiding, our hearts drift from communion to convenience.

Sensitivity to the Spirit's Leading

Spiritual sensitivity is sharpened by response. Every time we obey the Holy Spirit, our discernment grows. But the opposite is also true: every time we ignore His prompting, our awareness dulls. Jasmine's ability to recognize God's voice weakened—not because she lacked desire, but because she lacked space. What she once sensed clearly now felt vague. That's how discernment is lost—not stolen, but surrendered.

Trust in God's Timing and Pace

Jasmine had adopted a rhythm that didn't come from God. She lived by urgency, not by peace. Her internal pace was shaped by performance and obligation, not by the Spirit's flow. And when you no longer trust God's timing, you start managing life by your own clock. Salvation offers rest—but Jasmine was too busy to receive it.

Faith in Action

Jasmine didn't need to overhaul her entire life—she needed to realign it. God wasn't asking her to abandon her responsibilities or stop serving others. He was inviting her to come back to the still place where discernment is restored. Faith in action begins not with doing more, but with doing differently—slowing down, listening closely, and responding quickly to the One voice that truly matters.

Create intentional space for stillness

You can't hear a whisper when your life is filled with noise. Build moments of silence into your day—times when your phone is off, your calendar is closed, and your heart is open. Even a few minutes of stillness can reawaken your sensitivity to God's voice.

Respond to the promptings immediately

When the Holy Spirit nudges you—act. Don't wait for the right time, the perfect setting, or a better mood. Obedience grows sharper through practice. The more you respond in faith, the more clearly you'll begin to hear Him.

Obey—and trust God with the consequences

Sometimes the nudge to act will require you to drop everything. It may interrupt your plans, delay a deadline, or cost you something that feels important in the moment. But obedience is never wasted. When God calls you to move, He also takes full responsibility for the outcomes. Jasmine didn't know what would have happened if she had called—but God did. Faith means trusting that what seems like an inconvenience to us may be a rescue mission in His Kingdom. When obedience costs you something, God provides what you need on the other side of the sacrifice.

Evaluate what's driving your pace

Not all busyness is holy. Ask God to show you what commitments He called you to—and which ones you took on out of guilt, ambition, or fear. Let Him reorder your priorities. Peace is often waiting on the other side of no.

Reconnect with God relationally, not just functionally

Don't just check off spiritual boxes. Talk to God like a friend, not a supervisor. Ask Him questions. Invite Him into your schedule. Let your prayer life become conversational again—not just filled with requests, but marked by listening and stillness.

Prayer

Heavenly Father,

I've been moving too fast. I confess that I've let noise drown out Your voice and busyness distract me from Your presence. I haven't meant to ignore You—but I see now that I've often delayed when I should have obeyed. Forgive me for the times I've rationalized away Your promptings or treated them like interruptions instead of invitations.

Teach me to slow down. To be still. To hear You again. Sharpen my spiritual sensitivity and help me respond quickly, even when it's inconvenient. Reorder my priorities so that I live from a place of peace, not pressure. I don't want to just do things for You—I want to walk with You, moment by moment.

Speak, Lord. I'm listening.
In Jesus' name, Amen.

Areas of Study

1 Samuel 3 – God Calls Samuel

This chapter shows how the voice of God isn't always immediately recognizable, especially when we're unfamiliar with His ways. Samuel had to learn to distinguish God's voice—and so do we. His story reminds us that discernment begins with availability and a heart posture that says, "Speak, Lord, for your servant is listening."

Romans 8:14 – "For those who are led by the Spirit of God are the children of God."

Being led by the Spirit isn't just a sign of maturity—it's part of our identity as believers. This verse invites us to slow down, listen, and align our decisions with the Spirit's direction, even when it challenges our comfort or convenience.

Isaiah 30:21 – "Whether you turn to the right or to the left, your ears will hear a voice behind you, saying, 'This is the way; walk in it.'"

God promises guidance, but it often comes as a whisper—not a shout. This verse anchors the reality that His voice is consistent and directional, even when life is chaotic. The challenge is learning to hear it—and having the courage to follow it.

Luke 10:38–42 – Mary and Martha

Martha was busy serving Jesus, but Mary chose to sit at His feet and listen. Jesus said Mary had chosen what was better. This story offers a necessary recalibration: even good service can become a distraction if it takes us away from the better portion—His presence and voice.

Proverbs 3:5–6 – **"Trust in the Lord with all your heart and lean not on your own understanding…"**

Often, promptings from the Holy Spirit won't make logical sense. This passage reminds us that obedience doesn't always align with our reasoning—but it always aligns with His will. Trust means following even when we don't fully understand.

Closing Reflection

Jasmine didn't disobey out of defiance—she missed the moment because she didn't make space for it. And that's how it happens for so many of us. Not with loud rebellion, but with quiet neglect. We mean well. We love God. But when we live in constant motion, we trade sensitivity for survival. We stop noticing the whisper that was meant to guide us.

Maybe you've been there. Maybe you've ignored a prompting and regretted it. Maybe your days are so full that you can't remember the last time you felt clearly led by the Spirit. If so, let this chapter be your wake-up call—not to do more, but to slow down. To return to the still place where God's voice is not just heard, but honored.

You were never meant to live reactive. You were created to live responsive—to walk in step with the Holy Spirit, even in the smallest things.

CHAPTER 19

Striving or Surrender?
When You're Building Without God

———————•———————

"Unless the Lord builds the house, those who build it labor in vain. Unless the Lord watches over the city, the watchman stays awake in vain. It is in vain that you rise up early and go late to rest, eating the bread of anxious toil; for he gives to his beloved sleep." Psalm 127:1–2

There's a kind of exhaustion that sleep can't fix—the kind that comes from building in your own strength. You can be productive, successful, even admired by others—and still be completely out of alignment with God's will. That's what striving does. It wears the mask of diligence, but underneath is fear, control, and the need to prove something. The world rewards hustle. But Heaven responds to surrender. And when we chase results more than we chase God, we may find ourselves standing on a platform He never asked us to build. This chapter is about the quiet danger of spiritual independence—and the invitation to lay it all down.

Scenario

Manuel never planned to leave ministry—he just needed a break. He started young, full of energy, gifting, and ambition. The church where he was on staff was rapidly growing, and the team was small, so Manuel became the "go-to" guy for just about everything. After years of leading worship, organizing outreaches, managing volunteers, and mentoring young adults, he hit a wall. Spiritually dry, emotionally drained, and physically exhausted, he convinced himself that stepping away would be temporary.

So when a friend offered him a high-paying position at a real estate firm, it felt like a relief—maybe even a blessing. He had been praying for a financial breakthrough to support his growing family, and this opportunity seemed like God's provision. The enemy was quick to reinforce the decision with reasoning that sounded wise: *You need to reset. It's good to explore other gifts. You can still represent God in the marketplace. Ministry doesn't have to be your full-time job anymore. You've earned this break.*

Just for a season, he told himself. *I'll rest, regroup, save money, and come back stronger.*

But one year turned into two, and two into five. And just like before, he became the "go-to" guy—this time in a fast-paced sales environment. Promotions came quickly, and with them, more responsibility. The reasons for staying grew more convincing. He was providing well for his family—but spending a lot less time with them. He was able to tithe more generously—but had no time left to serve. His schedule was packed with closings, client calls, and late-night negotiations.

Manuel kept telling himself he liked this new life. He liked the pace, the income, the recognition. He liked closing deals and being seen as a leader outside the church. But the truth was, he was trying to sell himself a version of life that didn't fit. He missed the presence of God more than he admitted. He missed the joy that used to follow obedience. And the more he tried to convince himself he was fine, the more the pressure grew. It wasn't just the job that was exhausting—it was the act of pretending he was where he was meant to be. Every lie he told himself to justify staying on the wrong path only deepened the burnout.

But this burnout felt different. It wasn't coming from pouring himself out in obedience—it was coming from striving in his own strength. In ministry, the exhaustion had drawn him closer to God, reminding him to rely on grace. But in this new life, the exhaustion only pushed him further into self-preservation. The more depleted he felt, the more he pushed. The more disconnected he became, the harder he worked to prove he hadn't made a mistake.

And for a while, it seemed to work. His income kept increasing. His reputation in the industry was strong. But his spirit was dry, and his heart was restless. He no longer woke up with a sense of purpose—just pressure. God hadn't stopped speaking, but Manuel had become too busy and too burdened to listen. And now, the thought of returning to his original calling brought a new kind of fear.

How could he go back? He had built a life—one with a mortgage, private school tuition, and a standard of living his family had grown used to. Surrendering now would mean starting over. It would mean explaining a decision that didn't make financial sense. It would mean laying down everything he had worked for, just to pick up what he had once put down in the name of rest.

He still loved God. He still believed in the call. But surrender now felt costly in a way it never had before.

Key Choices

Manuel's story isn't just about burnout—it's about misalignment. He didn't fall into sin; he drifted into self-sufficiency. And when you've built a life around striving, surrender doesn't just feel inconvenient—it feels impossible. But this is where many believers find themselves: gifted, driven, and deeply out of sync with the Spirit. The question isn't whether God's calling still stands. It's whether we're willing to lay down what we've built in our strength to walk in what only He can sustain. These are the key choices Manuel—and many of us—must face.

1. Choosing to walk in grace vs. striving in your own strength

Manuel was already burned out before he left ministry—not because he was doing too much, but because he was doing it without God's strength. He had been relying on effort, not grace. But instead of learning to minister from a place of rest and dependence, he walked away—and stepped into an even heavier burden. In real estate, he was still striving, still proving, still pushing. Only now, he was outside of his assignment. The pressure didn't leave—it multiplied. God never designed us to live this way. His grace sustains what He's called us to do, but when we operate outside of that grace, we carry weight we were never meant to hold.

2. Choosing to pursue God's purpose vs. chasing worldly success

Manuel's initial decision to step away from ministry wasn't the issue—it could have been a season of realignment, a chance to learn how to rest in God's strength instead of striving in his own. But instead of seeking healing and understanding, he sought success. What began as a break turned into a pursuit of money, achievement, and control. He missed the opportunity to ask God, *What are You trying to show me in this season?* Instead, he forged ahead with his own plans. And while God can redeem even our detours, Manuel kept missing the invitation to slow down and be taught. The longer he chased success, the further he drifted from the very purpose he was meant to rediscover.

3. Choosing to justify the cost vs. facing the consequences

Manuel knew what he was giving up. He saw the long work hours cutting into time with his kids. He noticed how he no longer served at church, no longer led worship, no longer used the gifts that once brought him joy. Deep down, he knew this wasn't sustainable. But rather than confront the cost, he kept justifying it. *It's just for now. I'm doing this for my family. I can always go back later.* But every justification became a layer of insulation between him and conviction. He wasn't unaware—he was unwilling to stop long enough to face what his striving was truly costing him. The longer he avoided the consequences, the more they compounded. And eventually, the cost of staying where he was became greater than the cost of returning.

4. Choosing surrender vs. self-preservation

Manuel feared what he would lose if he said yes to God again. But in protecting the life he had built, he was forfeiting the one God had designed. Surrender always feels risky to the flesh—but it's safety to the soul. The longer we cling to what we've built in our own strength, the harder it becomes to receive what God wants to give.

Enemy Tactics

Manuel didn't wake up one day determined to abandon his calling. He simply started believing a lie he had lived under for years—that it was up to him to carry the weight of ministry. He was gifted, needed, and praised for how much he could handle. And that's where the enemy planted the seed: not in sin, but in overextension. Striving became normal. He confused productivity with faithfulness. So when burnout came, the enemy didn't have to introduce a new lie—he simply built on the one already in place. The tactics that followed weren't aggressive—they were calculated, targeting Manuel's tendency toward self-reliance, his unhealed need to prove himself, and his quiet fear of letting people down.

Targeting an unhealed identity: You are what you do

Manuel had learned early that his value came from how much he could contribute. The more he led, the more affirmation he received. But the enemy twisted that into an identity rooted in performance. *"They need you."* *"You're the one holding it all together."* When that identity went unchecked, it became a stronghold. Striving wasn't just a habit—it became how Manuel saw himself. So when the real estate opportunity came, he brought the same identity into a new arena—only now, there was no spiritual accountability to confront it.

Replacing dependency with self-sufficiency

In the early days, Manuel cried out to God for wisdom. But over time, results started to come through effort, systems, and strategy. That's when the enemy struck: *"See? You don't need to wait on God—you just need to work harder."* It sounded like discipline, but it was really pride. Dependency gave way to self-sufficiency, and striving replaced surrender. The more things "worked," the less Manuel paused to ask, *Is this still God's will?*

Reframing burnout as a calling problem

Burnout was real—but instead of leading Manuel to the feet of Jesus, the enemy reframed it as a sign that ministry was no longer a fit. *"This isn't who you are anymore."* *"You've outgrown that season."* *"You were never built for full-time ministry anyway."* What Manuel needed was healing and recalibration—but what he accepted was a shift in assignment, based not on God's voice, but on personal exhaustion.

Using success to validate misalignment

The enemy didn't oppose Manuel's success—he used it. Real estate rewarded his effort. The affirmations came in. The finances improved. And with each new milestone, obedience felt less urgent. *"You must be where God wants you—look how well it's going."* But earthly fruit doesn't confirm divine assignment. The enemy knows how to open doors too—especially when they lead you further from the one God asked you to walk through.

Counterfeit Outcome

Manuel didn't leave ministry to run from God—he left because he was running on empty. But instead of turning to God for rest, he ran toward what would reward his effort. That's how the enemy works. He doesn't always tempt us with rebellion—he tempts us with relief that doesn't require repentance. What started as a break became a counterfeit—a life built on striving instead of surrender. Manuel hadn't rejected his faith, but he had replaced intimacy with activity, and the voice he used to follow was now drowned out by one that told him what he wanted to hear.

Here is what happens when we keep striving:

We carry what we produce

Manuel's life was full of accomplishments, but they came with pressure God never asked him to bear. Without surrender, striving turns our victories into burdens. He wasn't building with God—he was building apart from Him. And what we build without God, we're forced to maintain without Him.

We confuse momentum with alignment

The more success Manuel experienced, the harder it became to admit he was off course. Striving creates movement, but not always in the right direction. Manuel was going somewhere—but not where God had originally called him. And the longer he kept going, the more difficult it felt to turn around.

We drift from our calling while appearing faithful

On the surface, Manuel still looked committed—he was generous, hardworking, and spiritually informed. But beneath it all, he had drifted far from obedience. His heart wasn't hardened; it was misaligned. He was living from pressure, not purpose.

We miss the rest we were promised

Striving always demands more. But God's design is rest—rest that comes not from inactivity, but from trust. Manuel worked harder than ever, yet felt emptier than ever. Because rest isn't found in results—it's found in relationship. And without that, no level of success could restore what was missing.

Areas of Salvation Impacted

A New Identity as a Child of God

Manuel's identity became wrapped up in performance. He no longer lived from the truth that he was a son first—called, loved, and accepted apart from his output. Instead, he measured his worth by results, promotions, and praise. When we strive to prove our value, we forget that our identity has already been secured in Christ.

Peace With God

Though Manuel still believed in God, the peace he once experienced in his spirit was replaced with pressure. Peace isn't the absence of activity—it's the presence of alignment. And when we walk outside of God's will, that peace gives way to striving, anxiety, and restlessness. Manuel's outward success masked an inner disconnection.

A New Heart and a Renewed Mind

Manuel's mindset never fully shifted from self-reliance to Spirit-dependence. Though saved, his thinking was still shaped by old patterns—work harder, prove yourself, carry the load. He had access to a renewed mind, but he continued operating under the pressure of self-made expectations. Transformation stalled because surrender was avoided.

Purpose, Calling, and Spiritual Gifts

Manuel didn't lose his calling—but he walked away from it. His gifts remained, but they were no longer submitted to Kingdom purpose. When we disconnect from the One who gave us our assignment, we begin to misuse or underuse what was meant to serve others and glorify God. Purpose becomes diluted, and eternal impact is minimized.

The Indwelling of the Holy Spirit

The Spirit never left Manuel, but Manuel stopped listening. The partnership that once marked his ministry was replaced by independence. The Holy Spirit speaks, leads, and empowers—but when we choose to operate in our own strength, we begin to ignore His voice. Manuel wasn't resisting the Spirit—he was drowning Him out.

Faith in Action

Manuel didn't need another promotion—he needed a reset. Not a career reset, but a spiritual one. The turning point wouldn't come by rearranging his schedule or scaling back responsibilities—it would come through repentance and realignment. Striving isn't broken by working harder; it's broken by surrender. And that begins when we stop asking, *How can I make this work?* and start asking, *Lord, what are You calling me to lay down?* Faith in action means exchanging control for trust—and choosing to follow, even if it costs us what we've built.

Recognize the striving and repent

The first step is honesty. Ask the Holy Spirit to reveal where you've been pushing in your own strength instead of resting in His. Repentance isn't just about wrongdoing—it's about misalignment. Invite God to expose any areas where you've drifted from dependence, even if they seem "successful."

Lay down what you've built

If what you're building requires you to carry the full weight of it alone, it may not be what God asked you to build. Faith means being willing to walk away from what's good in order to return to what's God. That might mean stepping back from a position, saying no to an opportunity, or releasing control over a future you planned without Him.

Recommit your gifts and calling to God

Your gifts haven't disappeared—but they need to be re-surrendered. Ask God to reignite the fire for what He originally called you to do. Whether that means returning to a past assignment or stepping into a new one, place your abilities back into His hands and trust Him to direct their use.

Restore a rhythm of rest and intimacy

Striving thrives in busyness. Break the cycle by rebuilding rhythms of rest—spiritual, emotional, and physical. Schedule silence. Prioritize presence. Set boundaries. Rest isn't laziness—it's obedience. And it's often in rest that God speaks most clearly.

Trust God with the consequences of obedience

The cost of surrender is real. But so is the reward. Obedience may require financial risk, humbling conversations, or letting go of a life others admire. But if God is calling you out of striving, He's also making provision for the path ahead. Trust that He can sustain what you submit.

Prayer

Father,

I'm tired—not just in body, but in soul. I confess that I've been striving in my own strength, chasing outcomes You never asked me to carry, and trying to build a life without fully consulting You. I've confused success with alignment, and I've relied on myself more than I've rested in You.

Forgive me for the ways I've drifted. Forgive me for replacing intimacy with activity, and calling it faithfulness. I don't want to live this way anymore.

I surrender the plans I've made, the pressure I've been under, and the path I've been pursuing apart from You. Show me where I need to let go.

Teach me how to trust You again—not just with my salvation, but with my daily steps, my calling, and my future.

Help me return to the joy of walking in step with You. Fill me with Your Spirit, reestablish Your voice as the one I follow, and give me the courage to obey—no matter the cost.

In Jesus' name, Amen.

Areas of Study

Matthew 11:28–30 – "Come to Me...and I will give you rest."

Jesus doesn't call us to carry everything—He calls us to come to Him. These verses contrast the heavy burdens of self-effort with the lightness that comes from walking in step with Christ. True rest isn't passive—it's a result of surrendered obedience.

Proverbs 3:5–6 – "Trust in the Lord with all your heart..."

This passage calls us away from self-reliance and back to trust. Manuel's journey mirrors what happens when we lean on our own understanding instead of seeking God in all our ways. Striving fades when we return to trust.

Isaiah 30:15 – "In repentance and rest is your salvation..."

This often-overlooked verse connects salvation directly to rest and quiet confidence. The people of Israel missed it because they chose action over surrender. Manuel did the same—and this verse invites us to reverse that pattern.

Hebrews 4:9–11 – "**There remains a Sabbath rest for the people of God…**"

This New Testament teaching reminds us that rest is not just a command—it's a promise. But entering that rest takes intentionality. Striving keeps us from experiencing what Christ already secured for us.

Jonah 1–3 – **Jonah's resistance to God's call**

Jonah's journey shows the cost of running from God's assignment, even when it's masked by logic or self-preservation. Like Manuel, Jonah learned that obedience is not optional—and that surrender is always the path to restoration.

Closing Reflection

Manuel didn't fall because of rebellion—he drifted because of striving. He didn't run from God—he just tried to outrun exhaustion. And that's the trap so many of us fall into. We work harder, achieve more, and tell ourselves we're doing it for good reasons. But when the Holy Spirit is no longer guiding the pace, even our best intentions can lead us off course.

You don't have to keep living that way.

If Manuel's story stirred something in you—if you've recognized patterns of striving, misplaced identity, or spiritual fatigue—it may be the Holy Spirit gently inviting you back to rest. Not the rest of quitting, but the rest of trusting. The rest of walking with God instead of ahead of Him. The rest of laying down what you've built so He can rebuild what's eternal.

You may feel like too much time has passed. Like there's too much to unravel. But surrender is never too late. Grace doesn't expire, and your calling hasn't been revoked.

The God who called you before you ever picked up the pace is still calling now. And He's not asking for more effort—He's asking for your yes.

CHAPTER 20

When God Says Wait: Trusting His Timing in the Tension of Delay

———•———

"But they who wait for the Lord shall renew their strength; they shall mount up with wings like eagles; they shall run and not be weary; they shall walk and not faint." Isaiah 40:31

As I wrote this book, I came under enemy attack. I was bombarded with negative and discouraging thoughts. A heaviness came upon me, and I battled through it—losing days of productivity in the process. Honestly, I should have expected it. This isn't content the enemy wants published, taught, or shared. It exposes his strategy, calls believers to repentance and action, and arms people with truth. Of course, he would come against it.

But I was able to keep writing because I'm no stranger to spiritual warfare. Over the past few years, I've gone through a deep and intense process of healing, mind renewal, and transformation. I've torn down strongholds, confronted lies, and fought daily to walk in obedience. It was early during that season—while doing the very kind of faith-in-action work I've laid out in this book—that I hit a point of deep weariness. I was doing everything God had asked of me, and yet I felt under constant pressure, like I was always at war. So I cried out to Him.

"Why does it feel like I'm always entangled in battle?"

God responded with a question of His own.
"What do warriors do?"
"They fight battles," I answered.
"You're a warrior. I've called you to fight battles," He said.

That moment didn't stop the warfare—but it shifted everything. God reminded me who I am: I'm a warrior, an overcomer, and more than a conqueror (Romans 8:37). And if you are in Christ, so are you.

My twenty years in the Marine Corps taught me that being a warrior is not about bravado—it's about discipline, training, and submission to authority. You don't just wear the uniform; you train and prepare for the battle. And in the Kingdom, the same is true. The Bible tells us that those who are called must be trained, tested, and proven. "It is God who arms me with strength and keeps my way secure" (Psalm 18:32, NIV). He prepares our hands for battle and our hearts for endurance.

That's why we can't confuse God's training, equipping, or pruning with the enemy's attacks. The refining fire is not the battlefield—it's the boot camp. But here's the truth: it's in these very seasons of refinement that the enemy often intensifies his assault. Why? Because he senses the growth. He sees the sharpening. He fears the fruit that's about to break through.

And this is where waiting comes in. Waiting is one of God's most powerful tools of formation. It's not punishment—it's preparation. God was showing me that *the waiting*—this long, slow, often painful delay in visible breakthrough I desired—is where warriors are forged. Not just to endure, but to become a match for the enemy.

Because the enemy doesn't give up. He is relentless, strategic, and tenacious. He studies us. He adapts. As we grow in truth, he refines his tactics. He becomes more devious and more subtle. He twists Scripture, manipulates timing, and weaponizes our very obedience to provoke doubt, frustration, and compromise. He waits for exhaustion. He counts on us losing heart. He wants to outlast us.

But that's exactly why God uses waiting as a weapon. Because in the waiting, He is forging what the enemy fears most: a believer who will not quit. A believer who listens longer, trusts deeper, prays harder, and obeys more precisely—not out of hesitation, but discernment. A believer who recognizes the enemy's voice even when it's wrapped in Scripture, and who clings to God's Word when it looks like it's not working.

That's who God is shaping me into.

That's what this final chapter is about.

Waiting is not weakness. It's not delay for delay's sake. It's divine strategy. And if you've found yourself in a prolonged season of obedience without visible breakthrough, this chapter is for you.

Personal Experience

God has been working in me and through me, building on what He seeded in me as a child through a prophetic vision, and what He anchored in my heart through the entrepreneurial vision He gave me. The moment came when He told me plainly: *You'll never become the entrepreneur I created you to be unless you go through the fire with Me.*

That was the moment I stepped into the furnace. What followed was an intense, sacred process of full submission and surrender. I entered focused on outcomes—but He fixed my eyes on Jesus instead. Over time, what I desired most shifted. My need for Him became greater than my desire for calling, purpose, or even vision. Those things didn't disappear—they just got properly reordered.

I learned what it means to *be* instead of just *do.* I discovered my true identity. He healed wounds I thought were permanent. He softened my heart and made it more like His—freer, fuller, whole. His Word came alive, and my faith grew deeper and stronger than I ever imagined it could.

I've trusted Him completely. I've said yes to every assignment, followed every prompt, written every word, spoken every truth—even when it cost me. I've built my business according to His leading, stewarding First Time Storytelling and Brave Action Ministry with obedience and conviction. I've given Him my whole life.

Internally, the breakthroughs and revelations have been tremendous and incredible. However, externally, it looks like I've gone backward. I even faced eviction—not from rebellion or disobedience, but in the very act of trusting Him as Provider. But even then, I didn't doubt Him. The eviction became a divine appointment, one that led to opportunities to serve in unexpected ways and reminded me once again: my provision doesn't come from platforms, people, or paychecks. It comes from Him.

I've seen more internal transformation than I ever dreamed possible. But I'm still waiting for the external shift—for the vision to be fulfilled, for the promises to manifest. I've prayed, obeyed, trusted—and still, I wait.

What the enemy does now is subtle but fierce. He reminds me of all the promises I believe, the trust I've placed in God, the greatness of the One I follow—not to encourage me, but to twist the truth and weaponize my faith against me. He can't take my calling, so he tries to wear me down in the waiting. He wants trust to become torment.

But I see him now. I see what he's after. And I see what God is doing. The waiting isn't weakening me—it's making me dangerous. He's sharpening my discernment, deepening my dependency, and forging endurance I didn't know I had. I'm not striving. I'm not shrinking back. I'm not giving in. I'm being forged in the wait.

Key Choices

This season of waiting has revealed more about my faith than any breakthrough ever could. It's exposed my motives, refined my trust, and stretched my obedience in ways I never anticipated. I didn't walk into it expecting comfort, but I also didn't expect it to last this long. And while I've grown in countless ways—I've still had to wrestle with the quiet thoughts that surface when delay lingers.

There have been moments I've asked, *What else am I supposed to do?* or *Did I mishear God?* But deep down, I know I didn't. I know I've obeyed. I know I've trusted. And yet, I'm still waiting. It's in this space— between what I know and what I see—that the most pivotal choices are made.

In the delay, we're confronted with choices that shape our character, test our convictions, and expose any lingering doubts about God's goodness. The enemy knows this. That's why waiting is one of his favorite battlegrounds—because it tempts us to take control, redefine obedience, or quietly give up. But if we can recognize the tension for what it is—a refining fire rather than a rejection—we'll see that every moment of waiting is a chance to deepen our faith or drift from it.

Here are the choices I've faced—and the same ones you may be facing if you're walking through the tension of delay.

1. Choosing surrender over striving

I've built. I've obeyed. I've poured myself out. But there came a point where I realized I was starting to strive again—not to prove something to God, but to feel like I was still moving forward. Striving made me feel useful. Surrender made me feel vulnerable. But God wasn't asking me to perform—He was asking me to rest. He reminded me that fruitfulness comes from abiding, not forcing. Striving might produce results, but only surrender produces peace.

The enemy tries to convince us that if we're not striving, we're falling behind. In the waiting, we often feel tempted to "make something happen" or help God out. But striving births Ishmaels, not Isaacs. True rest is found in trusting God to fulfill His promises without our manipulation.

2. Choosing to believe God's character vs. questioning His timing

The longer I've waited, the more tempting it's been to measure God's faithfulness by the pace of my progress. But the Holy Spirit keeps reminding me: *God is never late, and He's never withholding what is good.* I've had to choose to believe that God is still good, even when the wait feels unkind. His timing is an extension of His love—not a sign of neglect. Choosing to trust His character anchors me when everything else feels uncertain.

When breakthrough delays, it's easy to ask, *Why hasn't God done it yet?* But underneath that question often lies a deeper one: *Can I still trust Him?* David had to decide whether God's delay meant He had forgotten him—or whether it meant God was forming something deeper in him.

Every believer in a waiting season must choose to stand on who God is, not how things look. His timing is never random—it's redemptive.

3. Choosing to stay rooted in purpose vs. redefining it through pain

There have been days I've wondered if I missed it—if I misheard, misstepped, or misunderstood the vision. The temptation to downgrade my calling or rewrite the promise is real. But God keeps calling me back to what He said. Purpose doesn't change just because the timing does. I've learned to sit in the tension and hold the vision steady—even when it still feels out of reach.

Long delays can lead us to redefine what God said. These are the whispered lies that try to erode purpose in the wait. But staying rooted means holding onto the vision, even when the evidence hasn't caught up yet. God's promises don't expire with time. They mature with it.

4. Choosing hidden faithfulness over public fruitfulness

It's hard to keep showing up when no one sees it. It's hard to keep giving when it doesn't look like anything is growing. But God keeps reminding me that He watches in the hidden place. This is the season where I've learned that obedience isn't about applause—it's about alignment. The fruit will come in due time, but right now, I'm called to faithfulness in the soil, not the spotlight.

In a world that celebrates visibility, hidden seasons can feel like punishment. But God often develops us in private before He uses us in public. David had to continue obeying, building, and showing up even when no one was clapping, no doors were opening, and no progress could be seen. Choosing hidden faithfulness is choosing to honor God for who He is, not for what we hope He'll do next.

5. Choosing hope over resignation

I've felt the pull to lower my expectations—to stop hoping so I won't be disappointed. But hope is holy. It's not naïve. It's not foolish. It's a weapon. Choosing to hope again is my declaration that God is not finished and that His promises are still true. Resignation is easy, but it's not the life of faith. Hope requires courage, and by God's grace, I keep choosing it.

There's a weariness that tries to creep in when you've waited a long time. It tells you to lower your expectations, protect your heart, and stop hoping. Resignation says, *Maybe this will never happen.* Hope says, *Even if it hasn't yet, God is still who He says He is.*

Enemy Tactics

Waiting is a sacred space—designed by God to deepen our trust, refine our character, and anchor us in obedience. But the enemy sees it as prime territory for attack. He knows that while we wait, we're vulnerable to suggestion. And instead of overt temptation, he leverages the silence, the slowness, and the struggle to twist what God intended for good into something that feels like punishment. He doesn't just try to steal the promise—he goes after your perception of God, your sense of worth, and your will to persevere.

Here's how the enemy worked during my waiting—and how he often works in the lives of maturing believers:

Twisting truth into accusation

The enemy began using the very promises I believed to torment me. He didn't say God was a liar—he used Scripture to question *me.* *"You're doing all the right things—so why hasn't God come through? Maybe He's holding out on you."* He used truth out of context to breed doubt. That's what he does with mature believers—he stops arguing against the Bible and starts twisting it to erode trust in the Author.

Using delay to distort identity

In the absence of visible progress, the enemy tempted me to define myself by what hadn't happened yet. *"If you were really called, wouldn't there be fruit by now?"* He pushed me to attach my value to my outcomes instead of my obedience. But our identity isn't found in what we've achieved—it's rooted in who we belong to and what God has spoken over us.

Exploiting exhaustion to justify compromise

There were moments I was tired—spiritually, emotionally, physically. And in those moments, the enemy whispered, *"It's okay to lower the bar. You've done enough. Stop pressing in so hard."* He offered shortcuts that looked like self-care but were really spiritual retreat. When we're weary, he doesn't tell us to walk away—he tempts us to settle.

Offering distraction over discernment

In the wait, it became easy to chase "good" opportunities just to feel like I was moving. The enemy filled my inbox with distractions that looked helpful but would have misaligned my focus. He tempts mature believers not with blatant rebellion, but with busyness that leads to disobedience. Discernment becomes our greatest defense.

Targeting faith with fear masked as logic

The longer I waited, the more the enemy appealed to reason. *"Maybe you misunderstood. Maybe this isn't practical. You need a backup plan."* His goal wasn't to make me walk away—it was to get me to shift just enough to lean on logic instead of faith. But trusting God doesn't always make sense. Obedience often won't.

Counterfeit Outcome

Waiting with God strengthens us. But waiting without God—without anchoring ourselves in His voice, His Word, and His character—leaves us open to deception. That's when the enemy's lies take root. And if we're not careful, what was meant to strengthen us becomes the very season that defines us in all the wrong ways.

You begin to question God's goodness. Not because you stopped believing in Him—but because you started measuring His love by how fast He moves or how much He delivers. The enemy slowly convinces you that delay means denial—and that's where trust begins to fracture.

You settle for survival instead of contending for breakthrough. When the wait feels endless, you stop expecting and start enduring. You numb yourself with productivity, or comfort, or distraction. Hope gets replaced by routine, and faith becomes passive instead of active.

You perform instead of persevere. You keep doing the right things, but no longer out of love—just obligation. You pray, fast, serve, and give, hoping it will move God's hand. But striving is not the same as standing, and religious effort doesn't produce spiritual breakthrough.

You start listening to logic over the Lord. Slowly, the voice of God gets drowned out by the opinions of others and your own internal calculations. Instead of moving by faith, you make decisions based on what makes sense, feels safe, or looks wise to the world.

You forget who you are. The longer you wait, the more tempted you are to define yourself by what you lack, haven't seen, or still haven't received. Identity slips from "beloved child" to "unfinished project." The very season meant to affirm your identity in Christ becomes the breeding ground for spiritual amnesia.

The danger of delayed promises isn't just discouragement—it's distortion. When we stop standing in faith, we start slipping into a counterfeit version of ourselves: doubtful, hesitant, striving, and self-reliant. But God never asked us to wait alone. He calls us to wait *with Him*—trusting, listening, resting, and standing on what He said, not what we see.

Areas of Salvation Impacted

Peace With God

When delay is met with distrust, our peace is the first casualty. We may not realize it, but when we allow frustration, confusion, or anxiety to take root in the waiting, we begin to question the character of God. Instead of resting in Him, we wrestle against Him. Peace isn't the absence of waiting—it's the presence of trust in the One who holds time.

A New Heart and a Renewed Mind

Waiting reveals what still needs transformation. The longer the wait, the more our thoughts, motives, and beliefs are exposed. Will we allow the Holy Spirit to renew our thinking and purify our hearts? Or will we let disappointment harden us? God uses waiting to sanctify our desires—not to punish us, but to prepare us.

Purpose, Calling, and Spiritual Gifts

Delay doesn't mean disqualification. But if we let discouragement define us, we may abandon the very calling we were meant to fulfill. The enemy wants us to confuse delayed timing with denied purpose. But God often trains warriors in seasons of obscurity, refining their gifts and strengthening their endurance before the breakthrough comes.

Divine Provision

One of the most difficult aspects of waiting is provision. When circumstances look barren and resources are thin, the enemy whispers that God has forgotten. But our Provider is never late—He's teaching us to depend on Him, not the outcome. Waiting exposes whether we trust in God's hand or in our own ability to control outcomes.

The Indwelling of the Holy Spirit

The Holy Spirit is our Comforter, Guide, and Advocate in the waiting. But when we let delay turn into doubt, we tune out His voice and lean into our flesh. Seasons of delay are meant to train us to walk more closely with the Spirit—not to grow distant from Him. Intimacy deepens when we remain sensitive to His leading, even in silence.

Faith in Action

I've learned—and been reminded again and again—that waiting isn't passive. It's one of the most active, refining places of faith we'll ever stand. For me, it's been years, decades even, that I've been believing for a breakthrough in the very place He's called me: my entrepreneurial assignment. It's where I've seen the slowest results but it's also been the means for leading me to my most profound transformation. I don't have the language to fully express how challenging the waiting has been and what the waiting has done in me—how it's stripped me of self-reliance, awakened a fiercer trust, and taught me to worship without evidence. It's become sacred ground.

And while the world may see delay as failure or stagnation, heaven sees it as preparation. Every moment of waiting is a moment to reaffirm who God is, what He's said, and who you are becoming in the process. If you find yourself in a prolonged season of delay—still praying, still trusting, still holding on to promises that haven't yet come to pass—you're not forgotten. You're being formed.

Waiting has demanded not just patience, but bold, repeated choices—sometimes daily, sometimes moment by moment. Here are the decisions I've had to make—and the ones you'll likely face, too, if you're in a similar place of holy delay:

Speak truth over your delay.

Declare who God is, even when you don't feel Him near. Say the promises out loud. Rebuke the lie that nothing is happening. Speak faith until your heart catches up.

Stay faithful to what He last told you.

You don't need a new word—you need to keep walking in the last one. Delayed fruit doesn't mean a wrong assignment. It just means deeper roots are being established.

Submit your timeline again—and again.

Surrender doesn't just happen once. I've had to lay down my expectations a hundred times, and every time, I've found God's timing to be wiser than mine. Waiting isn't punishment—it's preparation.

Remember His faithfulness.

When discouragement whispers, I remember all He's already done. How He pursued me when I was running. How He healed wounds I thought would never mend. How He made me whole, renewed my mind, and transformed my heart. I want to see Him move through me—but I will not forget what He's already done *in* me. Those testimonies fuel my endurance and remind me: He's done it before, He'll do it again.

Prayer

Father,

You are not slow in keeping Your promises. You are wise in Your timing, perfect in Your ways, and faithful in all You do. I confess that I don't always understand Your delays. I've wrestled with doubt, weariness, and discouragement. But today, I choose to trust You again.

Forgive me for the times I've tried to rush the process, manipulate outcomes, or measure Your goodness by my timeline. Teach me to wait well. Make the waiting holy ground—not a place of despair, but of transformation. Strip me of self-reliance. Empty me of control. Fill me with unwavering trust.

When the enemy whispers lies, help me speak truth louder. When comparison creeps in, remind me of Your unique plan for my life. When silence feels unbearable, let Your Word anchor my soul.

I believe You are doing more than I can see. You are working behind the scenes, preparing me, stretching me, and strengthening me. Help me keep showing up in obedience. Help me worship without evidence. Help me stay rooted in Your love—even when the fruit hasn't come.

You are the Author of my story. You've never failed. And You won't start now.

In Jesus' name, Amen.

Areas of Study

Hebrews 10:35–36 – "So do not throw away your confidence; it will be richly rewarded. You need to persevere so that when you have done the will of God, you will receive what he has promised."

Study how perseverance is tied to obedience and reward. Reflect on how confidence must be maintained in the waiting, not just after the breakthrough.

Isaiah 40:31 – "But those who wait for the Lord shall renew their strength…"

Meditate on the exchange that happens in waiting—our weakness for His strength. Examine how this verse reframes waiting not as wasted time, but as divine renewal.

James 1:2–4 – "Consider it pure joy, my brothers and sisters, whenever you face trials of many kinds…"

Study how trials—including delays—test our faith and produce endurance. Look at the maturing work of patience and how God uses it to complete and equip us.

Psalm 27:13–14 – "I remain confident of this: I will see the goodness of the Lord… Wait for the Lord; be strong and take heart…"

Reflect on David's confidence in God's goodness amid delay. Study how strength and courage are cultivated not just in battle, but in patient expectation.

Lamentations 3:25–26 – "The Lord is good to those whose hope is in him, to the one who seeks him; it is good to wait quietly for the salvation of the Lord."

Explore how seeking and waiting are deeply linked. Waiting is not idle—it's a posture of hope, humility, and hunger for God.

Romans 4:18–21 – **Abraham's faith "did not waver through unbelief regarding the promise of God."**

Study how Abraham navigated the long wait for God's promise. Reflect on the connection between being "fully persuaded" and giving glory to God while waiting.

Luke 8:15 – **"But the seed on good soil stands for those... who hear the word, retain it, and by persevering produce a crop."**

Dig into the parable of the sower and how fruitfulness is tied not just to hearing but to persevering. Waiting is part of that perseverance that leads to harvest.

The Story of Joseph (Genesis 37–50)

Trace the timeline of Joseph's life—from betrayal to prison to promotion—and observe how God's favor and purpose were never absent in the delay. His story is a blueprint for how waiting prepares us for Kingdom responsibility.

Closing Reflection

Waiting has a way of exposing what we really believe—about God, about ourselves, and about the promises we've been given. And when the wait is long, it can start to feel like punishment instead of preparation. But I've come to see waiting as one of God's greatest tools for shaping warriors. Not because it's easy, but because it teaches us how to stand when nothing moves. It strips us of self-sufficiency, purifies our motives, and trains our hands for battle—not with doing, but with surrender.

The longer I wait, the more clearly I see: the goal was never the breakthrough itself. It was the becoming. The deepening. The anchoring of my identity in Christ, no matter what the outcome. And the greatest victory isn't that I finally get what I've been believing for—but that I've learned to believe even when I don't. That I've become relentless. That I've been made strong enough to stand against an enemy who never stops attacking because I now serve a God I'll never stop trusting.

Maybe you're in that place right now. The long delay. The silent middle. The stretch of obedience that doesn't seem to be producing anything visible. If so, let this be your reminder: You're not stuck. You're being shaped. You're not forgotten. You're being formed.

Keep worshiping. Keep trusting. Keep staying. The promise hasn't changed—and neither has the God who made it.

Section V Closing

We often imagine spiritual warfare as dramatic battles or sudden temptations—but the most dangerous ground is usually the ordinary. It's the everyday crossroads where obedience costs something. The moments where God asks us to wait, stay, surrender, or trust—and we're tempted to do the opposite in the name of progress, security, or relief.

In Section V, we stepped into those subtle battlegrounds. These final chapters revealed that the enemy doesn't need us to turn our backs on God to derail our destinies—he only needs us to drift. To choose striving over surrender. To pick comfort over calling. To keep building lives that look blessed but lack intimacy with the One who blesses.

Through the lives of those who compromised just a little, detoured just for a season, or delayed obedience just long enough, we saw how small decisions carry eternal weight. These chapters weren't about rebellion— they were about reluctance. And that's what makes them so relevant. Because most believers aren't running from God. They're just trying to balance faith with practicality, calling with comfort, trust with control.

But there is no middle ground in the Kingdom. There is no "just for now" with compromise. Every decision either draws us closer to the life God authored or deeper into the counterfeit life the enemy offers. That's why these final chapters matter so much—because they confront the everyday choices that shape our spiritual legacy.

As this section draws to a close, the invitation is clear:

Don't delay your obedience.

Don't downgrade your calling.

Don't despise the waiting.

Because these are the places where God refines us, defines us, and prepares us for His glory.

CHAPTER 21

From Counterfeit to Commissioned: Living Authored, Armored, and Faithfully

—————•—————

Throughout this book, we explored stories of counterfeit living, the choices that make it possible, and exposed the spiritual tactics behind them. You've seen how the enemy operates subtly through whispers of delay, distraction, deception, and distorted truth. We've traced how everyday decisions—seemingly harmless, spiritually delayed, or dressed up as wisdom—can over time form lives that appear full yet are out of alignment with the authored path God intended.

But this isn't just about living right. It's about living *empowered*.

Jesus didn't just come to save us—He came to commission us. And in John 14:12, He delivers one of the most staggering promises in all of Scripture:

> *"Truly, truly, I say to you, whoever believes in me will also do the works that I do; and greater works than these will he do, because I am going to the Father."*

Pause and let that sink in.

Greater works. Thank Jesus.

The One who healed the sick, calmed storms, cast out demons, fed thousands, and raised the dead—tells us we will do *greater* works.

This isn't religious hype—it's Kingdom reality. But it's only available to those who believe and become. To those who stop settling for the appearance of godliness and begin walking in the full authority of it. To those who reject the counterfeit and step fully into the authored.

Because that kind of power is not for the half-surrendered. It's for the fully yielded. The faithfully trained. The spiritually armed.

But this book was never meant to merely inform. It was meant to equip.

It was written as a field manual for those ready to reject the counterfeit and live intentionally authored lives—lives fully submitted and surrendered to God. Lives that don't just avoid sin but faithfully pursue purpose. Because power without purity leads to destruction, and authority without alignment leads to deception.

To walk in the "greater works," you must be grounded in greater truth. You must become mature enough to carry the weight of Kingdom responsibility. You must be rooted deep enough to endure testing without falling into pride, fear, or compromise.

That's why this book isn't just about freedom from sin. It's about formation into Christlikeness.

It's about training for the battlefield, not just surviving the struggle. It's about learning to discern the enemy's schemes and respond—not in panic, but in power. Not in human strength, but in Spirit-led wisdom, boldness, and unshakable faith.

You can't live authored if you're still unaware of the war being waged for your choices. You can't walk in victory if you're still flirting with what's counterfeit. And you can't bring healing to others if you're still believing the lies that keep you bound.

That's why God is calling you higher—not just into breakthrough, but into becoming. Because the world doesn't just need more Christians. The world needs warriors—those who reflect Christ, wield truth, and carry glory.

Engaging in Spiritual Warfare: Armor Up

But no warrior enters battle unarmed.

If you are going to stand in truth, walk in power, and advance God's Kingdom in a world full of compromise and confusion, you must be armored. Not occasionally, not when things get hard—always. Because the war isn't seasonal. The attacks aren't random. And the enemy doesn't wait until you feel ready.

> *"Put on the full armor of God, so that you can take your stand against the devil's schemes."*
> —Ephesians 6:11 (NIV)

This is not poetic language. This is spiritual instruction. This is God saying: *You are in a war—and here is how you survive it. Here is how you win it.*

Every piece of the armor has a purpose:

The Belt of Truth: because lies are the enemy's native language, and without truth, you will be swayed by every wind of culture and confusion.

The Breastplate of Righteousness: because your heart must be protected by holiness, not propped up by performance or self-justification.

The Shoes of Peace: because you are not just called to stand firm—you are called to *move* in obedience, ready to go wherever God sends you.

The Shield of Faith: because fiery darts will come—doubts, accusations, fears—and faith is what extinguishes them.

The Helmet of Salvation: because your mind is a battlefield, and your identity in Christ must guard every thought.

The Sword of the Spirit—the Word of God: because defense alone is not enough. You must go on the offense with the only weapon that never fails.

This armor is not metaphorical. It is spiritual. And it's not a one-time prayer—it's a daily posture.

But hear this clearly: The armor is not powered by your discipline—it is activated by your dependence on the Holy Spirit. You were never meant to do this in your own strength.

The Holy Spirit is your Helper, your Advocate, your Counselor. He reminds you of truth when the lies get loud. He convicts you when you drift. He strengthens you when you are weary. He leads you when you don't know what comes next.

So don't just ask God for strength—stay filled with the Spirit. Let Him guide your steps, purify your desires, and embolden your faith.

So don't leave your house spiritually naked. Don't walk through life unaware of the attacks forming against you.

Be armed. Be trained. Be ready.

Put on the armor—and keep it on. Let your language and prayers reflect that. Let your conversations, declarations, and intercessions be rooted in the reality that you are a soldier of Christ, led by the Spirit of God.

Because when you're armored and anointed, you don't just survive the enemy's schemes—
You advance in spite of them. You move forward when others retreat. You hold the line when others fall. You shine light where darkness has long prevailed. Because you don't fight alone—you fight in the power and authority of the One who already won.

Engaging in Spiritual Warfare: Faith in Action

Faith isn't passive. It's war-ready.

Every chapter in this book included a *Faith in Action* section—for a reason. Because faith is not just belief. Faith is movement. Faith is action. Faith takes the truth of God's Word and builds a life on it. Faith doesn't wait for emotions to catch up—it acts in obedience even when the heart is still trembling.

> *"As the body without the spirit is dead, so faith without deeds is dead."*—James 2:26 (NIV)

In spiritual warfare, what you believe matters—but what you do with what you believe is what builds your resistance, deepens your discernment, and anchors you in victory.

These were never meant to be read and skipped. If you bypassed the *Faith in Action* sections, go back. Revisit the recommendations. Reopen the conversation with the Holy Spirit. Because transformation doesn't come from reading—it comes from responding.

Don't rush past what stirred you. If conviction rose, let it lead to repentance. If revelation came, let it shape new rhythms. If wounds were exposed, let healing begin—not in isolation, but in partnership with God.

The Foundational Steps of Faith in Action

Here are five consistent practices that appeared again and again across these chapters. These aren't boxes to check—they are spiritual habits to build your life around:

1. Renewing the Mind

You cannot live authored while thinking like someone still enslaved. Every spiritual breakthrough begins with mental transformation. Lies must be replaced. Truth must be rehearsed. You must begin to think with the mind of Christ—daily. This is not a one-time epiphany. It is daily renewal.

Without it, you will drift. With it, you will discern.

2. Repentance

Repentance is not just for gross sin. It's for misalignment. It's for wrong motives, subtle pride, silent agreements with fear, shame, and control. Repentance repositions you under God's authority. It breaks the enemy's grip and opens the door to restoration. Repent quickly. Repent often. It's how you stay free.

3. Worship

Worship isn't just singing—it's realigning. When you worship, you shift your gaze from what's broken to the One who restores. Worship disarms bitterness. It breaks silence. It rebuilds awe.

When your emotions are numb and your mind is heavy—worship anyway.

4. Prayer

Prayer is not a routine—it's your weapon. Prayer aligns your heart, opens your ears, and positions you to receive strategy from Heaven. Don't just pray for breakthrough—pray for insight. Ask God: *What are You doing here? What am I not seeing? Where is the enemy trying to deceive me?* Prayer isn't a last resort—it's your first response.

5. Community

You cannot win this battle alone. Isolation is one of the enemy's oldest strategies—because alone, you're vulnerable. Healing, discernment, and strength often come through the body of Christ. Surround yourself with believers who will speak truth, call out compromise, pray without fear, and carry you when you can't carry yourself. Real connection is part of real warfare.

Faith in action is not a one-time surge of obedience—it's a lifestyle of surrender that evolves with every season. The battles may change. The assignments may shift. But the foundations—renewing your mind, repenting quickly, worshiping fully, praying continually, and staying rooted in community—never stop being essential. These aren't just beginner steps. They are *warrior basics.* And when we forget, drift, or fall, the way back isn't complicated. We return to the fundamentals. We start over—not in shame, but in trust, knowing God always meets us where we are to lead us where He's calling us. So if you ever find yourself lost, overwhelmed, or unsure of what to do next—go back to what you know is true. Start with truth. Start with repentance. Start with worship. Start again. And keep walking.

Engaging in Spiritual Warfare: The Word of God

The Word is Where It All Begins

Everything—every act of faith, every moment of discernment, every spiritual breakthrough—starts with the Word of God. It is the foundation, the mirror, the sword, and the light and lamp. Without it, there is no transformation. No lasting freedom. No victory in battle. If you try to engage in spiritual warfare without the Word, you're not just unarmed—you're exposed.

> *"For the word of God is living and active, sharper than any two-edged sword, piercing to the division of soul and of spirit, of joints and of marrow, and discerning the thoughts and intentions of the heart."*
> —Hebrews 4:12 (NIV)

The Word of God is what makes everything else possible.

The *Areas of Study* at the end of each chapter were not included as optional reading—they are high-value invitations to dig deeper. They are not for skimming. They are for breaking out your Bible, sitting with the text, and asking the Holy Spirit to reveal what you need to see. This is where your spiritual understanding is sharpened and your discernment strengthened. These studies are not just about learning what happened—

they help you see how God moves, how the enemy schemes, and how truth confronts lies.

But this isn't just about reading the Word. It's about letting the Word read you. Letting it expose, correct, comfort, instruct, and realign you. The Word isn't passive—it speaks. And when you open yourself to it, God speaks through it.

That's why, if you find yourself facing scenarios or choices similar to the ones shared throughout this book, don't just look for a feeling or a sign—go to the Word. The *Areas of Study* were designed with that very purpose in mind: to anchor you when you're confused, to guide you when you're conflicted, and to reestablish your footing when the counterfeit starts to feel convincing.

And once that Word takes root—protect it. Because the enemy will come for it. Every time.

Jesus warned us in the parable of the sower that the enemy comes immediately to steal the Word that was sown (Mark 4:15). Why? Because the Word is dangerous to the kingdom of darkness. If it's left alone, it will grow. It will bear fruit. It will transform your life. That's why the enemy attacks the seeding of the Word (through distraction), the watering of the Word (through doubt and busyness), and the growth of the Word (through temptation and persecution).

So guard it. Water it. Meditate on it. Don't just receive the Word—contend for it.

Because in spiritual warfare:

- Ignorance is not innocence—it's a weakness.
- Truth is not optional—it's survival.

- And Scripture is not supplemental—it's essential.

If you want to live in truth, you must abide in it.
If you want to defeat lies, you must know the truth.
If you want to live free, you must renew your mind daily.

The Word of God isn't just information—it's your weapon. It's your lens. It's your anchor. Open it. Study it. Meditate on it. Protect it. Let it read you. Let it form you. Let it lead you. Because without the Word, you won't just miss the truth—you'll mistake the counterfeit for it.

The Goal Isn't Just Clarity—It's Christlikeness

Ultimately, this book isn't about becoming more self-aware. It's about making the right choices towards becoming more like Christ.

It's about walking in the full power and authority of your identity in Him. About developing the character, mindset, and spiritual maturity required to live as a son or daughter of the King. It's about being transformed—not conformed.

This is the path of a Kingdom warrior.

It's not glamorous. It's not always celebrated. It's a path of pruning, purifying, persevering. But it's the only path that leads to true freedom and fruitfulness.

The real win isn't just rejecting the enemy's lies—it's becoming so grounded in truth that those lies can't even take root. It's living armored, faithful, and aligned.

You're Part of Something Bigger

This journey of turning away from the counterfeit life is personal—but it's never private.

My obedience and your obedience matters more than you know. The enemy's agenda isn't just to derail your calling—it's to weaken the Body of Christ, one compromised believer at a time. But when you rise up, when you armor up, when you choose truth over comfort, repentance over pride, and action over apathy—you don't just reclaim your life. You reclaim ground for the Kingdom.

We are in a generation that is starved for truth, numbed by noise, and drowning in distraction.
The world doesn't need more polished performances. It needs Spirit-filled warriors—people who walk in truth, lead with love, and carry the weight of glory without bending to the pressures of the age.

That's why this matters. That's why *you* matter.

A Closing Prayer of Commissioning

Father, I thank You for revealing what's counterfeit and for calling me back to what You've authored. I lay down every lie I've believed, every compromise I've tolerated, and every fear that has delayed my obedience. I receive Your truth. I receive Your grace. I receive the armor You've provided—and I choose to put it on and never take it off. I break agreement with distraction, deception, and despair. I choose to walk in alignment, in authority, and in love.

Holy Spirit, fill me afresh. Lead me in wisdom. Train my hands for battle and my heart for worship. Use my life to expose the darkness, to reflect the beauty of Christ, and to advance Your Kingdom. Let the story of my life reveal not just what I've overcome—but who I belong to.

In Jesus' mighty name, Amen.